ASSESSING AND MANAGING BEHAVIOR DISABILITIES

Norris G. Haring, Editor

Foreword by James M. Kauffman

Contributing Authors:
Norris G. Haring, University of Washington
John Jewell, Highline School District
James Kauffman, University of Virginia
Thomas Lehning, Education Law Project
Margaret J. McLaughlin, University of Maryland
Hill M. Walker and Ted R. Fabre, University of Oregon
Gregory J. Williams, Pacific Lutheran University

Assisted by:
Michael Boer, Assistant Editor
Susan Lewis, Word Processing Operator
Jane A. Kortemeier, Expediter

UNIVERSITY OF WASHINGTON PRESS
Seattle and London

Assessing and managing behavior disabilities / Norris G. Haring, editor; foreword by James M. Kauffman.
     p.   cm.
Includes bibliographies and index.
ISBN 0-295-96563-0. ISBN 295-96545-2 (pbk.)
1. Behavior disorders in children–United States. 2. Problem children–Education–United States. I. Haring, Norris Grover, 1923-   .
LC4802.A77 1987   87-16008
371.93–dc19   CIP

ACKNOWLEDGEMENTS

These acknowledgements apply to the extensive work involved in the SBD study and the preparation of two major reports to the Office of the Superintendent of Public Instruction. During the preparation of this report, working committees were organized for the purpose of examining the results, discussing additional areas of concern, studying the implications, and formulating the recommendations. The members of these working committees contributed a significant amount of time and their efforts have substantially strengthened this report.

Identification, Eligibility, and Assessment

Mike Jacobsen, Chair	William Moore
Rick Fuhrman	Christy Perkins
Virginia Hardiman	Donald Ray
Blanch LeBlanc	Dick Swenson

Comprehensive Management, Staff Development and Training

Judy Larson, Chair	Joe Harwood
Susan Ballard	C.M. Higby
Kirby Cleveland	Vern Leidle
Cliff Christiansen	Bill Lenth
Del Cross	William Moore
Kathryn Fantasia	Richard Neel
Genevieve Frankenberg	David Peterson
Karen Gross	Jan Thomas

Interagency Services

Paul Lichter, Chair	Paul Peterson
Cliff Christiansen	Carl Plonsky
John Dunne	Gary Snow
Faye Fuchs	Don Whitney
Mel Mangum	

Parent Advocacy

Renee Nowak, Chair	Dorothy Fouty
James Affleck	Martha Gentili
Mary Christie	Cecile Lindquist

OSPI Staff

Judy Schrag	Greg Kirsch

Special thanks to Rich Cole, Cliff Christiansen, Don Whitney, and Dick Swenson from ESD 121 and ESD 101 for serving as hosts for the Best Practices Colloquium.

Special thanks also to Cecile Lindquist, Chairperson of the SBD Task Force; Del Cross, Assistant Chairperson of the SBD Task Force; and James B. Pruess for assistance in manuscript preparation.

TABLE OF CONTENTS

FOREWORD: SOCIAL POLICY ISSUES IN SPECIAL EDUCATION AND RELATED SERVICES FOR EMOTIONALLY DISTURBED CHILDREN AND YOUTH[1]

James M. Kauffman

With respect to special education for emotionally disturbed children, there is today one overarching social policy issue. This issue rests on the problem of definition, and it involves this question: Can the right of all disturbed children to special education be assured by government decree? My belief is that that right cannot be guaranteed and that attempts to guarantee it are and will invariably be sham. My reasons for believing that the guarantee is necessarily sham are these: The definition of emotional disturbance is arbitrary; the current federal definition is very seriously flawed; the identification of disturbed children is subjective and somewhat unreliable even with the best definition one can construct; and the rights of handicapped persons present a set of policy problems that is essentially different from those presented by the rights of more objectively definable minority groups whose distinguishing characteristics are irrelevant to their participation in social institutions.

Current policy does not assure all disturbed children an appropriate education. The central issues involving definition, mandated services, and legal rights effectively preclude well-reasoned consideration of other policy questions, such as those regarding the nature of special education services, teacher training, and research. Answers to policy questions regarding services, training, and research are always hopelessly ambiguous when the definition of the population to be served is ambiguous and the children are unreliably identified.

The Arbitrariness of Definition

Emotional disturbance presents a peculiar set of problems for policy makers because it is, probably to a greater extent than any other type of exceptionality, a figment of social convention. Perhaps because psychiatry has been extremely influential in the formation of public attitudes and social policy, creating an assumption that "disturbed emotions" and "mental illness" are disease entities, current social policy does not reflect the arbitrariness of the definition of emotional disturbance. Scull (1975) has described how the medical profession gained control over the designation and management of certain types of social deviance during the 19th century, eventually fixing in the public mind the notion that much troubling social behavior is attributable to physiological causes or arcane intrapsychic features and is treatable only by medical science. But it is abundantly clear that emotional disturbance is not a disease in any usual sense of the term–it is not a separate, distinct entity that invades a person or can be assessed reliably without reference to the environment in which a person lives. Rather, it is, as suggested elsewhere (Kauffman, 1979, 1981a; Kauffman & Kneedler, 1981), a phenomenon involving complex interactions among what a person does, how that person perceives and evaluates his or her own behavior and the environment, and how the environment responds. And it is the failure to come to grips with this central problem of definition or description of emotional disturbance that leads to the primary policy issues today.

Conceptual confusion and disagreement have always been rife among professionals who deal with disturbed children. The lack of consensus about what the problem of such children really is and what can or should be done about it has been highlighted by numerous writers and several major projects, including the Conceptual Project in Emotional Disturbance (Rhodes & Head, 1974; Rhodes & Tracy, 1972a, 1972b) and the Project on the Classification of Children (Hobbs, 1975a, 1975b). Perhaps Rhodes and Paul have written the most succinct statement of the difficulty faced by scholars and policy makers:

> The epiphenomenal problem of deviance is complex and the definitions that exist are many. Each time a group of special children gain social and professional attention, a plethora of definitions of the problems of these children follow. The inconsistency is not, as is typically thought, simply in the definitions but rather in the primary view of the world from which the definition is derived. (1978, p. 137)

The differences among the world views of various influential individuals and groups are reflected both in terminological chaos and in current social policy that is starkly unsuccessful in meeting the needs of most disturbed children. There is no standard terminology for the problems of disturbed children or even for the general category "Seriously Emotionally Disturbed." In fact, it is not uncommon to hear extensive discourses on the differences between "emotional disturbance" and "behavior disordered" or between "emotional disturbance" and "social maladjustment." Moreover, the rules and regulations related to PL 94-142 contain, in the definition of seriously emotionally disturbed, an attempted distinction between emotional disturbance and social maladjustment. Certainly children can and do exhibit social deviance in many different ways. Nevertheless, attempts to distinguish between groups designated by many of the common labels for social deviance, including socially maladjusted and seriously emotionally disturbed, are useless (or worse) in formulating social policy.

Flaws in the Federal Definition

The problems of definition and terminology deserve close scrutiny because they are the beginning points for building a social policy. Current policy derives from a definition, with certain modifications, offered by Bower (1969). The definition of seriously emotionally disturbed included in federal rules reads as follows, with significant addenda to Bower's definition indicated by italics:

(i) The term means a condition exhibiting one or more of the following characteristics over a long period of time and to a marked degree *which adversely affects educational performance*:

    (a) An inability to learn which cannot be explained by intellectual, sensory, or health factors;

    (b) In inability to build or maintain satisfactory relationships with peers and teachers;

    (c) Inappropriate types of behavior or feelings under normal circumstances;

    (d) A general pervasive mood of unhappiness or depression; or

    (e) A tendency to develop physical symptoms or fears associated with personal or school problems.

(ii) *The term includes children who are schizophrenic or autistic. The term does not include children who are socially maladjusted, unless it is determined that they are seriously emotionally disturbed.* (Federal Register, 42(163), August 23, 1977, p. 42,478)

Bower's definition is probably as useful as any that has been written to date. It lists five characteristics that are likely to result in a child receiving a deviance label, and so it is useful in providing a general description of child behavior that is of concern to adults and that results in an educational handicap. But such description is not a sufficient basis for a social policy that mandates intervention for every disturbed child because it does not provide an unambiguous statement of who is and who is not disturbed. Consider, for example, the subjective interpretation that is required by some of the key terms and phrases in the definition: "to a marked extent," "over a long period time," "satisfactory interpersonal relationships," "inappropriate," "pervasive," and "tendency."

The addenda to Bower's definition do not clarify anything. They are, in fact, redundant and obfuscatory. The addition of the clause "which adversely affects educational performance" is particularly puzzling. It is redundant with characteristic (a), "An inability to learn ..." if educational performance is considered to mean academic achievement. Furthermore, it seems extremely unlikely that a child could exhibit one or more of the characteristics listed to a marked degree and for a long time without adverse effects on academic progress. But what of the child who exhibits, let us say, characteristic (d), "A general pervasive mood of unhappiness or depression," and is academically advanced for his or her age and grade? If educational performance is interpreted to mean academic achievement, then the child would seem to be excluded from the category of seriously emotionally disturbed. If, on the other hand, educational performance is interpreted to include personal and social satisfaction in the school setting, then the clause is superfluous.

At the outset, then, the federal addendum to part (i) of the definition confuses the issue of the type of problem that should be the concern of special educators. But an even greater confusion is created by part (ii) regarding schizophrenia and autism[2] (i.e., childhood psychosis), and social maladjustment in relation to serious emotional disturbance. It is clearly inconceivable that a psychotic child would not be included under the definition; any such child will exhibit one or more of the five characteristics, especially (b) and/or (c), to a marked degree and over a long period of time. Hence, the addendum is unnecessary.

One is forced to conclude that the federal definition is, if not claptrap, at least dangerously close to nonsense. It is not surprising that social policy based on such a definition is problematic. Two questions, then, present themselves: (a) Could the definition be significantly improved? (b) Would an improved definition resolve the social policy problems?

Definitions and the Problem of Identification

The federal definition could be improved considerably by omitting the addenda to Bower's characteristics. Removal of the addenda would eliminate the logical inconsistencies, terminological confusion, and redundancies, but it would not eliminate the most fundamental problem–the fact that emotional disturbance is whatever we choose to make it. This central problem is not unique to emotional disturbance. It is fundamental and unresolvable problem in mental retardation, learning disabilities, and other conditions defined by social convention; and it is a more obvious problem in the case of milder forms of social deviance. The problem in mental retardation was described pungently by Blatt:

> The most recent, little appreciated but astonishing revision of the American Association of Mental Deficiency definition of mental retardation to include theoretical eligibility–i.e., psychometric retardation–to from one to two standard deviations on the "wrong" side of the mean literally revolutionized the incidence, prevalence, and concept of mental retardation, all with the simple stroke of Herbert Grossman's pen. We cannot redefine measles, or cancer, or pregnancy with so easy and such external procedures. The Grossman Committee, sitting around a conference table, reduced enormously the incidence of mental retardation, never having to "see," or "dose," or deal with a client, only having to say that, hereinafter, mental retardation is such and such, rather than this or that. What, then, is mental retardation? (1975, p. 414)

The fact that emotional disturbance has no objective reality–like mental retardation, it is whatever we choose to make it–makes a social policy that mandates special services for all disturbed children and exacts penalities for noncompliance a tragic mockery. This would not necessarily be the case if there were highly reliable means of measuring the extent to which the children meet an arbitrary behavioral standard–that is, the problem is not inherent only in the arbitrariness of the definition, but also in the difficulty in determining whether a given individual meets a standard set by the definition.

A definition can be arbitrary, yet serve social policy purposes well. For example, 18 years and older arbitrarily defines the population that is voting age today, and the former arbitrary standard of 21 years was negated. But there is seldom serious doubt about whether or not a given individual is a certain age. Were the determination of age an unreliable process or were a much less objective criterion (e.g., "social maturity") chosen as the standard for defining the voting population, then a different set of policies regarding voter registration and voting rights would be required. The definition of emotional disturbance cannot be reduced merely to a set of objectively observable behaviors; subjective judgment of how the child functions in a given environment is always required (Kauffman, 1981a).   Hence, unreliability in identification can never be completely eliminated.

Definition, Identification, and Rights

The civil rights movement swept up the cause of the handicapped in the 1970s. Civil rights concerns led ultimately to the propositions of Section 504 and PL 94-142, some of which now appear to be untenable. The civil rights movement fostered the notion that any minority, however defined, can be rationally and responsibly guaranteed its rights, however its rights are defined. Thus, today we have a policy guaranteeing the right to appropriate education ("appropriate" being very ill defined) for populations that are defined in practice primarily by the exigencies of the moment. Special education for seriously emotionally disturbed children is guaranteed under PL 94-142, not because the population is well defined, but rather because the civil rights movement could not tolerate the exclusion of any population of the handicapped, no matter how poorly defined or how undefinable and no matter how absurd the notion that an ill-defined group can be assured its peculiar rights by the coercive pressure of government.

The implementation of civil rights legislation is a complex and arduous task. In cases involving minorities or other groups whose definition and identification are relatively unambiguous and whose members seldom can pass as members of a different class (e.g., races and sexes), civil rights can perhaps be effectively guaranteed by law. A new and complex dimension is added to the problem of civil rights implementation, however, when the very identification of an individual as a member of a special population or class (i.e., in "legalese," a "suspect class" deserving special protection of the law) is agreeable. Judgments about a child's behavior that lead to his identification as seriously emotionally disturbed are, unlike those defining race and sex, necessarily both arbitrary and subjective. Not only must one consider the accuracy of an individual's identification, but also the consequences of such identification. Identification of the child as disturbed bestows certain rights upon him (e.g., the right to an IEP, to due process hearings, to education in the least restrictive environment), whereas failure to identify him affords no special protection of the law, the assumption being that if he is not a handicapped child, then his rights are already sufficiently protected by laws governing the education of nonhandicapped children. The intent of Section 504 and PL 94-142 may have been to guarantee the rights of all seriously emotionally disturbed and other handicapped children to special education. But it will be particularly difficult, if not impossible, to fulfill that guarantee for emotionally disturbed children because their identification is subjective and can be avoided by school officials when it is in their own best interests to do so.

Effects of Current Policy and a Possible Policy Change

Given that handicapped children must be identified in order to receive special protection of the law and appropriate education and related services, but also that identification is a subjective and unreliable process, what is the result of a policy that not only requires identification of all disturbed children but demands as well that all identified children be served? The result is a disasterous hypocrisy. It cannot be otherwise. One must consider that current policy emphasizes punishment for noncompliance, not reward for approximations of full compliance. To require school officials to be perfectly candid about the number of emotionally disturbed children in their schools is to require their self-incrimination. Consider the facts that have been presented more extensively in other sources (e.g., Grosenick & Huntze, 1979; Kauffman, 1980, 1981a; Magliocca & Stephens, 1980). First, prevalence studies indicate that 2% is an extremely conservative estimate of the percentage of school age children and youth who are reasonably considered to be emotionally disturbed, yet only about one-third of that percentage (i.e., about 0.7%) are being served by special education–in spite of the fact that the law says that every handicapped child must be served.3 A conservative estimate of the additional cost of serving 2% of the school age population as emotionally disturbed is $2.3 billion per year, not more than 40% of which would be provided by the federal government. Even if the funds were made available, school officials could not find adequate personnel to staff the programs–the trained personnel do not exist and cannot be quickly obtained at any price.

In short, current policy has not resulted in services for anywhere near the number of disturbed children we have good reason to believe need special intervention. Our present policy does not take into consideration the arbitrary nature of the definition of emotional disturbance. It ignores the fact that most disturbed children can be classified as disturbed or normal for administrative convenience or out of necessity. It is blind to the fact that there are neither resources of money nor of trained personnel to serve all children who could reasonably be identified as disturbed. And it relies almost totally on coercion, on threatened negative consequences, to obtain a semblance of compliance with the law, a contingency system certain to foster avoidance or denial. It forces school officials to close their eyes to the needs of children if they don't have the resources to serve them, because to recognize the need without providing the appropriate service is to risk losing everything in the way of federal support. The policy is analogous to telling the destitute parents of a large family of hungry children who are receiving grants of food that they must feed all their children well, for if it is found that one of the children is hungry and not being fed, then all the food grants will be withheld. Under such circumstances, what would rational parents do if they had a hungry child and no more food? Probably they would vehemently deny their child's hunger to any inquirer. It is tragic that our current social policy regarding education of the handicapped is not more humane and consistent with principles of positive behavior management.

Social policy could be changed to support the growth of services for the emotionally disturbed, and services for other categories of mild and handicapped as well. Such a policy change should involve removal of the requirement of service for every child who has been identified as handicapped. Threats of withdrawal of funds or of other sanctions would be reserved for those cases in which there was an obvious lack of good faith effort to identify and serve disturbed children. Incentives for serving identified children would be provided. Such a policy would not guarantee service to all handicapped children. But as we have seen, such a policy change would be no great loss because the guarantee of appropriate service for every disturbed child is by necessity a sham. A more realistic and positive approach is to set goals and reward approximations of achieving them.

Policies on Intervention, Training, and Research

All indications are that the majority of emotionally disturbed children are not being served by special education (Kauffman, 1980, 1981a, 1981b). Most of them remain in regular classes with regular teachers who have no special training in how to deal with persistently disordered behavior. Under these circumstances it may seem necessary to formulate policies regarding intervention strategies, personal preparation, and research. But until the more fundamental issues of definition and mandated services are resolved, other issues are academic. Here, too, one faces a great dilemma: Lack of a clear policy also can have very undesirable outcomes. Social policy, as embodied in the law and judicial process, and behavorial science appear to have the common goal of enhancing the social order, but they often come into conflict in practice; legal victories ostensibly based on scientific evidence can have adverse effects on the very individuals they were designed to benefit (Baumeister, 1981; Townsend & Mattson, 1981). Thus, good intentions on the part of policy makers and behavioral scientists do not guarantee an ultimate outcome that is beneficial.

Townsend and Mattson (1981) have suggested that in the development of policy regarding the rights of the handicapped one must consider several interconnected sources of information and opinion: public attitudes, personal satisfaction, science and technology, laws and judicial interpretations, and political coalitions. To the extent that any one of these sources and its relationships to the others are ignored, social policy is likely to be unsuccessful. In the area of emotional disturbance as well as in special education in general, we have not fully considered the complexity of the problems we face in formulating policy that will be maximally beneficial but cannot work because they fail to account for the realities of others' perceptions, needs, and capabilities. In formulating such policy it would be prudent to think more carefully than we have in the past about the interests, perceptions, and likely reactions of people outside our professional enclave.

References

Baumeister, A. A. (1981). The right to habilitation: What does it mean? *Analysis and Intervention in Developmental Disabilities, 1*, 61-74.

Blatt, B. (1975). Toward an understanding of people with special needs. In J.M. Kauffman & J.S. Payne (Eds.), *Mental retardation: Introduction and personal perspectives*. Columbus, OH: Charles E. Merrill.

Bower, E. M. (1969). *Early identification of emotionally handicapped children in school* (2nd ed.). Springfield, IL: Charles C Thomas.

Bower, E. M. (1982). Defining emotional disturbance: Public policy and research. *Psychology in the Schools, 19*, 55-60.

Grosenick, J. K. & Huntze, S. L. (1979). *National needs analysis in behavior disorders*. Columbia: University of Missouri, Department of Special Education.

Hobbs, N. (Ed.). (1975a). *Issues in the classification of children* (Vols. 1 & 2). San Francisco: Jossey-Bass.

Hobbs, N. (1975b). *The futures of children*. San Francisco: Jossey-Bass.

Kauffman, J. M. (1979). An historical perspective on disordered behavior and an alternative conceptualization of exceptionality. In F. H. Wood & K. C. Lakin (Eds.), *Disturbing, disordered, or disturbed? Perspectives on the definition of problem behavior in educational settings*. Minneapolis: University of Minnesota, Department of Psychoeducational Studies.

Kauffman, J. M. (1980). Where special education for disturbed children is going: A personal view. *Exceptional Children, 46*, 522-527.

Kauffman, J. M. (1981a). *Characteristics of children's behavior disorders* (2nd ed.). Columbus, OH: Charles E. Merrill.

Kauffman, J. M. (1981b). Historical trends and contemporary issues in special education in the United States. In J. M. Kauffman & D.P. Hallahan (Eds.) *Handbook of special education.* Englewood Cliffs, NJ: Prentice-Hall.

Kauffman, J. M. & Kneedler, R. D. (1981). Behavior disorders. In J. M. Kauffman & D. P. Hallahan (Eds.), *Handbook of special education.* Englewood Cliffs, NJ: Prentice-Hall.

Magliocca, L. A. & Stephen, T. M. (1980). Child identification or child inventory? A critique of the federal design of child-identification systems implemented under PL 94-142. *Journal of Special Education, 14,* 23-36.

Rhodes, W. C. & Head, S. (Eds.). (1974). *A study of child variance* (Vol. 3: Service delivery systems). Ann Arbor: University of Michigan.

Rhodes, W. C. & Tracy, M. L. (Eds.). (1972a). *A study of child variance* (Vol. 1: Theories). Ann Arbor: University of Michigan.

Rhodes, W. C. & Tracy, M. L. (Eds.) (1972b). *A study of child variance* (Vol 2: Interventions). Ann Arbor: University of Michigan.

Scull, A. T. (1975). From madness to mental illness: Medical men as moral entrepreneurs. *Archives of European Sociology, 16,* 28-251.

Townsend, C. & Mattson, R. (1981). The interaction of law and special education: Observing the emperor's new clothes. *Analysis and Intervention in Developmental Disabilities, 1,* 75-89.

US Education Department. (1977). *Federal Register, 42* (163). Washington D.C.: US Government Printing Office.

Notes

[1]This article originally appeared in Margaret M. Noel and Norris G. Haring (Eds.), (1982), Progress or Change: Issues in Educating the Emotionally Disturbed, Volume 1: Identification and Program Planning; Seattle: University of Washington, Program Development Assistance System; produced under US Department of Education contract no. 300-79-0062; ERIC Document Reproduction Service ED 229 948.

[2]Federal rules and regulations have been changed. Autism has become a subcategory under "Other Health Impaired" rather than under "Serious Emotional Disturbance." Bower (1982) recently noted some of the policy problems presented by the exclusion of autism and social maladjustment.

[3]A report of the U.S General Accounting Office published in September 1981, Disparities Still Exist in Who Gets Special Education, indicated that

special education services for the majority of emotionally disturbed children are inadequate or nonexistent.

PREFACE

This volume was prompted initially by serious concerns expressed from members of the Washington Council of Administrators of Special Education and the Washington Association of School Administrators about the education of students with behavior disabilities in Washington State. These concerns were presented to Drs. Judy Schrag and Greg Kirsch of the office of the Superintendent of Public Instruction and they arranged funding for a comprehensive statewide study of the processes and procedures for identifying, classifying, placing, and serving children and youth who have serious behavior problems (SBD).

The study, which we will refer to as the SBD study, conducted over a period of eighteen months, involved opinions of administrators from 174 school districts including 2,542 (84%) of the 3,400 SBD students in the state. From these results, the project staff developed additional questionnaires designed to yield more detailed information. This considerably more intensive study involved interviews and questionnaires administered to a representative sample of all the districts in the state.

The administrators' questionnaire covered the topics of state and federal laws and definitions, assessment strategies, program settings, relationships with nonschool agencies, theoretical approaches, needs of students with mild/moderate behavior disabilities, inservice training priorities, and model practices. The special education teachers' questionnaire addressed the student population served, support services, curricula and materials used, assessment and evaluation procedures, intervention strategies, inservice training needs, model practices, and suggested improvements. The third questionnaire was designed for and addressed to the assessment/support personnel. The fourth questionnaire was sent to regular education personnel. This instrument was designed from the one used by special education teachers.

Following the systematic analyses carried out from the results of the questionnaires, certain target questions were used in a series of intensive in-person interviews with administrators, teachers, and support personnel, including school psychologists, school social workers, and counselors from a representative sample of school districts which were currently providing special services for SBD students. The results of these intensive interviews confirmed the results of the four questionnaires and served to validate those results.

The analyses of responses from the surveys revealed that we have significant needs in the following four areas:

1. A need for agreement in regard to identification and classification.

2. A need to develop and implement a statewide comprehensive assessment procedure.

3. A need to develop and implement a statewide comprehensive management plan.

4. A need to identify the nature, content, and dissemination methods of training for school staff.

Following the completion of the study, Judy Schrag has appointed Claudia Partlow coordinator for the serious behavior disability area who, in turn, has appointed a task force consisting of key members of the SBD advisory committee. The task force has met and is planning strategies for implementing many of the recommendations from the study.

This publication, then, is a response to the need to identify the nature, content, and dissemination of best practices which are available and which are known to improve conditions and provide more effective intervention. The body of this volume has been organized into two parts. Part I presents an overview and history of the classification and education of students with serious behavior disorders, the study itself, and a thorough discussion of the implications of the study to the organization and administration of services by John Jewell. Part II presents a careful selection of procedures and methodologies that teachers, administrators, and support personnel should find helpful in dealing with these students in educational environments.

The second half of this work begins with Walker's chapter on assessment. One of the most controversial issues in the study of behavior disorders is the identification of the population of concern. Drs. Walker and Fabre have reviewed the current and historical practices in assessment in the schools. The authors question many of the assumptions that currently influence assessment with the behaviorally disordered. They believe that some of these assumptions inhibit the use of tactics which are more functional as well as accurate and reliable in assessing these students. The authors follow this by a procedure that offers promise to the assessment of behavior disorders.

Following the chapter on assessment, Dr. McLaughlin's presentation includes an overview of public school programs for the behaviorally disordered. McLaughlin's chapter focuses sharply on the nature of public school education for this population. This chapter discusses the theoretical diversity that exists in the programming of the behaviorally disabled student. Further, the chapter offers an excellent discussion of general programming efforts as well as an overview of the major conceptual models that have developed within special education. Finally, examples of current programming strategies along with observations regarding future directions are discussed.

The Williams chapter gets right down to earth with the presentation of a series of vignettes which illustrate several behavior problem students. In each case, practical classroom strategies are implemented with varying degrees of success. Teachers should find this chapter particularly helpful as they plan interventions for their integrated behaviorally disordered students.

Finally, the Lehning chapter provides a knowledgeable presentation of a system for responding to the educational requirements of these individuals including discussions of: (1) types of alternative living settings, (2) service delivery systems and programs, (3) coordinating and administering services, and (4) a comprehensive management system for serving these individuals.

Norris G. Haring

ASSESSING AND MANAGING BEHAVIOR DISABILITIES

OVERVIEW

Norris G. Haring

Almost all students have behavior problems at some time during their lives. They may be short-term, or last a year or so. They may affect a small part or many aspects of their lives. Behavior problems from time to time are very common, but when the behavior disorders become chronic, and when maladaptive behavior occurs daily or intensely, it becomes a real problem for teachers, parents, and peers.

Strategies for intervening with and managing behavior disabilities are essential for educators and parents if educational programs are to be effective. Concensus on the theories of treatment and procedures for assessment and intervention is far from being achieved among professionals in special education, which creates more confusion about management of the problem than exists with other handicapping conditions. Our position generally is that what is good for educational progress is also good for social and emotional growth. Instructional programs that result in achievement and self-management are also therapeutic (Haring & Phillips, 1962). Clinical remediation of behavioral problems need not be established as an antecedent to education. The classroom, combined with a positive, supportive environment with steady progress in performance, can offer a major source of behavioral remediation.

During the past 30 years, various theoretical approaches to educating the behaviorally disabled have emerged, increasing the number of educational programs and treatment options. Out of these models have come a number of important perceptions that have influenced the development of educational service programs. These include the concept of structure and the effectiveness of direct behavioral intervention as well as a recognition of the importance of the student's family and the total ecology or environment (Kauffman, 1985).

The years of research and development have resulted in a large body of literature as well as the establishment of a separate, albeit not necessarily distinct, field within special education. Despite the amount of work that has been done, special education for the behaviorally disabled has been plagued with problems. Among these are what label should students whose behavior is maladaptive be given, and how should they be defined? The terms used to describe this population are numerous. Among these, the most commonly used are: seriously emotionally disturbed, behaviorally disordered, and emotionally impaired. Definitional problems, with the attendant difficulty in identification, seem to present the greatest obstruction to providing full educational services to these students (Kauffman, 1985).

Irrespective of the terminology and the concerns about eligibility, all professionals recognize that the needs of these students, as well as the challenges faced by the educational systems that must develop programs for them, are formidable and real. The concept of this volume has grown out of the concerns expressed by teachers and program administrators who work with the behaviorally disabled. Their concerns have focused on three major areas.   First are the problems of identification and assessment–for determining eligibility for services as well as for developing educational programs that address social, emotional, and academic needs.   Second, concerns centered on the organization of services, particularly in light of the diverse needs of the behaviorally disabled. The problems of dealing, within a public school program, with disordered families and community disruptions are frequently mentioned.   The third area is the lack of agreement among the various state agencies to cooperate with one another to provide full services. Other agencies are willing to say these students are of school age, so they are the schools' problem.

Separation of the emotional and social problems of behaviorally disabled students from their academic needs would disregard the basic principles of education. While the classroom has been transformed to provide a benign learning environment, these individuals need to have the positive aspects of education extended throughout the special services available outside the classroom.   A comprehensive system of management for intervention, coupled with the establishment of general partnerships with parents and service professionals, enables a systematic order to permeate their experiences. Through the continuous coordination of extended educational services, these children can be influenced by educational reality that extends through all facets of their lives.   The disparity between home life and educational instruction can be removed (Kauffman, 1985).

Student Profiles

From a very large perspective it is possible to classify all children and youth into two subcategories.   One is that large group who adapt to problems and conflicts they experience from very early on by consistently using an externalizing strategy. The second large subcategory is that group that cope by internalizing their problems (Walker, Severson, & Haring, 1985). An example of each is included below.[1]

Debbie: "A Typical ED Child"?

Debbie is 15 years old and currently lives in a private residential facility for emotionally disturbed children. Her history is marked with a number of placements, including both special and regular education settings. Her parents and brother reside in a large, suburban upper-middle-class community on the East Coast, reputed to have an excellent public school system.

Debbie's mother described her daughter as "a typical disturbed child" in that her behavior was, and is, totally unpredictable and inconsistent across program placements, management plans, and individual people. Despite the behavioral extremes and the learning problems, it was difficult for anyone to diagnose Debbie's problem. Her mother felt that something wasn't right by the time Debbie was 2 years old. For example, according to her mother, Debbie never crawled. At 8 1/2 months, she reportedly just stood up and walked. More noticeable were her severe temper tantrums and extreme activity. As her mother says, "She was into a lot of things and had to be closely watched." Debbie was adopted at 3 months of age and no prenatal histories were available. Therefore, while Debbie's mother saw some unusual development problems, there was no reason to suspect that anything was really wrong with her daughter.

Debbie's Case History

At age 3, Debbie was enrolled in a neighborhood nursery school where her behavior and motor problems soon became apparent. Debbie was clumsy; she also bit other children. The children quickly learned to avoid her, so that Debbie was basically socially isolated for the 2 years she managed to stay in nursery school.

At age 5, Debbie entered a public school kindergarten and quickly became a major management problem. Although she had been toilet trained for several years, she began to wet the bed and herself almost daily. This daily enuresis was to continue until Debbie was 13 years old. Debbie was also distractible, had a short attention span, and her clumsiness increased. The tantrums intensified, but only at home, and when Debbie's mother tried to talk to the kindergarten teacher, she was told to "just get on Debbie more."

In first grade, Debbie was referred to the reading specialist for evaluation because of problems in reading and math as well as for her motor problems. The reading teacher felt that Debbie had a "minor" perceptual motor problem, but recommended no follow-up or special assistance.

Neither Debbie's regular teacher nor her reading teacher saw any problem. Debbie was "a sweet little girl in school." Her mother, however, reported that Debbie was "totally unmanageable" at home.

The home behavior intensified during the next 2 years, and Debbie spent hours having tantrums. She practically had to be dressed by her mother and frequently was carried to school. Her academic performance in school was slipping, but the school did not consider her far enough below her peers to warrant an evaluation. Again, there were no behavior problems in school, although Debbie was considered withdrawn and had no friends. The school told the mother that Debbie's problems, if they even existed, were due to "problems in the home" and that the mother was not managing Debbie well and was too neurotic.

As Debbie's home behavior became more violent, she began to break things and punch holes in walls. Her mother became more adamant about having an evaluation. She went to Debbie's pediatrician, who told her that she needed to provide a more structured and controlled environment with time schedules and definite limits. At times Debbie would respond to the new limits, but at other times she would have an unprovoked major "blow up."

Her mother began to feel more and more insecure about her own parenting ability. "Everyone, even my own mother, felt that it was my fault. No one saw a problem. Finally, I said to my husband, 'If it's me, I need to know'." The parents contacted the pediatrician, who in turn recommended a private psychologist. Thus, at age 8, Debbie had her first psychological evaluation.

The psychological examination revealed a below-average IQ, which was considered inaccurate. Other test results led the psychologist to recommend a complete neurological exam. The sum of the evaluations was that the psychologist and neurologist agreed that Debbie was a "multiproblem child" who had definite signs of organic brain dysfunction and significant signs of a psychomotor seizure disorder. In addition, she was probably learning disabled. Debbie's mother said she was unsure and confused by all the tests and diagnoses, but "I was looking for anything that would stop the tantrums."

The parents had paid for both evaluations, but they decided to have a private educational evaluation through a local private special education center. The educational evaluation revealed that, at age 8, Debbie could neither spell nor write any letters past E. She was also functioning below the kindergarten level in reading and math. The evaluator felt that Debbie had developed highly refined coping skills and had managed to "cheat" or copy from her classmates. Furthermore, he felt that Debbie's IQ was probably above average, although she seemed to have some memory problems.

Armed with all of those test results, the parents confronted the public schools. Debbie was now at the end of third grade, and her parents wanted her retained at her grade level, but placed in a small, highly structured classroom and provided with tutoring. The public schools could not provide such a program, but agreed to an out-of-district placement in a private, albeit not special school. The parents accepted the placement and agreed to pay for the additional tutoring. At this same time, Debbie was placed on medication, initially Mellaril, and her parents began to send her to a private psychologist.

The first year at the new school, a repeat of third grade, basically went well as Debbie made some academic gains. But the social isolation remained, and the tantrums at home continued. Debbie had more EEGs done, each one showing some abnormal spiking, and medications were changed. Debbie's fantasy life, always present, became more apparent. She talked to herself often and began to play with things like garbage and scraps of paper. According to her mother, Debbie retreated more and more into her own world.

By age 10, after 2 years in the private school, the pressures began to show. Debbie's home tantrums increased markedly in frequency and intensity. Debbie's private therapist recommended special education, so her parents returned to the public schools to seek a special education placement. PL 94-142 was not yet in place and there were no state guidelines for placement. The only program for emotionally disturbed children in Debbie's school district was in a special school, and the school officials did not feel that Debbie had severe enough problems to be placed in the special school program. Not accepting the private psychological evaluation, the school requested their own psychological and educational evaluations, both of which agreed with the prior findings.

Thus, at age 11, Debbie was placed in the fifth grade class in the special school. The school staff immediately began to say that Debbie did not belong in the school and wanted her transferred to a regular public school program. However, the mother felt that Debbie was making progress and seemed to want to stay in the program; the parents resisted the transfer. "The staff kept telling us there was nothing wrong with our child. We alienated everyone at the school at this time. Teachers placated me and said they were intimidated by me or couldn't deal with me."

At the time that Debbie entered the special program, her mother began to attend parent groups run by a social worker on staff. Gradually, the mother reports, this social worker began to agree with both Debbie's mother and her private therapist about the seriousness of Debbie's problems. "She [social worker] kept telling the rest of the staff that she had observed

Debbie and worked with me, and the problems were real—complicated and subtle—but real."

Debbie completed the next year, attended summer school, and returned to the special school the next year for sixth grade. By this time, Debbie had matured sexually and by her mother's account was "gorgeous—a beautiful girl." She was placed into the sixth grade with 39 emotionally disturbed boys and no other girls. Her parents became concerned and asked about other placement options; they even contacted the superintendent of the district. The school's response was to do a computer search to find another girl for the program. None was found, however, and Debbie remained in the program.

By mid-year, Debbie began once again to deteriorate. Her academic progress began to slip and she continued to have no friends. Again, the violent home outbursts intensified, and Debbie began to refuse to go to school. Debbie's therapist felt that this pattern—one year of success followed by a deterioration in the second year—was due to the stress Debbie created for herself by trying to maintain an image as a good, compliant student.

In early January, the parents and the school met to discuss a placement for seventh grade. The school wanted to place Debbie in a partially mainstreamed program in a junior high school. The parents were concerned because, once again, Debbie would be the only girl in the program. They were also unsure of the amount of instructional time Debbie would receive, so they began to look at private schools with learning disabilities programs.

Debbie's outbursts at home were becoming more violent and destructive, particularly over the issue of going to school. One morning in the spring of that year, Debbie became particularly upset over having to go to school. She painted the floor with fingernail polish, overturned furniture, broke the telephone, and then attacked and bit her brother. When the distraught mother arrived at the school with her daughter, she happened to be met by the social worker who directed the parent group. Debbie's mother said that her account of the destruction and the violent outburst was met with the usual disbelief and suspicion. However, this time the social worker asked Debbie's mother to take her home and show her the damage. The social worker immediately went back to the school and began to advocate for Debbie's placement in a small, structured school environment, and confirmed the descriptions the parents had previously given.

By the next fall, PL 94-142 was in effect. The parents refused the junior high placement and requested alternative placement in a small local private school. The mother reported that the placement decision was made with no IEP meeting and that an IEP was sent to the parents for signature. Furthermore, there had been no multidisciplinary team evaluation.

Frustrated, the parents placed Debbie in the private school and then entered into administrative Due Process. At the review stage, the school began a thorough investigation into the family and home. The social worker was not allowed to testify, as she was considered too pro-family. The principal of the special school that Debbie had attended tried to convince the public schools to provide the money for the alternative placement. The psychologist who testified for the school district had never administered any tests to Debbie, nor in fact, was she certified as a child psychologist. According to actual records, she was a former psychiatric nurse who had no experience in child psychology.

Despite the testimony of Debbie's private psychologist and the support of professionals who had worked with Debbie, the county held firm, stating that "the junior high program is best for Debbie because her problems are not severe, and besides she is used to being the only girl among classes of boys." The parents lost at the first-level hearing, appealed for a state-level hearing and lost again. The mother reported that it cost the family $10,000 during that year for tuition, therapy, and attorney's fees. However, Debbie had done well in seventh grade and things were much calmer at home.

At the end of that year, the parents once again went to the public schools to discuss an eighth grade placement. Because things were going well, they wanted Debbie to remain in the private school, so they requested a full reevaluation. The school agreed and said they would have their "two top people" conduct the evaluation. This evaluation supported the parents and confirmed previous findings of neurological impairment and serious emotional disturbance with some learning disability. According to the mother, the whole attitude of the school people changed drastically after this evaluation. "We weren't treated like a plague anymore. The school was almost contrite."

An IEP meeting was held, the first ever, and the school offered placement in a learning disability program–reportedly against the advice of the teacher. The parents refused this placement and were prepared to ask for another hearing. Two weeks later, however, the public school, without explanation, agreed to provide for an out-of-district placement in the private school for one year only.

Thus Debbie, who was then 14 years old, began the eighth grade at her private school. However, all did not end well. In November the deterioration began again. Debbie's school behavior became worse, and she spent days at home crying, screaming, and begging not to go to school. The parents persevered until her theapist suggested hospitalization because of Debbie's "suicidal thoughts and wishes." The private school and the therapist recommended that Debbie be taken out of the program.

This time the public school responded quickly. They ordered a placement meeting immediately and recommended residential placement. Debbie remained at home until May while her parents and the public schools investigated residential options. Debbie was placed in an out-of-state residential program at public school expense. She has remained in this program for a year. Her parents feel that she is doing "OK," although there are still outbursts. She is making friends for the first time; however, she is not without problems—when she was home during her first vacation, she experimented with drugs and alcohol. In addition, although she was unlicensed, she took the family car without permission.

The family does not know what the future holds for Debbie or for them. They call her "a blessing in disguise" because they feel the family is stronger because they have had to work to survive. The mother also feels that it is only sheer luck that her older son, also adopted, is not on drugs, angry, or alienated. She feels that he lost out on much. "Debbie consumed our entire time and energy. We had to control her, get her to school, take her to doctors."

Although there is currently complete agreement and cooperation among the parents and the public school, the parents still feel angry about what they had to go through to secure appropriate services for Debbie. The mother wishes that they would have believed her or trusted her instead of trying to prove her wrong. She said the years of guilt were debilitating, and through it all, the school never looked at the whole situation, never attempted to investigate the problems. "They just assumed the problem was with us." Early on, Debbie's therapist told the parents that the only reason that Debbie was maintained in school and at home for so long was because of their support and effort. Lately, several other professionals have told the parents the same thing, and this has been reassuring.

When asked to make recommendations for improving parent-school relationships, Debbie's parents had strong opinions. The most important factor they cited was the need for emotional support. In particular, they mentioned the need for school staff to be trained to communicate with parents. School staff need to describe the problems or situations thoroughly, they need to be explicit about how they will deal with the problem, and they have to help the parents understand. The parents felt that the administration, in general, was unsupportive, but even worse, none of the teachers showed any understanding of Debbie or the complexity of her problems. They report that,

> All the teachers knew was behavior management. They focus on tantrums and acting out. They don't recognize tension, stress, or emotional states in children. The principal of Debbie's first elementary school once said to me that if she had thrown bricks they would have helped her.

According to Debbie's parents, a second major area that needs improvement is advocacy. They feel that the public schools should have someone on staff who can serve as an advocate, or at least objectively represent the interests of the child. This person should be someone who is not immediately involved with the child, because it is too dfficult for teachers and administrators to deal with errors or suggest reevaluations. Also related to advocacy, Debbie's parents stressed the need for educating parents about emotional disturbance, to remove the stigma and the guilt. Furthermore, parents need to develop communication skills and need to know what to ask of the schools.

Michael: "The Multiple Problem Child"

Michael, an only child, is 11 years old, physically healthy, intelligent, and is described by his mother as having a loving, generous, friendly, and inquisitive nature. He lives in a major city in the southern United States. He appreciates art, nature, architecture, history, and is a lover of books. He has an appreciation of and talent for music and plays the piano both for music therapy and for pure enjoyment. He has coordination and perceptual problems for which he receives occupational therapy.

Michael is described as fearful, anxious, nervous, timid, and having low self-esteem. He deals with these feelings by being bossy, by taking on the role of an adult, which alienates his peers, and occasionally by being aggressive. He is emotionally immature. When upset, he becomes verbally abusive. He falls apart, cries, hides in a corner, and brings more negative attention to himself. Mike has been diagnosed as having emotional disturbance (childhood schizophrenia), minimal brain dysfunction, hyperactivity, soft neurological signs, learning disabilities, visual-perceptual and motor handicaps, and multiple handicaps.

> Mike shows great courage each day, meeting the challenges even when the fear inside of him is at fever pitch. I have seen him face. summer camp day after day, knowing he would be taunted, knowing that he would have to face a swimming pool full of unruly boys and the ever-present bully ready to ridicule and torment. But he faces these nightmares at school, camp, scouts, and Sunday school again and again and manages, after the initial anger wears off, to keep a charitable heart for the ones inflicting pain. Last summer he was excluded from the second semester of camp because he hit one of his tormentors. It was a disappointment to be excluded after one and a half summers in a "normal" summer camp, but it was also a relief for us because he was spared the ordeal for the rest of the summer. We are deciding now about how he will spend his summer. His therapist feels, and we agree, that he needs exposure to other children and he needs to learn to manage his fears and handle his own problems. My heart aches when I think of what he goes through, but I know that someday he will be alone and will have to manage without our protection.

Mike does well academically and has the potential for superior academic performance. He has even been called "brilliant" by his teacher and by most of the people who have tested him.

Mike's Case History

Mike's mother reported that as an infant, Mike was alert and happy. Soon, however, little things began to disturb her. Mike was slow in turning over in bed, in sitting up, in crawling and in walking, but mostly he was extremely slow in talking. He did not speak until he was 3, except for a few words he mimicked. He did not initiate speech. Mike's mother repeatedly brought these delays to the attention of Mike's pediatrician and was told that he would "just grow out of it." She explained how Mike was not talking, how he looked through you when you were talking to him, how he banged his head, how he could not tolerate high pitched sounds like the vacuum, and how he was oblivious to other sounds. She also described his hyperactivity and the fact that she was insulted by every one of the nurses when Mike did not respond to their commands during office visits. When the pediatrician did not make any suggestions or diagnoses, Mike's mother became persistent. Finally, she was referred to a local speech and hearing center for evaluation.

The evaluation was incomplete because Mike was "not cooperative," although his hearing seemed to be normal. However, Mike was plagued by high fevers and ear infections until he was 3 years old, at which time drainage tubes were placed in his ears.

Mike's mother still considers that the pediatrician was a fine doctor who was just ill-equiped to recognize early signs of emotional disturbance and perhaps a little afraid of and repulsed by Mike's behavior. However, after 3years of wondering, Mike's mother struck out on her own. She wrote to Closer Look and began reading their newsletters, pamphlets, and other materials. These led her to other sources. She compiled two file cabinet drawers and several boxes of indexed information on organizations, legislative actions (and in some cases inactions), programs, books, laws, and research on the subject of emotional disturbance and learning disabilities. Despite her efforts, Mike's mother could find no programs or local information sources which pertained to children of Mike's age.

Finally she contacted the Director of the Developmental Disabilities Department at a local university medical center. The program was new, but the Director was very helpful. "I spoke to her about Mike's delayed speech, immature behavior, and other symptoms. She really seemed to understand and was not shocked or did not recoil–my hopes soared."

The evaluation at Developmental Disabilities was a drawn-out affair with appointments scheduled weeks apart with professionals from different disciplines. Mike had physical, dental, psychological, opthamological, and hearing examinations. He was given an educational evaluation and others that his mother cannot recall. The educational evaluation was the final appointment, and when it was over the examiner told his mother that Mike was learning disabled, not retarded–as she had feared–and was, in fact, very bright. A few weeks later, the parents met with the staff psychiatrist, who provided an interpretation of the evaluation.

The parents waited some time for the psychiatrist, who, when she arrived, had forgotten to bring any of Mike's test results. She gave the parents some general comments and diagnosed Mike as hyperactive and learning disabled. The sole recommendation was that Mike be seen by a social worker.

> She answered none of our questions adequately. We were given nothing in writing–no reports. Her attitude was one of superiority. She made us feel somehow at fault, but she did not explain how. This was our first encounter with such an attitude, but it has certainly not been our last.

During the next year and a half, Mike was seen by a social worker. He was never given a next appointment. Each time his mother had to call and convince the secretaries that the situation was serious and warranted an appointment. The appointments were always 1 to 2 months apart. The parents were never asked to talk to anyone about their feelings and were ignored or placated when they asked questions. Again, Mike's mother is not bitter. She feels that the social worker was a caring individual, but just did not understand Mike.

Later that year when Mike was 4, his pediatrician advised his parents to enroll him in a nursery school, hoping that contact with other children would help. After a month Mike was excluded from that nursery school for pushing other children who tried to make contact with him. The parents immediately enrolled him in another nursery school. The owner of this school, according to Mike's mother, was an intelligent and compassionate woman who understood children. She had patience with Mike and helped him a great deal. She worked with the Developmental Disabilities staff and when Mike was evaluated she was allowed to sit in on the staffing. The parents, however, were not allowed to attend. This exclusion would be encountered again and again. At the staffing it was decided to put Mike on Ritalin. He took the medication for about a week until his parents were called to the nursery because Mike was standing in a corner, glassy-eyed, frightened, and completely out of contact. Since that time, the parents have been told that Ritalin was totally inappropriate for Mike; they are grateful that they threw it away before it harmed him.

At this same time, the nursery home owner recommended that Mike's parents consult with another psychiatrist who was a friend of hers. This psychiatrist observed Mike in the nursery school and informed the parents that he was badly in need of help. He referred them to a church-affiliated social service clinic where he consulted, as the parents could not afford his regular fee, and prescribed a tranquilizer, Mellaril, for Mike. He accompanied Mike through the intake process. For the next 2 years Mike was seen by a social worker at the clinic twice a month. Again the parents were excluded and had only two meetings with the social worker during the entire time.

It was during this time that Mike was diagnosed as a "childhood schizophrenic." However, the parents were never given an explanation of the term. The mother, after years of searching the libraries and Mike's records, still says she has only a limited understanding of the implications of this diagnosis.

When the time came for Mike to go to school, his social worker recommended a local treatment center, which was a special, private school serving children with emotional problems and learning disabilities. The tuition was over $1,000 per month, but included the educational program and related services. In Mike's case this meant individual psychotherapy and family counseling.

At that time, because there were no programs for emotionally disturbed children, the state had funds available for private placements. Parents paid tuition on a sliding scale and the state provided the balance. However, many of the emotionally disturbed children were being sent to schools in other states. Mike's parents had him evaluated by the treatment center, enrolled him, and then applied for tuition support. It was then that the mother says she began her education in

> the cold, cold world of state politics, school board deceit and double talk, and bureaucratic red tape. I learned to recognize when I was being put off, put down, and when I was being lied to. Unfortunately, recognizing it is easier than doing something about it. The feelings of helplessness are overwhelming and serve to enforce the intimidation.

Mike's mother continued several months of what she called "game playing" with the school board. Finally, with school about to begin and no placement for Mike, his mother began to call the school board, the state special education director, local politicians, state legislators, and finally the governor's ofice. She had written letters to all of these people earlier, and many had contacted the school board, but still the school board took no action. She felt she was "begging" for services and describes that period as humiliating and very depressing.

The call to the governor apparently set things in motion, for the parents were informed that Mike could receive funds for the special school and so he was enrolled. However, for several months, the parents would receive conflicting letters—one saying Mike had tuition, another denying funds. Because of this uncertainty, the parents began to explore parochial schools. Mike was turned down at each school. Furthermore, Mike's mother felt that the various principals were totally unsympathetic. While they had programs for the mentally retarded, learning disabled, and neglected children, no one would take an emotionally disturbed child.

Mike's mother was particularly upset about the general insensitivity of the churches to their plight. Mike was even denied Sunday school in their own church beause of his behavior, and his mother had to arrange a special Sunday school class taught by a special education teacher from the congregation.

Mike was able to remain in the special school and did well. The principal and teachers were described by his mother as excellent and dedicated. Mike's teacher was very helpful to his parents. For the first time they were kept informed of Mike's progress, including his therapy. Also, the teacher spent much time helping them understand Mike and how to work with him. His mother said that she began to gain confidence in her ability to deal with Mike.

During Mike's second year at this school, PL 94-142 came into effect and the school board began to remove children from the private schools. Mike's mother became involved with other parents in an extensive lobbying effort to keep the schools open. They wrote letters, sent telegrams, and met with state legislators. They organized a number of fund-raising events, both to help the school and to create public awareness. Mike's mother remembers one meeting in particular. It was with the Assistant Superintendent of Special Education for the state who told the parents that certain state legislators were furious at them, that the name of their parent organization was too similar to another parent group and they probably were going to be sued, and generally intimidated and "bullied" the parents. Again Mike's mother said that she was humiliated and angry.

Despite the parents' efforts, the private treatment center closed, and Mike's parents had to face the ordeal of finding a placement in the public schools. A year before the closure of the private school, Mike's first IEP was done, which his mother describes as an "assembly-line" procedure. When the parents arrived for their appointment, they found the lobby full of waiting parents. Each parent was handed a form that essentially asked him or her to agree to a placement. There was no IEP nor was any placement specified. Mike's parents refused to sign and were told that an IEP meeting could not be held until Mike had an evaluation. When the meeting was held, the school board attempted to change Mike's diagnosis as well as his placement. However, the principal, teacher, and therapist from the private school were able to prevail and Mike was allowed to return to the private school.

As harrowing an experience as that was, Mike's mother said the next year's IEP meeting proved even more difficult. Despite the parents' efforts, the private school had closed. The parents had exhausted all of their options and had no choice but to try for the best possible placement in the public schools.

> We must have gained a reputation because they brought out their heaviest "guns." There were three or four supervisors present at our IEP, each with expertise in some related area pertinent to our case. We too had our heavy ammunition. We had the principal, Mike's two teachers, Mike's therapist, our counselor, Mike's private psychiatrist (who monitors his medication), and Mike's private occupational therapists. It was a grueling 3 hours of fighting on each point. We knew we had to compromise and compromise we did.

The parents agreed to provide private psychotherapy and occupational therapy as well as any family counseling. The school board agreed to place Mike in a new model school program in a neighboring school district, but the parents had to provide their own transportation. The schools did agree to provide minimal occupational therapy; however, this was inconsistent, and in a year Mike had only three sessions. Several years ago, during a meeting of a local parent organization, Mike's mother questioned a school board member about this issue of related services. She was told that parents should not expect "Cadillac treatment."

Mike remains in the public school program and is surviving. However, his mother feels that he is not performing well academically. While his grades are good, he is doing work that he did 3 years ago at his private school. Mike's mother feels that the special education students are not taken seriously and are not challenged academically. Not only are there academic problems with Mike's school program, but the general environment of the school is filled with violence, including students' use of knives and guns. Mike has suffered abusive taunting at the hands of schoolmates and his life has been threatened. Not only do Mike's parents fear for his safety, but even for their own when they pick him up from school. Mike's mother arrives at school 15 minutes before the end of the day to avoid encountering the general student body.

In addition, Mike's first home-room placement was into a class including violent behaviorally disordered children who had been in trouble with the police; one student was on parole. Mike has since been placed into a more appropriate home-room setting, but the overall school environment remains threatening.

Mike sees a private psychiatrist once a month to monitor his medication. After episodes involving detrimental side effects of various medications, Mike's parents have learned that medications must be diligently monitored, not only for behavioral effects, but also for potential physiological damage. He also has weekly therapy sessions with a private social worker. His parents pay for these services, and over the past few years have approached the school about providing therapy, but to no avail. Once, when they pushed the issue, they were told in a threatening manner that if Mike really needed these services so badly, he could be institutionalized. The threat of institutionalization was posed by various professionals to not only Mike's parents, but to other parents who also "pushed" the system for what they felt were appropriate services.

Overall, Mike's parents remain hopeful that effective treatment for Mike's condition will be discovered. However, they are bitter about what they see as lack of movement in the professional fields associated with mental illness. His mother comments:

> I am hurt by their apparent lack of caring. I am outraged by their lack of movement as a body of professionals to try to improve the conditions of the lives of their patients. They could do much to dispel the fear and hatred that the public feels for mental patients. This fear and hatred is demonstrated every day in movies, TV presentations, etc., which depict mentally ill patients inaccurately and with no compassion. They, in my opinion, discourage the joining together of families of mental patients to work for changes. But most important, some pressure needs to be put on government to provide programs that are needed. More money is spent on dental research than on the cause and cure for mental illness. Insurance is unfair to mental patients (our insurance pays one-half of one visit to the psychiatrist with a limit of $12.00 each month–12 per year only). Not one penny of the social worker's bill is paid and this is disgraceful. Mental illness is just that, an illness, but is treated like a crime. Even treatment for alcoholism is paid for by most insurance companies–surely a disease as debilitating as schizophrenia should be covered.

With respect to education professionals, Mike's mother considers that the major problem is with administrative personnel, most of whom she feels are ineffective and unwilling to help. "Mike has had some fine teachers, but the administrators are too concerned with their images, their budgets and their careers to care for the children." She also resents the lack of communication over the past years. The most helpful people have been those who are direct and honest. "It would have saved a lot of pain and perhaps meant more rapid progress if we had been dealt with as adults with honesty and candor. We would have liked it if the terms they were throwing at us had been explained."

Mike's parents have spent a great deal of time working with him at home. His mother reads to him daily as she has since he was 2 years old.

She spends several hours a day with him listening to music or playing. Mike is becoming more withdrawn, and it is more difficult to make contact with him, but his parents continue to keep him involved in scouting, concerts, movies, and exposing him to new experiences.

> I enjoy my child and even his illness has not diminished the joy and enrichment he has brought into my life. Yes, we do get tired of the therapy appointments, the problems with schools, the times when he is in crisis, the demand on our time, but he is a great kid and we enjoy having him in our lives–work and all. Having Mike, with his problems, was a factor in our decision not to have more children. We felt, and still feel, we have a responsibility to do the best we can for him. We try to keep a balance and sometimes it is hard, as it would be for any one-child family. We chose to have Mike, he was not an accident. So we are ready for the responsibility and we accept it. We enjoy every stage of his development, we savor every phase–raising a child is what we wanted to do. Yes, there is pain when we think about his future–Will he be able to have a life of his own? Will he be able to marry? Should he have children? Will we miss out on being grandparents? These things are painful to think about. But we have Mike now and we try to live now and do the best we can and try to have as happy a life as we can NOW.

The greatest concern for the parents at this time is for Mike's safety in school. They feel that he is vulnerable, and that the public school presents a life-threatening situation, filled with violence and abuse. This setting is totally inappropriate for Mike, characterized by his mother as "gentle and docile." Private and parochial schools offer no hope, as they do not have programs for emotionally disturbed children. Their next major concern is for his education. They feel that Mike is not being equipped to function in life. They fear that he will have no job skills and might not be able to be independent as an adult.

The foremost recommendation made by Mike's parents was for honest and open communication between schools and parents. They feel that parents should be trusted and not discounted. Professionals should learn to value parents' perceptions and experiences. In turn, parents need information so that they don't fall prey to "quacks" and fads. They also need to understand their rights and those of their children better. For if they are informed, parents can make better decisions and better judgments about what is best for their children. Children are parents' responsibility, not some school's or agency's, and parents cannot fulfill this responsibility if they remain ignorant.

Nature of the Problem

Teachers generally receive very little training in how to manage children with behavior problems in the regular classroom. Yet we see greater numbers of children with problem behaviors in the regular grades. The policy to integrate the mildly handicapped and some children with even more serious behavior problems in regular education has begun to significantly impact many classrooms with a wide variety of very difficult management conditions. In the past, social and emotional behavior disabilities have been thought to be beyond the responsibility of regular teachers. When unexpected and maladaptive behavior such as an attack on another child, the destruction of property, or persistent noncompliance occurs, this creates a serious upset to the normal proceedings of any classroom. Yet these incidents are occurring at an alarming rate in the schools. The loss of time for instruction under these circumstances is having a significant, measurable effect on the academic progress of students. The kinds of attention and the objectivity of information about the relationship between the child's behavior and the attention are critical in understanding the causes of maladaptive behavior and how to manage the environment and social exchanges to direct the child toward adaptive and productive behavior (Reeve & Kauffman, 1978).

Teachers do have a variety of theories and models to choose from to guide them to effect intervention; however, the practical application of these rather abstract guides has been disappointing in many instances. It is difficult to determine the exact reason for the poor results in the schools, but certainly a variety of conditions seem to be associated with the problems in managing behavior. The following is an abbreviated list of the problems teachers express:

1. Too many students with behavior disabilities are integrated in the classrooms without a reduction of class enrollment;

2. Adequate and reliable assessment information is lacking; such information is needed to guide the instructional program;

3. The inservice training is not adequate and often not relevant to the actual problems presented by having several students with behavior disabilities in regular classes;

4. There is a lack of effective, systematic strategies for teaching students with a wide variety of behavior disorders;

5. There is insufficient support from other disciplines which represent, or at least should represent, the expertise necessary to manage behavior disabilities;

6. The building administrators seem overwhelmed with the problems presented by these students and often suggest untried rather than effective changes;

7. The parents are unwilling, in many instances, to become involved and participate regularly in home/school cooperative intervention programs.

While these are only a few of the complaints teachers present, many of these problems can be responded to in productive ways. It has been shown that if we, as professional educators, support professionals, and parents, respond as well-organized intervention teams, almost all students can be educated in the schools with greatly improved results. The suggestions that appear in the pages of this volume have been tried with successful results by the authors or have been seen to be effective in practice within the classrooms we visited.

Definition

The majority of the categories within which the handicapped have been placed have more precise and objective definitions than those for behavioral disabilities. The mentally retarded, for example, can be defined by the results of measures of intellectual ability and social adequacy. Learning disabilities are slightly more complex; however, academic achievement plus a systematic, comprehensive analysis of performance patterns can provide substantial evidence of learning problems.

At present there are not reliable objective measures of emotional and/or behavioral disabilities. The closest approximations, at least for the purposes of education, are teacher-administered rating scales and teacher timed, recorded, and charted observations.

In addition to problems of definition presented by the lack of measurement of the disability, defining behavioral disabilities is complicated by different expectations for behavior established by different societies and cultures. Behavior that is adaptive and functional in one society may be considered disturbed by another. The norms for inner-city street behavior differ dramatically from those seen in middle-class suburbia. Certainly, social and cultural expectations need to be considered in defining behavior disabilities.

A survey of a number of definitions used by state departments of education (Cullinan & Epstein, 1979) revealed common components, as seen in the following child behaviors:

1. disorders of emotions and/or behavior,

2. interpersonal problems,

3. inability to learn or achieve at school,

4. behavior differing from a norm or age-appropriate expectation,

5. problems of long standing,

6. problems that are severe, and

7. a need for special education.

Certainly, among many definitions, the one which has had the greatest influence has been Eli M. Bower's (1969) definition. He defined "emotionally handicapped" as exhibiting one or more of the following five characteristics "to a marked extent, over a period of time."

1. an inability to learn which cannot be explained by intellectual, sensory, or health factors;

2. an inability to build or maintain satisfactory interpersonal relationships with peers and teachers;

3. inappropriate types of behavior or feelings under normal conditions;

4. a general, pervasive mood of unhappiness or depression;

5. a tendency to develop physical symptoms, pains, or fears associated with personal or school problems (pp. 22-23).

Bower's definition was included, with certain modifications (as discussed in Kauffman's preface to this volume), in the rules and regulations which serve as the basis for the implementation of PL 94-142, Section 121a.5.

In order to define and subsequently to identify these students, it is necessary to go beyond the way the behavior looks. The behavior of disabled students is topographically similar to the behavior of nonhandicapped students. Almost all students at one time or another do most of the things disabled children do. They laugh, cry, noncomply, flap their hands, hit others, bite themselves, write on their arms and hands, and destroy their work. There are, however, ways to discriminate the behavior of disabled students from the nondisabled:

1. Disabled children have long-standing problems.

2. The disabled student's behavior is grossly inappropriate for the time and the place in which it occurs.

3. The rate of occurrence of the maladaptive behavior is the most important distinguishing feature of the student's behavior.

4. The behaviors of the behaviorally disabled student are of greater or lesser magnitude/intensity than the nondisabled.

5. The behaviorally disabled child exhibits numerous problem behaviors.

Classification

Classifying the particular type of behavioral disability the child exhibits once the problem has been defined is many times more complex. Students are classified in terms of the category of handicapped such as mental retardation, visually impaired, and so forth. In addition, each handicap may be classified in what might be referred to as a subclassification. Problems even exist in finding agreement on what system is appropriate for education. Some of the problems which arise in developing a functional method of classifying these students are seen in the following:

1. The various systems now used for classifying behaviorally disabled children and youth have serious reliability and validity problems (i.e., behavior is classified differently from childhood to adulthood); different classifications may result from using different methods.

2. Classifications are useful when there is an established etiological basis–in the case of behavioral disabilities, a single cause is difficult to pinpoint.

3. In certain categories, legal terms, such as juvenile delinquent, runaway, incorrigible, or psychotic, are involved with the behavior disabilities.

4. The classification of a behavior disability may change as a child reaches adulthood such as in the case of autism to schizophrenia, which occurs quite often.

It is reasonable to say, for better or for worse, that the medical profession has developed more agreement in the classification of children's behavior disorders. There is an increasing trend toward the adoption of the *Diagnostic and Statistical Manual of Mental Disorders* developed by the American Psychiatric Association (DSM-III, 1980). Several categories in the DSM-III are used for children's disorders (see Table 1).

Table 1

DSM-III Categories for Disorders of Infancy, Childhood, and Adolescence

Behavioral (overt)
  Attention Deficit Disorder
    With hyperactivity
    Without hyperactivity
    Residual Type
  Conduct Disorder
    Undersocialized, aggressive
    Undersocialized, nonaggressive
    Socialized, aggressive
    Socialized, nonaggressive
    Atypical
Emotional
  Anxiety Disorders of Childhood or Adolescence
    Separation anxiety disorder
    Avoidance disorder of childhood or adolesence
    Overanxious disorder
  Other Disorders of Infancy, Childhood or Adolescence
    Reactive attachment disorder of infancy
    Schizoid disorder of childhood or adolesence
    Elective mutism
    Oppositional disorder
    Identity Disorder
Physical
  Eating Disorders
    Anorexia nervosa
    Bulimia
    Pica
    Rumination disorder of infancy
    Atypical eating disorder
  Stereotyped Movement Disorders
    Transient tic disorder
    Chronic motor tic disorder
    Tourette's disorder
    Atypical tic disorder
    Atypical stereotyped movement disorder
  Other Disorders with Physical Manifestations
    Stuttering
    Functional enuresis
    Functional encopresis
    Sleepwalking disorder
    Sleep terror disorder
Developmental
  Pervasive Developmental Disorders
    Infantile autism
    Childhood onset pervasive developmental disorder
    Atypical
  Specific Developmental Disorders

Prevalence and Head Count

"Prevalence" refers to estimated proportions of the student population based on surveys within a specified period of time. Estimates of the national prevalence of behavior disabilities vary from 1% to 20%. The available evidence indicates that the estimate of 2% is too conservative, although that figure has been used for more than 2 decades by the US Office of Special Education and Rehabilitative Services (OSERS). More recent estimates by Achenbach and Edelbrock (1981) and Cullinan, Epstein, and Kauffman (1986) would place the prevalance at 6% to 10%. However, based on reports of the service population, the US Office of Special Education Programs (SEP) is reducing the estimate of prevalence to a range from 1.2% to 2.0%.

"Head count" is not an estimate of the population; it is an actual count of the children with behavior disabilities being served during a particular reporting period. For example, OSERS reported that the total number of children and youth served under PL 94-142 and PL 89-313 during the 1980-81 school year was 349,788 which represented 8.3% of all handicapped individuals served. This represents 0.72% of the total population served between ages 5-17 years.

Many states have actually decreased the number of SBD students they are serving. Washington, for example, has reported serving 33% less students over the past few years, while during the same period the SEP reported a national increase of 25% in the population served. Obviously there are inconsistencies throughout the states in increases and decreases they have reported over the last few years in the number of children they have served. As we discussed earlier, some of the problems with these inconsistencies in head count are associated with the problems that are experienced by using several different and often contrasting definitions and classifications. In addition to that, some states may simply be maintaining SBD students who are manageable within regular classrooms.

These unserved students come primarily from two sources: (1) a large number of underserved students are coming from a population of children with serious behavioral disabilities who are known by the school district but who have not been specifically identified as a target of focus because the district does not have adequate facilities, trained personnel, and resources available to provide the service; and (2) another large source of unserved SBD students remain in regular education or have withdrawn from school and hence are not served or are largely underserved and are students who utilize internalizing strategies for coping with their problems. We predict that we will continue to underserve this population in the future until systematic screening and assessment procedures are standardized throughout the states and are widely used for identifying this population.

Educational Classifications

Unlike the medical discipline, education does not have a single classification system that prevails. In fact, educators use numerous terminology and classifications. An approach that has gained usage and does offer greater functional application involves identifying behavioral dimensions based upon clusters of highly intercorrelated behaviors (Kauffman, 1978). Based on a large number of studies using factor-analytic techniques, with data ranging from problem checklists to information obtained from life-history ratings and questionnaires, three behavior patterns emerge (Quay, 1975). These behavioral dimensions are:

1. Conduct problem: a tendency to express impulses against society.

2. Personality problem (neuroticism): a low self-esteem, social withdrawal, and dysphonic mood.

3. Inadequacy (immaturity): involving preoccupation, daydreaming, passivity, and inattention.

Apparently these dimensions are reasonably stable from early childhood through adolescence (O'Leary, 1972).

A very promising approach to a functional classification system is being developed by Hill Walker and his colleagues (Walker, Severson, Haring, & Williams, in press). This procedure, which ultimately leads to classification and placement, involves three stages of standardized screening, identification, and assessment. The first stage involves teachers ranking the children in their classes on two dimensions: externalizing and internalizing behaviors. In this stage, each student is rated separately on very critical behaviors in each of the two dimensions. Check lists are provided which include externalizing behaviors such as (a) "Is physically aggressive with other students or adults," (b) "Damages others' property," (c) "Makes lewd or obscene gestures," and (d) "Uses obscene language or swears," and internalizing behaviors such as (a) "Exhibits sad affect, depression, and feeling of worthlessness," (b) "Has auditory or visual hallucinations," (c) "Demonstrates obsessive-compulsive behaviors," and (d) "Is teased, neglected, and/or avoided by peers."

The second stage involves teacher judgment of child behavior and requires that students who ranked highest in Stage One be rated in Stage Two in terms of the content of their behavior problems. The three highest ranked externalizing students and the three highest ranked internalizing students are rated for frequency of adaptive behaviors such as (a) "Is considerate of the feelings of others," (b) "Produces work of acceptable quality," (c) "Gains peers' attention in an appropriate manner," and (d) "Cooperates with peers in group activities or situation," and maladaptive behaviors such as (a) "Requires punishment (or threat of same) before s/he will terminate an inappropriate activity or behavior," (b) "Avoids or withdraws from social contact with peers," (c) "Behaves inappropriately in class when corrected," and (d) "Uses coercive tactics to force the submission of peers.".

Both Stages One and Two rely totally on teacher rankings and ratings of student behavior. In Stage Three, direct observation of student behaviors are independently recorded in school settings by personnel other than the teacher (e.g., school psychologist, counselor, aide, or other support professionls). Students who meet the criteria on the two rating tasks in Stage Two are observed in the classroom and another setting (e.g., playground) on two separate occasions each. Observations recorded in the classroom provide a direct measure of the student's behavior and are relevant to (a) the requirements of an academic setting and (b) teacher behavioral expectations. Those recorded during recess periods on the playground provide a measure of the student's social adjustment and peer interaction in less structured situations.

Early identification, classification, and intervention of students exhibiting excessive behaviors on externalizing or internalizing dimensions is critical to the effective management of children with behavior disabilities. The fact is that, once established, maladaptive behavior has a long term influence on the adaptive strategies used to solve conflicts, whether those behaviors be excessively externalizing or internalizing (Foff, Sells, & Golden, 1972; Waldrop & Halverson, 1975).

History of Educational Programs

Looking back, one can identify those psychological bases from which educators have devised specific strategies and interventions within direct service settings. The actual history of education for the behavior disabled, however, can hardly be seen as an incremental series of progressively better educational practices. Rather, in sorting through the primary and secondary reports of educational practices in documents and textbooks, one finds that the history of the education of these individuals (up to circa 1950) resembles a dance step--one step forward, two steps back. Only as educators realized the effectiveness of applying behavioral pinciples to the intervention and education of children and youth with emotional disorders have educational approaches become more systematic. 2 Educators have produced their most comprehensive and effective intervention and management programs when they have worked together with professionals from the field of special education.

Influence of Learning and Behavior Theory

Learning theory was the foundation for behavior modification. Research in conditioning, reflexology, and comparative psychology stimulated the objective study of behavior, and methodological advances made in these areas were applied to the field of behavior intervention in general. The basis of behaviorism is the emphasis on overt behaviors rather than private experience. John Watson was the first behaviorist of record (1913). He was strongly opposed to the dominant school of psychology and its focus on covert mental processes, not observable behavior. Even though Watson had done some important work in instinctive behavior, he became impressed by the human organism's capacity for learning. He made some rather extreme claims about the potential of the human infant, without factual support at the time. However, many of his claims have subsequently been borne out (Kazdin, 1978).

B. F. Skinner was responsible in large part for establishing the facts that Watson lacked; his work also made possible the development and refinement of behaviorism into a technology. Skinner's work clarified the learning paradigms developed by Pavlov and Thorndike. He distinguished between these two models on the basis of the type of response and the type of conditioning (Skinner, 1937). Responses that were termed respondent are elicited and are often referred to as reflex responses, such as salivation and knee jerk in response to patellar tap. Operant responses are spontaneous, and no eliciting stimuli may be observed. Operant responses may be more difficult to explain immediately because their causes are not detectable without further analysis. Skinner concentrated much of his research on operant conditioning, using an investigative procedure known as the experimental analysis of behavior.

The Historical Use of Reinforcement Principles

Many systems for consequating desired behavior can be found in early school programs. While it is quite obvious that these applications of reinforcement were not based on the systematic findings of the behavioral laboratory, the functional value of reinforcement has been recognized for many years. Long before the laboratory confirmation of operant conditions, reinforcement principles were used widely. In the earliest examples of teaching, educators used reward systems of one variety or another. An illustration is the use of the pretzel, shaped to represent a child's arms folded in prayer, which was invented in the seventh century A.D., as a reward to children for learning their prayers. Nuts, honey, and figs were given as rewards for learning religious lessons in Europe during the 1100s (Birnbaum, 1962).

Just as rewards have been used throughout history to strengthen desired behavior, punishment has been used in elaborate ways to discourage undesired behavior. Many forms of rewards and punishments were used in education, the military, politics, and business thousands of years before Skinner "discovered" the principles of reinforcement in his laboratory.

One of the most systematic applications of rewards in education was Lancaster's Monitorial System (Lancaster, 1805; Salmon, 1904), developed by Joseph Lancaster (1778-1838) for use in the education of disadvantaged children. Given large numbers of these children, limited facilities, and a lack of personnel, Lancaster developed a peer-teacher monitoring system using academically advanced students from the program (Kaestle, 1973). These student monitors were assigned to a variety of teaching tasks, including taking attendance, distributing and collecting completed work, scoring responses, instructing individual students, and even recommending promotion to the next academic level. Student monitors were assigned to each group of 10-12 students. The goal was advancement to a higher level within the group and eventually to a group at a higher academic level. The Lancaster monitoring system had a fairly elaborate positive reinforcement system. Based on competition, students were rewarded for correct responses. The student in each group with the highest score in all subjects received the highest rank and a ticket of merit. If he or she was surpassed by another student, the ticket had to be exchanged for a merit, stating that the student had achieved, but did not still hold, first place.

Another early (circa 1880) classroom application of reinforcement was the Excelsior School System (Ulman & Klem, 1975). This system provided merits for such appropriate behaviors as punctuality, orderliness, and studiousness. These rewards, called "excellents" or "perfects," were in the form of tokens. They could be exchanged for a special certificate of outstanding behavior and academic performance. The Excelsior system contained a commercially prepared set of materials, including tokens in different denominations, instructions, certificates, and report-to-parent forms. Thousands of teachers throughout the United States used this system.

Educational Models

Several models for the education of behavior disabled children have been developed over the past three decades. These models draw from psychological theories, but have concentrated upon techniques for educating these students. In some instances, the specific model or approach is derived directly from one school of thought, with strict interpretations of the philosophical basis; others, however, are more eclectic in nature, and are broader in their educational application. The first detailed analyses of the various approaches and their theoretical bases were performed by Rhodes and Tracy (1972a, b). Of the models identified by Rhodes and his colleagues, those that have had the most impact on educational service delivery have been the psychoeducational and ecological approaches, and applied behavioral analysis.

The Psychoeducational Approach

The psychoeducational approach is an eclectic combination of psychodynamic theory and prescriptive education. Many of its concepts are common to the child guidance movement, but it also includes direct educational intervention. It evolved from within the mental health areas as a pragmatic means for understanding behavior disorders. A number of excellent child clinicians developed this approach, based not on research, but on many years of clinical research.

The most influential of these were William Morse, Fritz Redl, Dave Wineman, and Ruth Newman. Morse and his colleagues were very active in conducting demonstration and professional training programs in the 1950s and early 1960s (e.g., Morse, 1953). Two main management strategies, Redl's Life Space Interview and Morse's Crisis Teacher, characterize the major work of this group. Many of Morse's students, among them Peter Knoblock, Peggy Wood, and Nicholas Long, continued the basic assumptions of the psychoeducational approach, adding their own variations and adaptations.

The basic psychoeducational approach focuses on the cognitive and affective domains and considers the existence of instincts, needs, and drives in disordered behavior. Through treatment, the individual gains insight into and control over his or her maladaptive behavior. The following diagram, adapted from Kauffman (1985, p. 227), illustrates how the process of the psychoeducational approach works to change maladaptive behavior.

Instincts	Cognitive and			Behavior
Drives —>	Affective —>	Intervention —>	Insight —>	Change
Needs	Problems			

The psychoeducational model is child centered, as it assumes that the nature of disordered behavior resides in an internal, unconscious state. In contrast, the ecological approach views the problem of behavior disorders as a result of the interaction among the child, the people, and systems in his or her environment.

The Ecological Approach

The ecological approach is based on the premise that disturbed children require change and intervention in many aspects of their environment--home, school, and community. The most extensive application of ecological techniques has been in the work of Nicholas Hobbs and his program, Project Re-Ed.

Project Re-Ed was a weekday residential program in which the teacher-counselors planned and implemented children's day and evening programs and served as their counselors, recreation planners, and friends. Efforts were made to improve the children's environment by psychiatric social workers who worked with the children's family both during and after the children's treatment. A liaison teacher maintained contact with the children's school programs in their communities.

The basic elements of the Re-Ed model focus on

1. Educational intervention stressing mental health rather than illness;

2. Teaching rather than treatment;

3. Learning and acquisition of skills rather than personality reorganization;

4. The present and the future rather than the past; and

5. Intervention in the child's total social system and not just educational or intrapsychic process. (Hobbs, 1965)

Other goals included re-establishing disturbed children's trust in significant adults within their environment and helping children develop a sense of identification and belonging within their communities. Children were also helped to unlearn undesirable behaviors, to learn desirable ones, to set goals, and to gain cognitive control over problem areas.

Applied Behavior Analysis

Of all the early behaviorists, Skinner, with his work in operant conditioning, has had the greatest influence on education of the behavior disabled. He used the principles discovered in his laboratory in practical life situations, and his writings have practical application to the classroom. In addition, many of his students, including Charles Ferster, Ogden Lindsley, and Sidney Bijou, have applied his work to behavioral intervention with seriously behaviorally disabled children and adults. From the late 1950s on, the behavioral approach began to have a major impact on the management philosophy and procedures used in programs for the behaviorally disabled.

Paul Fuller (1949), while a graduate student at the University of Indiana, was among the first to apply operant conditioning to human behavior. He demonstrated considerable behavior changes with a profoundly handicapped young adult. Ogden Lindsley was the first to develop a series of operant conditioning programs applied to human behavior. While on the staff at Harvard University in the early 1950s, Lindsley studied the behavior of psychotics at Metropolitan State Hospital. Extensions of operant techniques in applied settings increased in the late 1950s and early 1960s. An example is the work of Ayllon and Michael (1959), who collaborated in a study involving 19 psychotic patients whose behaviors, such as violent acts, psychotic talk, and hoarding, were modified through operant procedures.

In 1962, following a year's study with Skinner, Sidney Bijou established an experimental classroom at the Rainier School in Buckley, Washington. Mentally retarded school-age children were given programmed instructional material and were provided reinforcement for work completed correctly. At about the same time, Montrose Wolf designed a token system, and Donald Baer applied those procedures to modify a number of behaviors in natural settings. Ivar Lovaas, a graduate of the University of Washington, began a series of studies wth autistic children at the University of California at Los Angeles.

During this same period, Gerald Patterson, at the University of Oregon, conducted studies with school children who were hyperactive in classroom settings (1965a). One of these studies involved reinforcement of a child's attending behavior with a light as a signal and the advance of a counter on the child's desk. The points on the counter were "cashed in" for pennies. In another study Patterson used social reinforcement (i.e., praise) with a 7-year-old child who was experiencing school phobia (1965b). Concomitant to these developments, other psychologists conducted similar applied research with children possessing a variety of behavior disorders in natural settings, including classrooms.

Operant conditioning in special classrooms.

During the time that researchers were refining the methodology, special educators were extending the application of systematic operant procedures and reinforcement in a number of special and regular classrooms. These early attempts by special educators were less sophisticated than those of the psychologists, but the activities they used were more adaptable to natural settings with children. Probably the first application of reinforcement by a special educator in a systematically arranged classroom environment was conducted by the author and Lakin Phillips. In this service-oriented application, two special classrooms in Arlington County, Virginia were established for 15 behaviorally disabled children. One was a primary class (i.e., ages 7 to 9), the other an intermediate class (i.e., ages 9 to 11). These classes provided a highly structured educational setting in which each child was individually programmed with specified work objectives for each day. Minutes of free time were scheduled at certain times each day, depending on work completed correctly (Haring & Phillips, 1962; Phillips & Haring, 1959).

In 1960 the author was appointed Educational Director of the Children's Rehabilitation Unit at the University of Kansas Medical Center and invited Ogden Lindsley to apply his knowledge of operant conditioning and technical skill to education. In the process of arranging behavioral procedures for classroom instruction, Lindsley developed precision teaching, a technique based on the precise measurement of behavior, including pinpointing the behavior to be changed, counting and charting behaviors on the standard behavior chart, and making instructional decisions based on performance data.

Two other special educators who contributed to the development of behavioral technology in special education were Richard Whelan and Vance Hall. Whelan began graduate studies in special education with the author at the University of Kansas in 1962. Whelan had developed a behaviorally oriented program for behaviorally disabled children while at the Southard School at the Menninger Foundation Clinic. He developed and refined operant procedures to increase their use by teachers in regular and special classrooms. Hall made a substantial contribution to the classroom application of operant techniques. Since moving from the University of Washington to the University of Kansas in 1965, he has been teaching teachers to use reinforcement techniques to modify children's behaviors in regular classroom settings.

Another application of a behavioral program for the behaviorally disabled was developed by Frank Hewett in 1968. His program, known as the Engineered Classroom, was initiated in the Santa Monica Public Schools and has been widely replicated. Hewett's work involved the developmental sequencing of educational tasks necessary to lead the child from the first stage of the educative process (i.e., attention) to the final stage (i.e., mastery).

By the 1970s the application of reinforcement principles had spread rapidly throughout school programs for the behavior disabled. The procedures, based on hundreds of case studies with school age children, became commonplace in the school, and many teachers skilled in applied behavioral analysis have done meaningful classroom research.

Other Developments

While the procedures of applied behavior analysis dominate programming for the behaviorally disabled, alternative approaches are proving successful in the management of disordered behavior. Two schools of thought, social learning theory and cognitive behavior modification, are contributing to the knowledge and practice within the field. Both are derived from the larger learning theory model, but have also been influenced by the principles of cognitive psychology. They have broadened the concept of behaviorism by emphasizing cognitive development and the role of cognition in overt behavior. Each approach has a distinct set of intervention procedures associated with it, but both are founded in basic behavioral technology.

Cognitive Behavior Modification

The cognitive behaviorists' approach to intervention involves the attempt to change overt behavior by altering thoughts, interpretations, assumptions, and strategies of responding (Kazdin, 1978). Cognitive behavior modification evolved from the operant conditioning model. However, those researchers and practitioners who use cognitive processes to change behavior differ significantly from behaviorists. Cognitive behaviorists emphasize the person's perception and interpretation of environmental events, and are willing to employ internal, private, implicit, or covert events as intervention techniques. They do not limit intervention to the arrangement or rearrangement of the environment.

The great debates from the early development of learning theory about what learning is, how learning occurs, and what role mediating variables play may be reduced to cognitive versus stimulus-response explanations of learning (Kazdin, 1978; Spence, 1950). The basic role of cognition in learning was first discussed by Tolman (1952), who maintained that the individual learns strategies of responding and perceives general relationships in the environment. Earlier, Thorndike (1935) had written that cognitive processes may facilitate learning but are not essential. Dissatisfaction with the strict operant model resulted in the development of intervention strategies that fall under the rubric of cognitive mediation.

Evidence that individuals can and do learn to control behavior as a result of this process is steadily increasing. Because overt behaviors are not always the essential problem, the individual's thoughts, specifically self-concept and self-evaluations, as well as feelings and verbalizations may become the target for change. Changes in cognition, then, influence behaviors. In human conditioning, researchers have noted that humans seem to form perceptions that complicate the experimental results (Grings, 1965). In a variety of learning experiments researchers have noted that human subjects provide self-instructions that increase cognitive activity. There is little doubt about the importance of thought in many aspects of behavioral research.

Cognitive processes have been used in behavior modification for some time. Wolpe (1958) refers to "thought-stopping," which has been used in behavior therapy. In that intervention the therapist shouts "Stop!" to interrupt the subject's obsessing. The subject repeats "Stop!" to him- or herself to control thoughts.

Lloyd Homme discussed another application of cognitive behaviorism in "Control of Coverants: The Operants of the Mind" (1965). Homme coined the term "coverant" by combining "covert" with "operant." Coverants are private events--thoughts, images, reflections, and fantasies. According to Homme, controlling coverants need not be impaired by overt responses or consequences. Individuals know best when they experience private events (i.e., coverants) that have been selected for change and they can apply consequences. Accordingly, in order to change an overt or covert behavior, individuals select a behavor such as smoking, determine the behavior objective, and provide the reinforcing consequence when the target consequence is reached. Other techniques have been developed by psychologists including Mahoney (1974), Meichenbaum (1977), and Mischel (1973), and include rational-emotive therapy, self-instruction training, cognitive therapy, problem-solving, and self-control.

Self-Control Techniques

The development of procedures to enhance self-control are of particular interest to educators. In these procedures, stimulus control techniques are used to modify a behavior that the client wishes to change, that is socially inappropriate, or not controlled by a narrow range of stimuli (e.g., overeating). Behavior is systematically associated with stimuli until it comes under the control of the stimuli. Self-control may be enhanced by self-observation and the self-recording of data on the behavior to be changed.

Self-observation is often successfully supported by self-reinforcement and self-punishment. The individual determines the responses to be reinforced and can reinforce him- or herself at any time. Clients are taught the basic principles of operant conditioning, and an external agent may initially implement the contingencies. Self-reinforcement has been used successfully in elementary classrooms to improve attention and studying and to reduce disruptive behavor (Kazdin, 1975). Self-control may also involve alternate response training, such as replacing anxiety with relaxation.

Opinions vary concerning the effect of external forces on self-control operations, and the design of most self-control studies prevents total exclusion of external forces. Also, individuals often reinforce their own behavior leniently or noncontingently, and some researchers have introduced external reinforcement to encourage strict self-reinforcement. Self-control techniques have been carried out primarily on adult outpatients. However, studies have been conducted with children and adolescents and the procedures have the potential for becoming a major intervention strategy.

Social Learning Theory

As noted earlier, the conceptual rationale for the social learning model draws heavily on research in behavioral and cognitive psychology. The basis of this theory relates environmental and cognitive events to behavior. The bulk of the theoretical and applied research in this area has been conducted by Bandura (1969, 1977), who has developed a comprehensive theory that, although derived from behavioral principles, considers cognitive variables. Bandura's research focuses on the role of cognitive processes in observational (i.e., vicarious) learning. According to Bandura, an individual can learn to respond correctly by watching another person perform the task, thus, he has given considerable attention to the importance of imitation in learning. The instructional strategy of imitation has been widely applied to handicapped individuals in the classrooms.

The social learning theorists have a pragmatic, functional view of social development. They define a socially well-adjusted child or adult as one who interacts with the environment in a way that produces satisfying and rewarding consequences and minimizes the occurrence of aversive or punishing events. The optimal balance between the negative and positive interactions will vary according to the characteristics of a given person and the characteristics and limitations of a given environment. Therefore, the "optimal" behavior of different people will vary, both within and across settings.

Social learning theorists believe that people's experiences in interacting with their environment affect their behavior. They reject the conceptual framework of "stages" described by developmental psychologists which focuses on hierarchical development of behavior. In the social learning paradigm, the appropriateness of behavior is evaluated through either the person's self-evaluation of a given behavior or a value judgment of other persons in the position of power; the emphasis of intervention is to change behavior so it will be more adaptive and so that others in the environment will reinforce it. Thus, social interactions are directed more positively and the natural opportunities for reinforcement are increased.

Wood, Spence, and Rutherford (1982) have provided seven principles from social learning theory which can be used to guide the implementation of educational programs for the behaviorally disabled. The authors summarized the following principles from a comprehensive review of social learning theory:

1. Behavior occurs in a continuously interactive system.

2. Cognitive and affective factors are hyposthesized to play an important role in human behavior, but observable actions remain our primary data.

3. For purposes of analysis and planning, it is useful to speak of fundamental "behavior contingency units."

4. Much social behavior is learned by observing the behavior of real or symbolic models.

5. A key instructional tool for social learning interventions is the restructuring of the special program environment to elicit and reinforce the social behavior the teacher wishes the student to learn and use.

6. The goal of social learning interventions is to have students learn, produce, and practice approved behavior at all times.

7. Generalization of approved behavior is planned. (pp. 240-243)

Both social learning theory and cognitive behavior modification are important extensions of applied behavioral analysis and represent promising new interventions for behaviorally disturbed children.

Conclusion

In many states throughout the nation, children with rather severe behavior problems are having an impact on regular classrooms. This is resulting in serious concerns among regular educators as they are faced with the increased challenge of providing quality education and increased academic achievement. Their concerns arise from the challenge of, on the one hand, maintaining high academic standards and, on the other, the management of seemingly insurmountable behavior problems in regular classrooms.

The problems exhibited and encountered by Debbie and Mike are typical of the serious behavior disabilities encountered in our schools, but certainly do not represent the entire universe of variables that school systems must be prepared to cope with. We know that both externalizing and internalizing students need our help, and the various approaches that have been developed through research and practical experience have provided many excellent options. However, we are still having difficulties with identifying which students need which services.

In the next chapter, we take a detailed look at these problems and present a series of recommendations that have come from a systematic survey of urban, suburban, and rural school districts in the state of Washington.

References

Ayllon, T., & Michael, J. (1959). The pscyhiatric nurse as a behavior engineer. *Journal of the Experimental Analysis of Behavior*, 2, 323-334.

Bandura, A. (1969). *Principles of behavior modification*. New York: Rinehart and Winston.

Bandura, A. (1977). *Social learning theory*. Englewood Bliffs, NJ: Prentice-Hall.

Birnbaum, P. (Ed.). (1962). *A treasury of Judaism*. New York: Hebrew Publishing.

Fuller, P.R. (1949). Operant conditioning of a begetative human organism. *American Journal of Psychology, 62*, 587-590.

Grings, W. W. (1965). Verbal-perceptual factors in the conditioning of automonic responses. In W. F. Prokasy (Ed.), *Classical conditioning: A symposium.* New York: Appleton-Centry-Crofts.

Haring, N. G. (1982). Perspectives on the develompent of educational programs for the emotionallydisturbed. In N.G. Haring & M. M. Noel (Eds.), *Progress of change: Issues in educating the emotionally disturbed, Vol.1: Identification and program planning.* Seattle, WA: Universityof Washington, College of Education. (ERIC Document Reproduction Service No. ED 229 949)

Hewett, F. M. (1968). *The emotionally disturbed child in the classroom.* Boston: Allyn & Bacon.

Hobbs, N. (1965). How the Re-ED plan developed. In N. J. Long, W. C. Morse, & R. G. Newman (Eds), *Conflict in the classroom.* Belmont, CA: Wadsworth.

Homme, L. (1965). Perspectives in psychology: XXIV. Control of coverants, the operants of the mind. *Psychological Record, 15*, 501-511.

Kaestle,C. F. (Ed.). (1973). *Joseph Lancaster and the monitorial school movement: A documentary history.* New York: Teachers College Press.

Kauffman, J. M. (1985). *Characteristics of children's behavior disorders.* (3rd ed.). Columbus, OH: Charles E. Merrill.

Kazdin, A. E. (1975). *Behavior modification in applied settings.* Homewood, IL: Dorsey.

Kazdin, A. E. (1978). *History of behavior modification: Experimental foundations of contemporary research.* Baltimore: University Park Press.

Lancaster, J. (1805). *Improvements in education, as it respects the industrious classes of the community, containing, among other important particulars, an account of the institution for the education of one thousand poor children, Borough Road, Southwark, and of the new system of education on which it is conducted* (3rd ed.). London: Darton & Harvey.

Mahoney, J. J. (1974). *Cognition and behavior modification.* Cambridge, MA: Ballinger.

Meichenbaum, D. M. (1977). *Cognitive behavior modification.* New York: Plenum Press.

Mischel, W. (1973). Toward a cognitive social learning reconceptualization of personality. *Psychological Review, 80*, 252-283.

Morse, W. C. (1953). The development of a mental hygiene milieu in a camp program for disturbed boys. *American Journal of Orthopsychiatry, 23*, 826-833.

Noel, M. M. (1982). Parenting the emotionally disturbed child: Personal perspectives. In N. G. Haring & M. M. Noel (Eds.), *Progress of change: Issues in educating the emotionally disturbed, Vol. 2: Service delivery.* Seattle, WA: University of Washington, College of Education. (ERIC Document Reproduction Service No. ED 229 950)

Patterson, G. R. (1965a). An application of conditioning techniques to the control of a hyperactive child. In L. P. Ullmann & L. Krasner (Eds.), *Case studies in behavior modification.* New York: Holt, Rinehart & Winston.

Patterson, G. R. (1965b). A learning theory approach to the treatment of the school phobic child. In L. P. Ullmann & L. Krasner (Eds.), *Case Studies in behavior modification.* New York: Holt, Rinehart & Winston.

Phillips, E. L., & Haring, N. G. (1959). Results from special techniques for teaching emotionally disturbed children. *Excetional Chidlren, 26*, 64-67.

Rhodes, W. C., & Tracy, M. L. (Eds.). (1972a). *A study of child variance, Vol 1: Theories.* Ann Arbor: The University of Michigan Press.

Rhodes, W. C., & Tracy, M. L. (Eds.). (1972b). *A study of child variance, Vol 2: Interventions.* Ann Arbor: The University of Michigan Press.

Salmon, D. (1904). *Joseph Lancaster.* London: Longmans, Green.

Skinner, B. F. (1937). Two types of conditioned reflex: A reply to Knorski and Miller. *Journal of General Psychology, 16*, 272-279.

Spence, K. W. (1950). Cognitive versus stimulus-response theories of learning. *Psychological Review, 57*, 159-172.

Thorndike, E. L. (1935). *The psychology of wants, interests, and attitudes.* New York: Appleton-Century-Crofts.

Tolman, E. C. (1952). A cognitive motivational model. *Psychological Review, 59*, 389-400.

Ulman, J. D., & Klem, J. L. (1975). Communication. *Journal of Applied Behavior Analysis, 8*, 210.

Walker, H. M., Severson, H., Haring, N. G., & Williams, G. (in press). Standardized screening and identification of behavior disordered pupils in the elementary age range: A multiple gating approach. *Direct Instruction News.*

Watson, J. B. (1913). Psychology as the behaviorist views it. *Psychological Review, 20*, 158-177.

Wolpe, J. (1958). *Psychotherapy by reciprocal inhibition.* Stanford: Stanford University Press.

Wood, F. H., Spence, J., & Rutherford, R. B. (1982). An intervention program for emotionally disturbed students based on social learning principles. In R. L. McDowell, G. W. Adamson, & F. H. Wood (Eds.), *Teaching emotionally disturbed children.* Boston: Little, Brown, & Company.

Notes

[1]Case histories presented here were originally compiled by Noel (1982) and are used here with permission of the author.

[2] Material on the history of the various educational approaches is based on Haring (1982, pp. 101-110).

RESEARCH ON SEVERE BEHAVIOR DISORDERS: A STUDY OF STATEWIDE IDENTIFICATION AND SERVICE DELIVERY TO CHILDREN AND YOUTH[1]

Norris Haring, John Jewell, Thomas Lehning, Greg Williams, and Owen White

Members of the Washington Council of Administrators of Special Education (WCASE) and of the Washington Association of School Administrators (WASA) have voiced a variety of concerns related to the education of students with serious behavior disabilities (SBD)[2] in Washington. Pointing to such problems as academic failure, drop-out rates, and classroom discipline, these organizations have stressed that the failure of our schools to adequately identify and serve the SBD population is an issue of pressing local, state, and national importance. Their statements were based on the experiences and concerns not only of administrators but of teachers, parents, and state legislators as well.

The issues have been well documented. The US Department of Education's Office of Special Education and Rehabilitative Services has declared behavior disabilities to be a top focus of investigation. The Sixth Annual Report to Congress on Implementation of PL 94-142: The Education for All Handicapped Children Act (US Department of Education, 1984, Table 3C1) revealed that segregated special classes are still the most common program option for this population and that 52% of all SBD students continue to be placed in restrictive programs (e.g., separate classes, schools, or other institutions) as compared to 38% of the total handicapped student population. An estimated 741,000 students nationwide are still in need of behavior-related special education services but do not receive them and many existing programs are inappropriate or of poor quality due to the lack of adequately trained staff (Grosenick & Huntze, 1980).

Historical Background

A variety of studies contribute to the conclusion that "the public schools do not have either a strong history or adequate record in serving this population of children" (Walker, Reavis, Rhode, & Jenson, 1985). That history has, for many years, been one of exclusion, separation, and lack of services. In the past, behavioral disabilities in children were seen as the responsibility of mental health professionals, rather than educators. Treatment involved removal of the child from the school setting–whether for short-term therapies or long-term placement in special schools and institutions.

Beginning in the 1950s, this approach came under increasing criticism for a number of reasons. Out-of-school treatments were disruptive to students and their families, depriving students of the beneficial effects of more normal relationships. The mental health system was seen as incapable of responding to the wide range of students' needs. Studies showed only weak evidence for the effectiveness of treatment. The illness model used by the mental health profession was seen as inappropriate in an educational context. Pressure shifted to the schools to provide more appropriate integrated services with an educational emphasis (Haring & Phillips, 1962; Paul & Warnock, 1980).

Nationally, the number of school-sponsored programs increased throughout the 1960s and 70s and continued, certainly, to grow after passage of the Education for All Handicapped Children Act, PL 94-142. But large numbers of children remained unserved, and those services which existed were neither consistent nor systematic. While the number of children with serious behavior disabilities reported by the states increased nationwide by 25% from 1976-1983 (US Department of Education, 1984), during the same period the state of Washington reported a decrease in this population of 33% (Office of Superintendent of Public Instruction, 1984). At both the state and the federal levels, it has become an educational priority to identify the causes of these incongruities and to develop and implement adequate solutions.

Project Guidelines and Objectives

In response to the suggestions of WCASE and WASA, and nationally identified concerns, the Office of the Superintendent of Public Instruction (OSPI) provided grant support to the University of Washington and the Highline School District to conduct a study of statewide identification and service delivery to children and youth with serious behavior disabilities. The project guidelines from OSPI included a request for the following information: a general description of the problem, an investigation of the assumption that these students are unserved or underserved, a description of the current state of the art and emerging technology, the adequacy of service delivery within the state, exemplary programs nationwide, means of promoting comprehensive management, recommendations regarding interagency agreements, and means of improving the quality of programs and services in the state. Project staff developed five specific objectives in order to meet OSPI's guidelines:

1. To estimate the number of children and youth with serious behavior disabilities in Washington who are not being served or who are being served inadequately or inappropriately.

2. To examine current Washington practices for educating students with SBD.

3. To investigate nationwide model practices for educating students with SBD which might have a positive impact in Washington.

4. To examine the role and relationship between schools and agencies in order to identify those practices most likely to promote successful cooperative management.

5. To assemble a final report including analysis of all available data and recommendations for program improvement.

Statewide Task Force and Working Committees

A task force was assembled at the beginning of the project to provide leadership and technical expertise as the project progressed. Members included representatives of state professional organizations, parent groups, advocacy organizations, agencies, the Washington legislature, and institutions of higher learning in Washington. The task force met quarterly; the recommendations in this report are the result of nearly 2 years' effort on the part of task force members and support staff.

In 1985, project staff and members of the task force formed four working committees to assist the task force in making final recommendations. Each committee was exclusively concerned with one of the following topics: (a) parent advocacy, (b) interagency services, (c) identification and assessment, and (d) comprehensive management, staff development, and training. Members of these committees (which included parents, child advocates, professors, administrators, and other professionals with expertise and experience) were recommended by the task force, who invited them to participate in a series of meetings to address these topics. This chapter includes the recommendations of the working committees.

Research Design

In order to provide the information required to meet the objectives of this study, project staff conducted a survey of individuals involved with the SBD population in school districts around the state. Questionnaires were developed for surveys of district administrators, teachers (both special education and regular education), and assessment personnel (psychologists and social workers). The project staff also visited school districts and other agencies around the state and visited agencies in four other states.

Needs Assessment Questionnaire

The first questionnaire was designed to elicit general data (e.g., common needs, priorities, opinions, issues, and concerns) related to the education of SBD students in Washington. This questionnaire (see Exhibit 1) was sent out in March 1984 to administrators in each of the 241 districts which reported offering programs for these students. It consisted of 22 items, primarily open-ended questions, in 10 content areas: agreements with nonpublic school agencies, support services offered, characteristics of the district's SBD population, strategies used, staffing, funding, theoretical models, inservice training and needs, and exemplary features of existing programs. The selection of questionnaire items began with suggestions from special education directors at the ESD regional meetings around the state. These suggestions were then forwarded to a subcommittee of 12 administrators. After brainstorm and review sessions, subcommittee members developed and refined the final questionnaire content from an initial list of 200 possible items.

Of the 241 questionnaires mailed, 146 were returned. Because some of them included information on students served in cooperative programs, the total actually represented the opinions of administrators representing 174 school districts and 2,842 (84%) of the 3,400 SBD students reported during the 1983-84 school year (OSPI, 1984).

Questionnaires for Administrators and Teachers

Project staff analyzed the responses to the needs assessment questionnaire and used them as the basis for developing additional questionnaires that would yield more detailed and specific information. Three groups were asked to contribute 100 possible questions. These groups were the project task force, the subcommittee of 12 who had developed the first instrument, and project staff. Their 100 suggested items were then sent to 7 school districts, 2 ESDs, and OSPI for review. Through this process, the list was cut first to 50 questions and then to 25. The remaining 25 questions were next reviewed by project staff and by research staff at the University of Washington. This last phase resulted in preparation of an administrator's questionnaire with 24 items (Exhibit 2) and a teacher's questionnaire of 22 items (Exhibit 3). The administrators' survey addressed topics in the areas of state and federal laws and definitions, assessment strategies, program settings, relations with nonschool agencies, theoretical approaches, needs of students with mild/moderate behavior disabilities, inservice training priorities, and model practices. The teacher survey covered student population served, support services, curricula and materials used, assessment and evaluation procedures, intervention strategies, inservice training needs, model practices and suggested improvements.

These questionnaires were mailed in May 1984 to administrators and special education teachers in 63 selected school districts and 2 ESDs. The 65 were selected based on two types of criteria:

1. Fourteen districts and one ESD were selected based on the presence of program components such as a planning process, written objectives, and some way of measuring results, in addition to location and size (Group A).

2. Forty-nine districts and one ESD were randomly selected to provide a representative sample of small, medium, and large districts in all geographic areas of the state (Group B).

The total sample included 20 small districts (i.e., 0-3,000 students), 31 medium districts (3,001-13,000 students), 12 large ones (over 13,000 students), and 2 ESDs. Each mailing included one administrator questionnaire and one to five teacher questionnaires (one each to small districts, two to medium districts, and five to large districts). The number of administrators' and teachers' questionnaires sent and received are summarized in Table 1. When significant differences were found between Group A and Group B districts, those differences are reported in the text.

Assessment Personnel Questionnaire

Project staff also prepared a questionnaire for assessment personnel. This questionnaire was identical to the administrators' questionnaire except for six additional questions (Exhibit 4), which were requested by assessment personnel members of the task force. These questions elicited information related to the role and function of the school psychologist and the school social worker. In 1985, a total of 450 questionnaires were mailed to assessment personnel in school districts and ESDs across Washington; 175 (39%) of these questionnaires were completed and returned. Analysis of returns indicated that the large districts (e.g., Seattle, Tacoma) were well represented. Returns from smaller districts, however, were sparse. Because

Table 1
Numbers and Distributions of Questionnaires Sent and Returned

Administrators' Questionnaire

	Group A (select)	Group B (random)	Total
Number Sent to Districts			
Small (0-3,000)	2	18	20
Medium (3,001-13,000)	11	20	31
Large (13,001 or more)	2	10	12
ESDs		2	2
Total	15	50	65
(Total SBD Students)	(803)	(2,219)	(3,022)

	Group A (select)	Group B (random)	Total
Number Returned			
Small (0-3,000)	2	8	10
Medium (3,001-13,000)	11	13	24
Large (13,001 or more)	2	10	12
ESDs	1		1
Total	15	32	47
SBD Students Represented in return = 82%	(803)	(1,984)	(2,787)

Teachers' Questionnaire

	Group A (select)	Group B (random)	Total
Number Sent to Districts			
Small (5 @ 0-3,000)	2	18	20
Medium (2 @ 3,001-13,000)	22	40	62
Large (5 @ 3,001 or more)	10	50	60
ESDs (none)			
Total	34	108	142

	Group A (select)	Group B (random)	Total
Number Returned (55%)			
Small (0-3,000)		7	7
Medium (3,001-13,000)	8	13	28
Large (13,001 or more)	9	10	37
ESDs			
Unidentified Size			6
Total	17	55	78

of this low return rate from the smaller, rural districts, generalization of the questionnaire results would perhaps be problematic. Accordingly, project staff randomly selected 20 assessment personnel from these low participating districts, and requested that they complete the questionnaire. These respondents had not completed the questionnaire previously. This procedure was initiated to insure that statements made from the original returned questionnaires could be generalized across all districts in the state. In fact, responses to this sample of 20 did reveal the same trends that were identified in the larger sample.

Survey of Regular Education Teachers

In response to concerns voiced by task force members regarding the need to obtain information from regular educators, project staff surveyed regular education teachers in Group A districts who had regular contact with SBD students in their classrooms or schools. These teachers received a questionnaire (Exhibit 5) that was similar to that distributed to special education teachers. In May 1985, the questionnaires were mailed to 110 teachers; 31 were completed and returned.

Site Visits

The analysis of responses to the needs assessment questionnaire resulted in the identification of four areas of need, which also appear in the results of similar investigations at the national level:

1. A need for agreement in regard to eligibility criteria for students with serious behavior disabilities.

2. A need to develop and implement a statewide comprehensive assessment procedure.

3. A need to identify the components of a comprehensive management plan.

4. A need to identify the nature, content, and dissemination methods of training for school staff.

In order to compare these responses and the results of the administrators' and teachers' questionnaires, project staff visited the fifteen Group A districts. Interviews were conducted with the special education director in each district. Each interview was also attended by one or two of the district's assessment personnel. These interviews elicited additional information in regard to the four areas listed above and the responses to interview questions confirmed the needs in these areas. Project staff also examined randomly selected files of SBD children in the schools in these districts, in order to gather information on the type of assessment used, type of student (i.e., externalizing or internalizing), and the nature of the management plan in effect for each student's program. A total of 368 student files were reviewed.

Programs in Washington and Other States

In addition to obtaining data through questionnaires supplemented by selective on-site interviewing, project staff wished to learn about current practices that existed in specific service delivery programs for students with serious behavior disabilities. The identification of such programs, in both Washington and elsewhere, would satisfy Objectives 2 and 3 of the study, and provide models to guide the deliberations and recommendations of the task force and working committees. In regard to Washington, the task force's joint subcommittee on comprehensive management and inservice training convened two meetings which would give school district and agency personnel an opportunity to share "best practices" occurring in both the eastern and western regions of the state. School districts or agencies that served children and youth with serious behavior disabilities were invited to participate in these meetings by presenting brief overviews of their programs. These presentations were to include (a) a description of the population served; (b) procedures for screening, referral, and assessment; (c) placement options and intervention strategies; (d) goals and objectives of the delivery model; (e) curricula, special materials, and instructional methods; (f) a description of any assistance received from noneducation agencies; (g) provisions for family and community involvement; and (h) a summary of the program's distinctive features. On May 21, 1985, twelve programs from eastern Washington were presented at a meeting held in Spokane; on May 22, 1985, twelve presentations took place during the western Washington meeting in Burien. Task force members and project staff reviewed each of the programs according to criteria that included systematic screening, multidisciplinary assessment, variety of placement options, behavioral objectives for students, procedures for monitoring progress, data-based decision-making, special instructional procedures and curricula, parent and community involvement, systematic transition of students into work or regular education environments, inservice training for staff, and periodic program evaluation. Summaries of these programs based on the presentations and reviews are shown in Exhibit 6.

In order to discover what kinds of best practices existed outside Washington, project staff sent letters of inquiry to special education directors in all of the other states. These letters requested information about existing programs and services for children and youth with SBD. Twenty-two states responded. Based on the criteria established by Grosenick and Huntze (1983) for exemplary programs, project staff selected six of these states for site visits. During these visits, project staff interviewed special education administrators and teachers, and also obtained relevant program descriptions and curricular materials. Four of these states (Colorado, Georgia, Idaho, and Vermont) shared a number of features listed by Grosenick and Huntze for the delivery of comprehensive services to special needs children and youth. Summaries of practices in these states are shown in Exhibit 7.

Limitations

Several limitations are inherent in any project which addresses what people know, believe, feel, or want. For this particular project a standardized questionnaire was presented to several groups of respondents (e.g., administrators, special education teachers, regular education teachers, assessment personnel). For each group, the same questionnaire was presented to all respondents. Across the groups of respondents slightly different questionnaires were designed–attempting to measure each group's perceptions of salient issues concerning SBD children and youth.

A limitation with the use of questionnaires is the type of questions presented. Ambiguity, double-negatives, etc. can cloud data gleaned from these responses. Project staff utilized rigidly standardized, fixed alternative, and open-ended questions to best ascertain valid responses across all respondent groupings.

Another limitation of the study could be the initial low return rate of, in particular, the assessment personnel questionnaire. Project staff addressed this problem by probing a group of nonrespondents from those districts with especially low return rates. This second sampling confirmed those trends established in the initial sampling. In addition, even though the percent of questionnaires was low, 25% of all school psychologists in Washington were represented.

Generally speaking, validity of results can be questionned given concerns about sampling procedures, subjects sample, const ruction of questionnaires, etc. Project staff addressed these concerns by sampling perceptions across different groups of individuals who are all involved in education for children and youth with SBD. By assessing these different groups with similar instruments, a striking degree of consistency was obtained in responses. This lends credence to the identification of trends established not only for respondents from one group, but across groups as well. This consistency of responding indicates that different groups of people perceive the same problems concerning children and youth with SBD, substantiating validity of the assessment methodology.

Results

Trends Identified Through the Needs Assessment Questionnaire

An analysis of responses to the needs assessment questionnaire yielded four identifiable trends. Further discussion with task force members and selected special education directors from local school districts and ESDs as well as more in-depth analysis of responses confirmed that these trends were valid. The four trends that emerged were (a) concerns regarding identification and eligibility, (b) lack of consistent and systematic assessment procedures from district to district, (c) absence of an organizing framework or model for delivery of services, and (d) requests for statewide inservice training in methods and strategies for identifying and teaching students with SBD.

Analysis of the Subsequent Questionnaires

The subsequent questionnaires were constructed to accomplish three goals:

1. To obtain Washington data that could be compared with similar national findings.

2. To provide specific data that would either support or negate the four initially identified trends.

3. To compare the responses to specific issues as a means of validating the information received.

Data derived from these questionnaires were tabulated and processed in the following manner.

Responses to open-ended questions were organized in clusters of consistent meaning. Percentage of agreement was calculated and percentages were examined for evidence of trends. Other data were tabulated and graphed. Where appropriate, a series of chi-square analyses were conducted to determine whether there were actual differences between what would be expected to prevail among our subject population and what actually did occur. In particular, we were interested in analyzing the responses of those districts in Group A, which were selected based on having demonstrated experience in the education of SBD students, and those of Group B, which were randomly selected and included some more conventional programs. Major concerns were to determine whether there were any differences between these groups and whether those differences were significant. In some cases, a chi-square analysis was also carried out on the responses from small, medium, and large districts and from teachers and administrators–where those two groups were asked to respond to the same question.

Administrators' Questionnaire

We can summarize the responses to the administrators' questionnaire under the following topic headings: Definition and Eligibility, Assessment, Service Delivery, Intervention and Educational Approaches, Service for Non-Eligible Students, Inservice Needs, and Innovative Practices.

1. Definition and Eligibility Criteria

Administrators responded to questions that requested their opinions concerning the state and federal definitions of "serious behavior disabilities" (see Table 2). They were also asked to indicate the eligibility criteria they currently used and to write their own "best definition" and eligibility criteria for "serious behavior disabilities."

Responses to the questionnaire revealed very little consensus regarding the adequacy of Washington Administrative Code (WAC) 392-171-386 in terms of the definition and eligibility criteria for SBD (see Figure 1). The majority of the respondents (88%, 31/35) suggested changes that would improve WAC 392-171-386 by clarifying the definition of the SBD population. Almost all of them requested clarification among behavior disabilities, learning disabilities, and socially maladjusted/delinquent behavior. Circa 73% agreed that services are insufficiently prescribed in the WAC. Overall, one must conclude that the present WAC does not provide sufficient guidance for a sizable proportion of the administrators surveyed.

In regard to the national definition and criteria, there was also some degree of disagreement among respondents (Figure 2). However, on three issues, consensus among administrators appeared strong: (a) PL 94-142 clearly guarantees the right of handicapped students to special education (95%), (b) state criteria used for definition and assessment procedures do not always correspond precisely to federal law (74%)–when there is a

Table 2
State and Federal Definitions

STATE DEFINITION

WAC 392-171-386

Definition and eligibility for seriously behaviorally disabled.

(1) Seriously behaviorally disabled students are those who exhibit one or more of the following characteristics over a long period of time and to a marked degree, which adversely affects their own educational performance:

    (a) An inability to learn which cannot be explained by intellectual, sensory or health factors;

    (b) An inability to build or maintain satisfactory interpersonal relationsips with peers and teachers;

    (c) Inappropriate types of behavior or feelings under normal circumstances;

    (d) A general pervasive mood of unhappiness or depression; or

    (e) A tendency to develop physical symptoms or fears associated with personal or school problems.

(2) The term includes students who are schizophrenic or autistic. The term does not include students who are socially maladjusted, unless it is determined that they are also seriously behaviorally disabled.

Students whose primary disability is identified in another handicapping category do not qualify as seriously behaviorally disabled.

(3) All students considered for initial placement in special education as seriously behaviorally disabled shall be assessed by a multidisciplinary team including at least one school psychologist or school social worker and determined as eligible for special education and related services according to the following:

    (a) A current school district evaluation which concludes that the student has a serious behavioral disability and which considers and describes the student's social and emotional beaviors and provides any implications for educational planning.

        (i) For the purposes of establishing that the student has a behavioral disability, the evaluation shall describe behaviors which distinguish between common disciplinary problem behaviors and serious behavioral disabilities. Common disciplinary problem behaviors (e.g., truancy, smoking, breaking school conduct rules) may exist in conjunction with serious behavioral disabilities, but cannot be used as the sole criteria for recommending special education and related services.

        (ii) The evaluation must include:

            (A) Dated and signed documented anecdotal records of behavioral observations made by two or more persons at separate times and places, each of which cite and corroborate specific behaviors which, in the aggregate, provide foundation for probable concern for serious behavioral disability. Multiple settings are required (e.g., in addition to the classroom setting consider playground, cafeteria, school bus, hallway, etc.); and

(B) Dated and signed documented evidence of at least two intervention techniques that have been tried and the effect of each. These interventions may include, but are not limited to, changes in student's regular class schedule, and/or curriculum, and/or teacher; school counseling or community agency therapy or counseling; and

(C) A social or developmental history compiled directly from the parent(s) and/or records, when parents are not available.

(b) Current assessment of level of academic or cognitive achievement as measured by standardized tests appropriate to age level and administered individually.

(c) A current vision and hearing screening report. EXCEPTION: Provided that the required academic assessment and vison and hearing screening are concluded, and provided that there are documented and dated anecdotal records of behavioral observations showing that the student's disability is evidenced in the school environment, the following evaluation reports may be substituted for the school district's evaluation:

(i) A current psychiatric evaluation whcih considers and describes the student's social and emotional behaviors, which concudes and describes a serious behavioral disability and where implications for educational planning are provided, the multidisciplinary team must consider these implications in planning and implementing the student's educational program; or

(ii) A current psychological evaluation by a nonpublic school mental health professional who holds a degree in a recognized mental health specialty that considers and describes the student's social and emotional behaviors, which concludes that the student has serious behavioral disability, the consequences of which entail the necessity for active, on-going therapy and/or counseling, and where implications for educational planning are provided, the multidisciplinary team must consider these implications in planning and implementing the student's educational program. (Statutory Authority: RCW 28A.12.070(7). 80-11-054 (Order 80-31), S 392-171-386, filed 8/19/80.)

FEDERAL DEFINITION

"Seriously emotionally disturbed" is defined as follows: The term means a condition exhibiting one or more of the following characteristics over a ong period of time and to a marked degree, which adversely affects educationa performance: (A) An inability to learn which cannot be explained by intellectual, sensory or health factors; (B) An inability to build or maintain satisfactory interpersonal relationsips with peers and teachers; (C) Inappropriate types of behavior or feelings under normal circumstances; (D) A general pervasive mood of unhappiness or depression; or (E) A tendency to develop physical symptoms or fears associated with personal or school problems. (ii) The term includes students who are schizophrenic or autistic. The term does not include students who are socially maladjusted, unless it is determined that they are also seriously behaviorally disturbed.

Figure 1

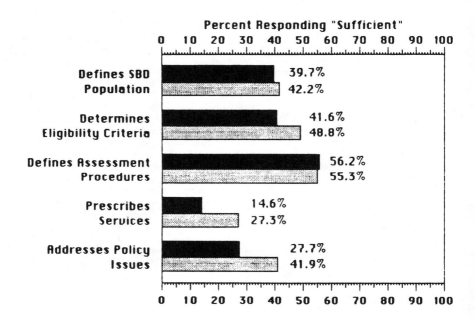

Percent of Responding Assessment Personnel ▬▬ and
Administrators ▨▨▨ Indicating that WAC Delineations of
Various Issues are "Sufficient"

Percent Responding "Sufficient"

Figure 2

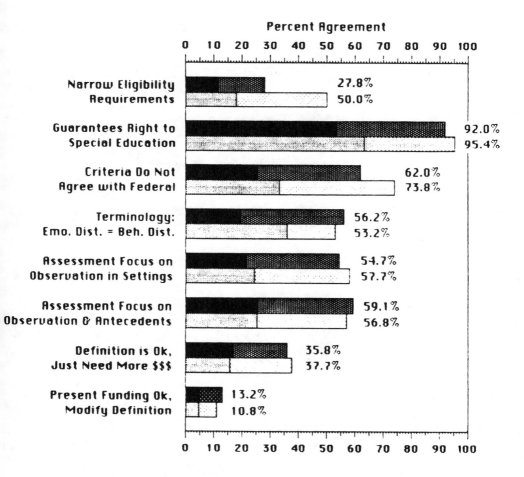

Percent of Responding Assessment Personnel ▭ and
Administrators ▬ Agreeing Moderately (lighter shade)
or Strongly (darker shade) with Statements
Concerning Federal Definitions (PL94-142)

Figure 3

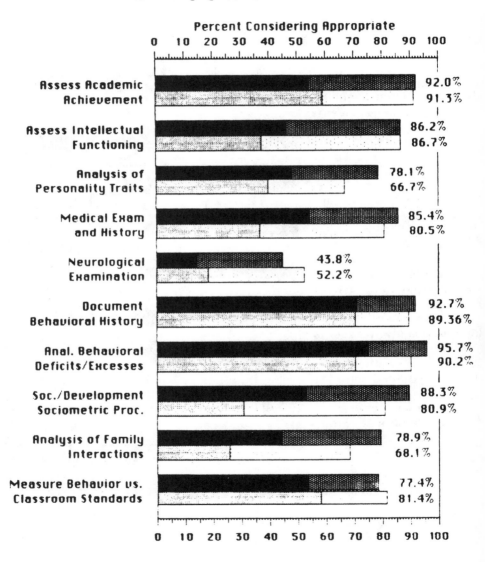

Percent of Assessment Personnel ▰▰▰ and
Administrators ▱▱▱ Indicating that Various Assessment
Strategies for the SBD are "Somewhat Appropriate" (lighter
shade) or "Highly Appropriate" (darker shade)

perceived difference on the part of district and school administrators, there is a question of which regulations to follow, and (c) the present level of funding is a concern (76%). Forty-eight percent (16/33) want major changes in the eligibility criteria. The majority of respondents (28/47 or 60%) indicated they currently use some type of criteria to differentiate between moderate and severe behavior disabilities, the most common being multidisciplinary team (MDT) input. Nineteen percent (9/47) do not differentiate between moderate and severe BD and another 19% do not serve moderately affected students in SBD programs.

2. Formal Assessment

The way we use assessments has much to do with the identification and eligibility issues discussed above. The needs assessment questionnaire pointed to two problematic areas: the need for a consistent strategy for assessment and an effective means of discriminating between those students who qualify for special education and those who do not. The subsequent, more detailed questionnaire asked administrators to rate the appropriateness of different assessment strategies. Results are displayed in Figure 3.

Each of the assessment strategies appears to have a reasonable number of advocates. The least favored strategy (i.e., neurological examination) is considered somewhat or highly appropriate by over 52% of the responding administrators and more than 43% of the assessment personnel; other strategies are considered appropriate by 66% or more of the respondents. Two strategies in particular are rated "highly appropriate" by a substantial proportion of the respondents: "documentation of long term behavior that is counterproductive to learning" and "analysis of behavioral deficits or excesses" were both identified by circa 71% of the administrators as "highly appropriate."

It is reasonable to assume that both valid and reliable assessment strategies exist (Smith, 1985; Walker, Reavis, Rhode, & Jenson, 1985). It would be beneficial for the state to develop a comprehensive statewide assessment procedure, using these strategies, which would reliably identify a consistent SBD population in districts across the state.

3. Service Delivery to SBD Students by Nonpublic School Agencies

The questionnaire included three open-ended questions designed to identify those districts which had entered into cooperative relationships. Sixty-eight percent of the respondents (37/47) indicated that their programs relied upon nonpublic school agencies for service delivery to SBD students, while 36% (17/47) reported having some type of cooperative agreements with nonpublic school agencies. Twenty-six percent (12/47) indicated problems such as bargaining, funding, or the simple unavailability of agencies.

4. Education and Intervention Approaches

Administrators were given descriptions of five approaches to educating SBD students and were asked to rate each of them according to its appropriateness (Question 13). Generally the results suggest that respondents would tend to combine various conceptual models rather than relying on a single one. Three approaches in particular won a high level of acceptance: the behavioral model (74.4%), the ecological model (78.7%), and the consultant/support model (90.7%). In fact, all three of these models share many components and are not mutually exclusive, nor do they single out any one learning theory.

These results were confirmed by the comments of teachers, who identified the same three models (i.e., behavioral, ecological, and consultant) as those most often used. According to the survey, teachers tend to use behavioral techniques in their own special classrooms; to use the ecological model in their work with psychologists, counselors, and other specialists; and to serve as consultants to other teachers.

This statewide survey seems to support findings from national studies that show a trend toward increasing use of cooperative models, such as the interactive (ecological) tactic and the consulting role for special education teachers (as defined in the questionnaire, see Exhibit 2, pp. 7-8). Although certain key trends seem to be emerging, there is still no single organizing framework or model with a consensus of support. Nationally, in the area of SBD, there is little consistent or uniform agreement among professionals in regard to assessment and intervention, which often serves as a source of controversy about the best educational practices for behaviorally disturbed students.

5. Service Delivery Needs for Students With Behavior Disabilities Who Do Not Meet Eligibility Criteria for Special Education

From national statistics, we know that SBD students are frequently unserved or underserved. A primary objective of this project was to assess the extent of this problem in Washington. Administrators were asked to estimate the number of students in their districts with mild or moderate behaviors that adversely affect their educational performance to the degree that they have special service needs but are not eligible for special education programs/services (Question 14). The results indicate that if an

Figure 4

Percent of Districts Currently Offering Various Services to SBD Students & Percent of Districts that Would Offer Services if State Funds Were Provided

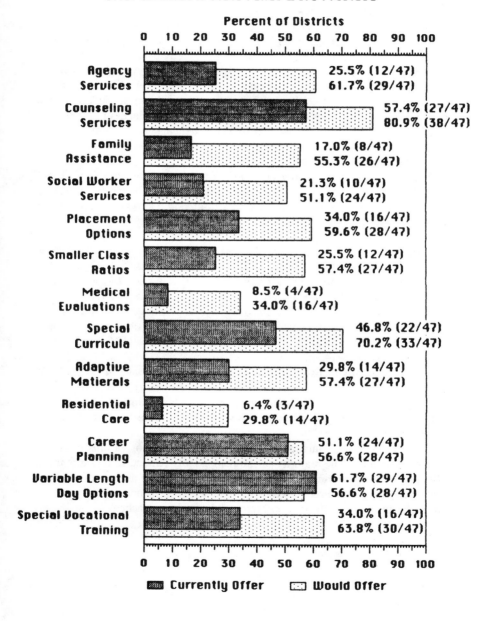

additional 1% of the students in the district were provided with SBD services, about 37% of the reporting districts would seem to be serving their entire estimated SBD population. If 2% more of the student population were served, about 55% of the reporting districts would be serving all their students with SBD.

The questionnaire further requested that respondents check the services their districts currently offer mild or moderate SBD students from funds other than special education and those that the district would offer mild or moderate SBD students if state funds were provided. The results are indicated in Figure 4. When asked what factors prevent school districts from adequately serving students with serious behavior disabilities (Question 17), 69% (32/47) of the respondents identified funding as a major factor. Next highest, with 38% (18/47) was lack of adequately trained staff. Thirty-four percent (16/47) listed lack of a comprehensive management plan and 30% (14/47) indicated lack of understanding or willingness on the part of regular staff.

Results of this survey show that some services are already being offered to those students who are seen as having behavior problems but who are not eligible for special education. However, no single service is consistently available in all districts or programs.

6.   Inservice Needs of Special Education Personnel

The responses of the administrators confirmed the need for professional development and inservice training described by Edgar and Hart (1984) for personnel providing services to SBD students in Washington. Ninety-seven percent (36/37) of those responding expressed a need for more effective classroom management/intervention systems, while 33% (12/36) requested a social skills curriculum. Seventy-six percent (28/37) listed the need for training in comprehensive management planning, and 43% (16/37) indicated inservice needs regarding definition, eligibility, and assessment. Twenty-three percent (11/47) did not respond. Maximum responses varied from item to item due to some participants' failure to answer some questions.

In addition, the administrators rated the effectiveness of various inservice delivery methods. The majority of the respondents seemed to feel it is more effective to keep training within the district and to use a form of training that maximizes contact between individuals (e.g., consultants, visiting particular programs, informal problem solving among teachers).

7. Innovative Practices

The questionnaire asked administrators to list innovative practices introduced into their districts for students with SBD. Most of the administrators mentioned resource rooms combined with mainstreaming as a means for bringing these students back into regular classrooms, although some administrators (30% of the sample) never removed them from regular classrooms in the first place. In regard to interactions between resource classrooms and other classrooms, 55% (26/47) either did not respond or indicated limited interactions, while the remainder of the sample reported using a regular education or special education classroom as a setting for these interactions, or nonacademic settings and activities (e.g., art, PE, lunch, recess).

The administrators were asked to describe examples of model behavioral management practices: 47% (22/47) listed reinforcement, behavior modification, modeling, and natural consequences, while 40% (19/47) listed model practices in the areas of educational programming, team teaching, program settings, or "other." However, the responses showed no consistency to any one model practice.

Similarly, when asked to respond to the question about changes or additions they would make if they had more funds, the administrators' suggestions for improvement ranged across 23 sub-areas (e.g., smaller class size, more counseling, more reliance on behavior management).

In summary, there was no clear evidence from the analysis of responses to these questions that systematic instructional and behavioral technology is being effectively used to accommodate SBD students in less restrictive environments. Over half of the administrators did not respond when asked to describe examples of model practices. The responses clearly did not offer evidence of common approaches, although nationally there is evidence of increasing consensus on SBD programming (Kauffman, 1982; Stainback & Stainback, 1984).

Special Education Teachers' Questionnaire

Based on the assumption that teachers who see students on a daily basis might have different views than administrators, a separate survey (Exhibit 3) was developed and distributed to special education teachers and regular education teachers in each district. There were several reasons for doing this: to check the consistency of responses between administrators and teachers and to glean specific information that teachers possess about the tactics and strategies used in management, frequency of behaviors, ways of measuring and recording behaviors, and making decisions based on the data collected. Finally, teacher experiences with students are crucial in forming recommendations about procedures for identification, assessment, instructional management, student/teacher ratios, classroom organization, and service settings.

1. Teacher Background and Students Served

No substantial demographic differences were found between the Group A (hand-picked) and Group B (randomly selected) districts. Figure 5 represents the number of SBD students served in each of the grade level categories. Figure 6 shows that roughly similar proportions of students are served for two hours or less, 2-4 hours, or more than four hours a day.

Figure 7 shows that the three behavioral characteristics most often reported by teachers (i.e., disruptive, socially inadequate/immature, aggressive) are examples of "acting out," or externalizing types of behavior that would involve at least one other person, whereas the internalizing behaviors less frequently noted (i.e., social withdrawal, self-stimulation, self-injurious behavior) would not necessarily directly affect the teacher or other students in the class.

Overall, one could say that a wide range of experience is represented in both groups of teacher respondents (A, the group of districts with certain program refinements, and B, the randomly selected comparison group) and that the two are not substantially different from one another. The data also suggest that many of the teachers have been working with SBD students since they started teaching.

There is a discrepancy when comparing the number of students with SBD served as reported by the teacher respondents, 7:1 to 10:1 with the pupil/teacher ratio reported by the state to the US Department of Education, Office of Special Education, of 18:1 to 21:1. However, the teacher-reported ratio is closer to the US and Territories ratio of 14:1 (US Department of Education, 1984).

Recent research studies indicate it is more likely that children with intrusive, externalizing types of behavior disorders will have access to available school service via the referral process than students with other problem behaviors. Students with internalizing behaviors frequently are not referred, even though their needs for services are just as great (Hersh & Walker, 1983; Walker, in press; Walker & Rankin, 1983). This again supports the need for systematic screening procedures in order to give all children an equal chance to be screened and identified for special education services.

Figure 5

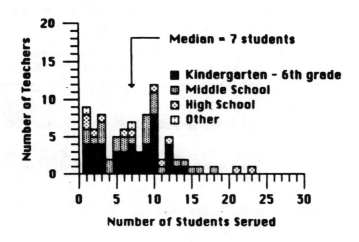

Number of SBD Students Served at Each Level of School

Figure 6

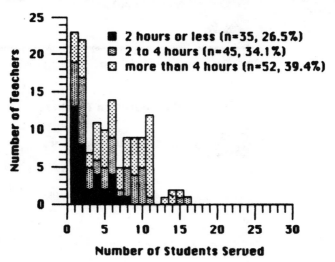

Number of SBD Students Served for Various Time Periods

Figure 7

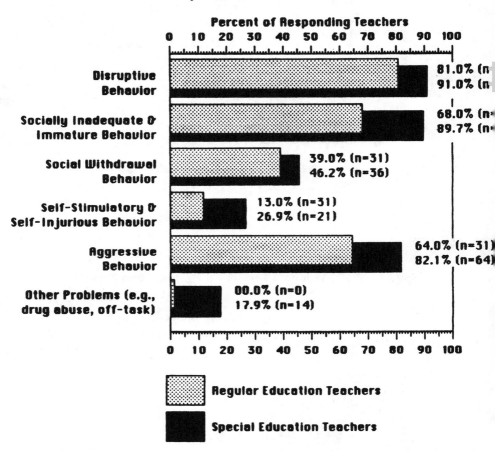

Percentage of Reporting Teachers with One or More SBD Students Exhibiting Behaviors Which Adversely Impact Academic Performance

2. Support/Assistance for Special Education Teachers

Teachers were asked to rate the types of support services they received in terms of importance (Figure 8). All of the services listed appeared to be considered important by a fair proportion of the teachers responding. "Other" forms of assistance that were positively valued included administrative support, psychological services, parental assistance, learning centers, and other teachers. With the possible exception of administrative support, these forms of assistance might be viewed as a means of providing direct services to the student without necessarily involving teacher time.

Statistically reliable subgroup differences were found in two cases. First, a much higher proportion of A-group respondents felt that specially designed curricula and materials were a valuable resource than B-group respondents (75% vs. circa 19%). Second, none of the smaller districts rated social workers as an important resource, as opposed to between 67% and 64% of the other respondents. This could be attributed to a lack of experience, in the smaller districts, with social work services in the school setting.

3. Description of Current Curricula

Special education teachers were asked to list any special curricula, materials, and equipment they used. The responses indicated a preference toward direct instruction and behavioral curricula. Of the more cognitive-based approaches, those materials and activities which strengthen social skills and self-concept were most often mentioned. This is interesting, since Gaylord-Ross and Pitts-Conway (1984) and other recent contributors to the literature have emphasized the importance of developing social interaction. Perhaps the most important of the general trends noted in response to this question was teachers' preference for strategies (i.e., social interaction) that build and strengthen adaptive behaviors.

4. Description of Instructional Practices

Teachers were asked to indicate which type of assessment procedures and intervention strategies they used. They were also given open-ended questions about methods used to measure target behavior, the average number of academic and/or social behavior change objectives per student on a typical day, and the average number of minutes spent daily in direct teacher/student instruction per objective (Questions 12-14).

Figure 8

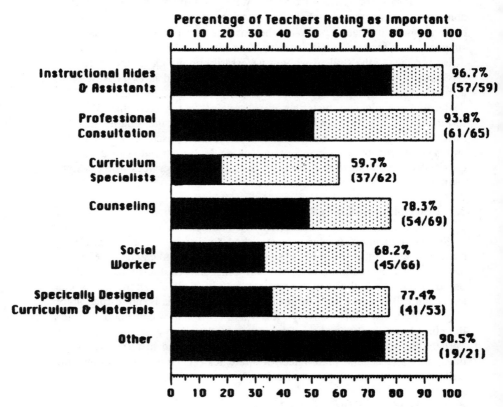

**Percentage of Responding Teachers Rating Various
Support Services They Utilize as
"Somewhat Important" (⊡ = 4 on a 5 point scale) or
"Highly Important" (■ = 5 on a 5 point scale)**

Percentage of Teachers Rating as Important

Figure 9 indicates that observation and referral information were most frequently reported for the purpose of identifying students.

Figure 10 shows the most popular intervention strategies used in programming for behavior changes. In response to a question eliciting ways of measuring behavior changes, 81% (63/78) indicated that they measured behavior changes by rating each student on change variables daily or weekly, based on counts of the behavior or a point system. Twenty-one percent (16/78) liked the use of daily self-monitoring by students. The third most frequently listed procedure was the use of direct observation by the teacher (10/78). Other strategies mentioned were student/teacher communication (6/78), folders and diaries (3/78). None of the other listed ways of measuring behavior change received more than one response.

The majority of respondents (32/48) reported setting, on average, between four and six academic and/or behavior change objectives per student per day, while the average number of minutes spent daily in direct instruction per objective ranged from 2 minutes to over 4 hours, with 5 minutes most often reported.

Overall, the responses indicate that many of the teachers are using instructional practices found in effective model programs (Noel, 1982). However, analysis of responses to questions about model practices in both the administrators' and the teachers' questionnaire, indicates no clear evidence that these practices are being systematically applied by teachers throughout the state.

5. Inservice Needs of Teachers Serving SBD Students

In regard to inservice training, teachers and administrators were given virtually identical questions. The four areas that special education teachers prioritized for inservice training are (a) behavior management strategies (60/78), (b) social skills training (20/78), (c) counseling techniques (14/78), and (d) mainstreaming strategies (13/78). Other inservice training topics montioned were task analysis, self-concept techniques, comprehensive planning, MDT planning, and stress management.

Figure 11 represents teacher ratings of inservice delivery methods. Several subgroup analyses proved significant. First, a greater proportion of Groups A teachers perceived classroom-based training as valuable than Group B teachers (93% vs. 59%). Second, all of the Group A teachers rated the use of consultants as at least somewhat effective, while only 71% (32/45) of the Group B teachers rated consultants as highly effective. Third, about 71% of the Group A teachers found visiting other programs highly effective, but only 34% of the Group B teachers provided similar ratings.

Figure 9

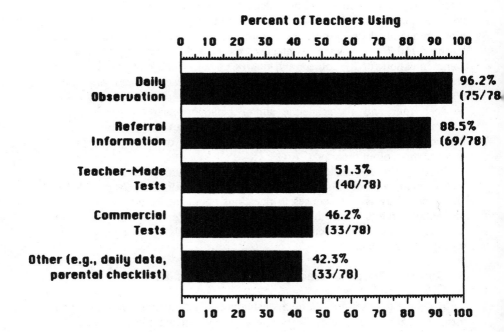

**Percent of Teachers Indicating They Use Various
Assessment Tools and/or Procedures to Identify
Student Behaviors for Intervention**

Figure 10

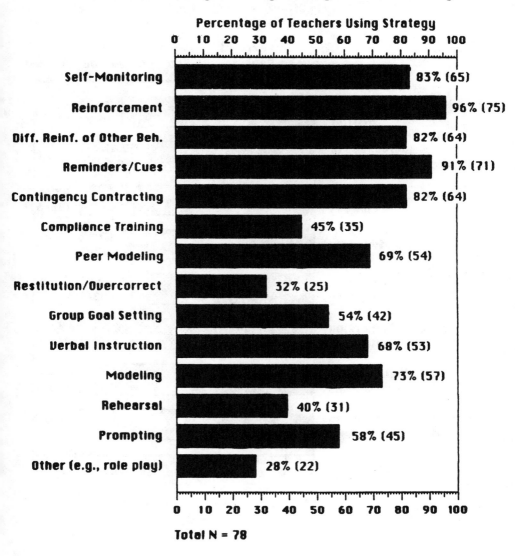

**Percentage of Teachers Indicating They Use Various
Intervention Strategies in Programming for Behavior Changes**

Percentage of Teachers Using Strategy

Strategy	Percentage
Self-Monitoring	83% (65)
Reinforcement	96% (75)
Diff. Reinf. of Other Beh.	82% (64)
Reminders/Cues	91% (71)
Contingency Contracting	82% (64)
Compliance Training	45% (35)
Peer Modeling	69% (54)
Restitution/Overcorrect	32% (25)
Group Goal Setting	54% (42)
Verbal Instruction	68% (53)
Modeling	73% (57)
Rehearsal	40% (31)
Prompting	58% (45)
Other (e.g., role play)	28% (22)

Total N = 78

Figure 11

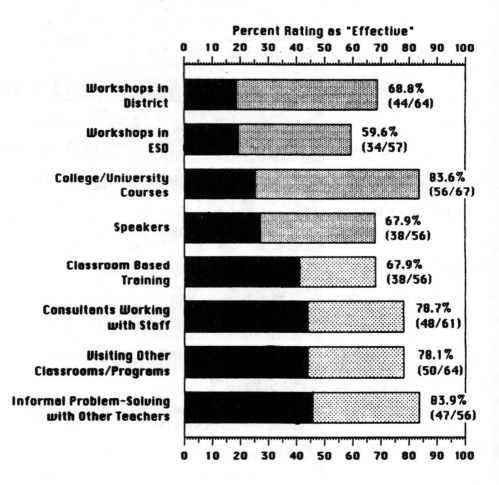

Percentage of Teachers Rating the Effectiveness of
Various Inservice Training Methods as
"Somewhat Effective" (▨ = 4 on a 5 point scale) or
"Highly Effective" (■ = 5 on a 5 point scale)

Data analysis revealed statistically significant differences between teachers' and administrators' responses for the following items:

> *Workshops in districts*: Teachers rated in-district workshops as effective less often than administrators (69% vs. 89%), chi-square = 6.6 with 1 degree of freedom; which was significant at the .01 level.

> *Consultants*: 78.7% of the teachers and 93% of the administrators though consultants were at least somewhat effective. Chi-square = 3.98 with 1 degree of freedom; significant at the .05 level.

Teachers rated college/university courses much higher than administrators (83.6% as compared to 60.5%). On other inservice delivery methods, teacher and administrator ratings were roughly parallel, with their closest agreement on the effectiveness of informal problem-solving with other teachers (about 84% and 88%, respectively).

Some differences among subgroups are worthy of mention, all related to the size of the district:

> *Workshops in District*: 22.2% and 30% of the small and large districts respectively rated workshops within the district as "highly effective," but more than 71% of the administrators from medium-sized districts rated such workshops as highly effective. The reasons for those discrepancies are not clear, since there is no small-to-large pattern. The chi-square for those differences is 9.367 with 2 degrees of freedom, which is significant at the .025 level.

> *Workshops in ESD*: All small district administrators rated ESD workshops as "somewhat effective" or "effective;" 73.9% of the medium-sized districts but only 45.5% of the large districts did so. The chi-square for that distribution of responses is 6.404 with 2 degrees of freedom and is significant at the .05 level. The interpretation of this pattern, presumably, is that smaller districts must rely more heavily on resources outside the district for inservice training.

6. Innovative Practices

Four questions (18, 19, 20, and 22) on this topic were identical to those on the administrators' questionnaire. In addition, teachers were asked to describe examples of communication systems between special education teachers, parents, and regular education teachers (Question 21).

Both administrators and teachers mentioned many of the same strategies, particularly in the area of behavior management. Both groups pointed to the need for support staff, including counselors, aides, and psychologists.

As a group, teachers didn't show a consensus on any one of several practices that could be considered innovative. However, small groups of teachers listed innovative practices such as flexibility of placement during the day, behavioral contracting and self-monitoring, joint planning on management strategies and settings with regular classroom teachers, flexibility in length of day allowing for gradual increase of time for students, peer tutoring, and team teaching.

At least some of the teachers mentioned almost all the strategies currently being used successfully with SBD students--both in Washington and nationally (Gaylord-Ross & Pitts-Conway, 1984; Kauffman, 1980, 1982; Stainback & Stainback, 1984).

Comparison of Teachers' and Administrators' Questionnaires

For the most part, the information sought from administrators was somewhat different from that requested of teachers. However, two sections of the teachers' and administrators' questionnaires were quite similar–those on inservice training needs and innovative practices.

Most of the questions in these sections were open-ended, which makes them rather difficult to compare, but a few conclusions can be drawn. Both teachers and administrators identified behavior management as the top priority for inservice training, with social skills strategies as the second priority. Both groups seemed to express similar tactics for reintegrating SBD students into regular classrooms and arranging interactions with their peers. Both mentioned a number of behavioral strategies under the topic of innovative practices, but as administrators, in general, were more reluctant to respond to the model practices questions, there are few data to compare. One difference worth noting is this: While 90% of responding teachers mentioned additional support staff under changes/improvements they would make if more funds were available, this was not a major concern of administrators (although about 30% of them did mention increased counseling services).

In one case, teachers and administrators were asked to respond to similar checklists on effectiveness of various means of inservice delivery. As summarized above, administrators rated in-district workshops and consultants significantly higher than teachers, while teachers gave higher ratings to university classes.

Except for these few differences, the information derived from the two questionnaires can be seen as complementary.

Assessment Personnel Questionnaire

In this section, we discuss the results obtained from the school psychologists and social workers who responded to the assessment personnel questionnaire. Except for six additional questions (see Exhibit 4), this questionnaire was identical to the administrators' questionnaire. Discussion of the results will thus appear under similar topic headings (i.e., Definition and Eligibility Criteria, Assessment, Program Setting Options, Intervention and Educational Approaches, Inservice Needs). The graphic displays of data from the Administrators' Questionnaire also show the percentages of responses from assessment personnel (most of whom were school psychologists) in order to facilitate comparison between the two groups of respondents.

1. Definition and Eligibility Criteria

Assessment personnel responded to six questions designed to obtain their opinions concerning state and federal definitions and ways to improve them. They were also asked to indicate the eligibility criteria they currently used and to write their "best definition" of "serious behavior disabilities" and eligibility criteria.

Regarding the clarity of the WAC definition on five issues, there was neither strong agreement nor disagreement on the first three issues. However, nearly 86% of the respondents believed that services were not sufficiently prescribed by the law. Similarly, around 73% felt that the law failed to address any policy issues, a more vehement response than that of the administrators to the same item.

Assessment personnel were also asked to register their agreement or disagreement with certain summary statements about PL 94-142, the Education for All Handicapped Children Act. Their responses were similar to those of the administrators (see Figure 2). There was strong agreement in regard to the law's specific "guarantee of a right to special education." Two of the summary statements dealt with the issue of funding levels. One proposed that the definition is adequate and that lack of funds is the only problem; the other that funding is adequate but the definition needs to be changed. The majority of the respondents failed to agree with either statement, which suggests that both funding and criteria are concerns for assessment personnel as well as for administrators.

When asked to write their own "best definition," most respondents (47%) suggested major changes in the current definition, 13%

recommended minor changes, and 40% no change at all. There was little agreement regarding their own eligibility criteria: 27% recommended major changes, 33% minor changes, and 40% no change.

2.   Formal Assessment

The responses of those in charge of conducting assessments were often similar to the responses of those who make decisions about assessment policy (see Figure 3). Fewer assessment personnel felt that neurological examinations were appropriate, and more of them than administrators indicated that the analysis of family interactions was an appropriate strategy. In addition, more of them advocated the use of personality data (78% vs. 67%). Nevertheless, the results revealed that a variety of assessments are being used with SBD populations, and that there is disagreement as to which strategies are best, thus supporting the results from the administrators on the same issue. In the *Results of Site Visits* section, below, we return to this issue of the variety of assessment procedures being used to identify different populations from one district to another across the state.

3.   Program Setting Options

Assessment personnel responded to several questions concerning program settings for SBD students. First, they were asked to rate the appropriateness of five kinds of settings most often used in their own districts. The greatest consensus of opinion occurred in regard to the third option, special education services within a public school setting. The assessment personnel were less enthusiastic than the administrators about endorsing the other options, especially the segregated special facility setting.

4.   Education and Intervention Approaches

Assessment personnel rated each of five approaches to educating SBD students according to its appropriateness (Question 13). The results seem to support the opinions of administrators and special education teachers, with two exceptions. Assessment personnel were more positive in regard to the "ecological model" (where the special education teacher plays the role of "interactionist") and considerably less enthusiastic (48% vs. 74%) about the appropriateness of the "behavioral model" (where the teacher is merely a "learning specialist"). However, the responses of the assessment personnel provide additional confirmation of a service delivery trend that we noted earlier–the trend toward an increasing reliance upon cooperative models that emphasize interactionist tactics, ecological sensitivity, and the consultant role for special education teachers. In addition, the responses seem to reflect a lack of consensus in regard to a single organizing framework, model, or system for meeting the needs of students in their classroom and community environments.

5. Inservice Needs of Assessment Personnel

Assessment personnel were asked to list the areas of inservice training needed in their districts and for their own personal benefit, and then to rate the effectiveness of various inservice delivery methods. The majority of assessment personnel felt a need for training in the areas of behavior modification and procedures for identifying SBD students. In general, the responses of the assessment personnel are in agreement with the opinions of administrators and special education teachers on this issue: Inservice training should occur within the district and should maximize contact between individuals in related positions (e.g., consultants and staff, psychologists and teachers, etc.). However, a higher proportion of the teachers (84%) than assessment personnel (56%) rated academic coursework as an effective means of inservice.

Regular Education Teacher Questionnaire

In cooperation with the Washington Education Association, the task force developed a separate survey (Exhibit 5), designed to sample regular education teachers' opinions, perspectives, and practices. Project staff distributed this survey to districts across Washington. It was intended to provide information to the task force on management tactics and strategies, types of problematic behaviors exhibited by SBD mainstreamed students, inservice needs/preferences, and teacher/student characteristics related to the education of SBD children in mainstream settings.

1. Teacher Background and Students Served

The first six items on the regular education teacher questionnaire sought information on teacher experience, students taught, and student time in regular classes. Overall teaching experience varied from 1 to 33 years. Mean years of teaching experience was 15.3, median years experience was 16. The responding teachers' experience in working with special education children is substantially less than their overall teaching experience. Overall experience with special education students was 9.7 years with a range from

0-25. Median length of time was 11 years. Information was gathered on the length of time spent teaching SBD children in regular classrooms. The overall range of experience with these children is substantially less than that for special education in general, with a mean length of 5.6 and a range from 0-20 (median = 2 years).

In regard to the number of SBD students taught at different grade levels, the data indicate that the majority of children are mainstreamed at the elementary level (14 teachers reporting 28 students), with somewhat less at the middle/junior high school level (9 teachers reporting 28 students), and substantially fewer at the high school level (4 teachers reporting 15 students).

The majority of students (43/71) are served in regular education classes 2 hours or less per day. Substantially fewer (17/71, 13/71) are served 2-4 hours, or greater than 4 hours per day, respectively.

As Figure 7 illustrates, the predominant behavior characteristic reported by regular education teachers was "Disruptive Behavior" (reported by 26/31, 84%) with "Socially Inadequate" (23/31, 74%) and "Aggressive Behavior" (20/31, 65%) reported as the next highest, respectively.

It is apparent that a wide range of experience is represented in this group of respondents. Of interest is the information obtained on the number of years these regular education teachers have been working with special education students in general. The range was 0-25 years, with a mean of 9.7 and a median of 11. This represents a considerable drop from the median years teaching, indicating that for these teachers, mainstreaming of students did not begin in earnest until Washington's Education of All Handicapped Children (HB 90) legislation was passed. The data on the number of years teaching these students were also interesting. Median length of time was 2 years, the mean 5.6, with a range from 0-20. This lends credence to the fact that these students tend to be served in more restrictive settings. Most teachers have had these students included in their regular classes only in the last 6 years (median = 5 years). In addition, the majority of these students are being served for 2 hours or less per day—indicating a continued tendency toward exclusion.

The three behavioral characteristics of the students reported most often served were all examples of acting out, externalizing types of behavior: being disruptive, socially inadequate, and aggressive. Internalizing behavioral problems were noted less frequently by the respondents. These results parallel recent research which indicates that students with externalizing behavioral problems are more likely to be identified.

2.   Support/Assistance for Regular Education Teachers

Teachers were asked to rate the types of support services they receive from special education. In response to a question about sufficient support from special education in maintaining SBD students in regular education classes, 52% indicated that support/assistance was "sufficient." Teachers were asked to rate the types of service they presently use in terms of importance. Highest, both in terms of the number of teachers rating "highly important" and the overall proportion rating as "highly" or "somewhat important" was the use of the special education teacher. Next was counseling followed by professional consultation.

A series of open-ended questions was designed to elicit comments regarding successful practices that facilitate integration of SBD students into regular classes. Teachers indicated that parental and administrative support, along with professional consultants, was useful. Smaller class loads, special education personnel support, and time allotted for communication with special education personnel were also noted. The use of behavioral/classroom management technologies and specialized curricula was also effective.

The teachers were asked to report the types of communication systems they utilize with parents and teachers in order to insure student success. Daily communication between parents and teachers through either notes or phone calls was most often mentioned. Memos, conferences, and group meetings were also noted. The respondents also mentioned regularly scheduled observations of the student by special education personnel in regular classes.

One question asked teachers to indicate crucial changes they felt would significantly improve the quality and effectiveness of the SBD program. Inservice training in the area of classroom/behavior management (with time allotted for special education personnel to work with regular education teachers), early intervention, and increased parental involvement were all noted.

The most important finding from this series of questions is that only a slim majority of the respondents (52%) felt that support/assistance from special education was sufficient. It seems obvious, given this response, that special education must do a better job of supporting regular education personnel when SBD students are placed in less restrictive settings.

In terms of types of services they receive, the highest ratings were given to the services provided by special education teachers. Counseling for the student was also rated highly, as was use of special education instructional aides and professional consultation. Those types of services receiving the lowest ratings were curriculum specialists, social workers, and specially designed curriculum and materials.

It was also noted that regular educators want administrative and parental support when they are faced with these children in their classes. Regular teachers feel that consistent communicating with all involved parties is essential to ensure the success of the student in the mainstream.

3.   Description of Instructional Practices

The next questions were designed to elicit descriptions of current instructional practices, curricula, special materials, and equipment used in serving SBD students.

Respondents indicated that, for the most part, strategies that reduced or minimized the interruptive behavior of students were the most often used—for example, preferential seating (e.g., seating in front of class), individualized instruction, and direct instructional methodologies. Curriculum modification, the practice of breaking down large units of academic work into smaller subunits to facilitate task completion, was also mentioned. Special curricula utilized were those that teach basic (or survival) skills. Social skills instruction was also mentioned. Special materials/equipment were comprised mainly of visual aids (e.g., overhead projectors, filmstrips, video tapes) and computers to maintain high interest and facilitate learning.

4.   Inservice Needs of Regular Education Teachers

In the area of inservice training, regular teachers were questioned on needs of those teachers who have SBD children in their classes. The priority areas for inservice training were:

1.   Behavior management strategies (12/31–39%)

2.   Modification of curricula to meet the SBD child's needs (7/31–23%)

3.   Developing motivation in the SBD child (5/31–16%).

Teachers were also asked to rate the effectiveness of delivery methods used to conduct inservice training. Those service delivery modes receiving "highly" or "somewhat" important ratings were:

1. Informal meetings with other teachers and support professionals for problem sharing/solving (19/31–61%)

2. Classroom based training (17/31–54%)

3. Consultants working with staff (14/31–45%)

4. Visiting other classrooms/programs (12/31–38%).

The three areas which regular education teachers felt were highest priorities for inservice training (i.e., behavior management strategies, curriculum modification, developing motivation) are related to the desire of teachers not only to help students complete more work and become more motivated, but also to manage disruptive behavior more adequately.

In achieving these goals, regular education teachers felt that inservice based upon informal meetings with other teachers/support personnel was most effective. This approach coupled with classroom-based training and the use of consultants working with staff were those approaches that received the highest ratings. A number of respondents also preferred having the opportunity to visit other classrooms/programs.

Results of Site Visits

This section discusses the conclusions derived from site interviews and random checks of student files at each of the Group A school districts. Project staff conducted these site interviews and random file checks in order to obtain anecdotal information and data to support the overall profile of results from the questionnaires.

1. Screening and Eligibility Criteria

The analysis of the site interviews that took place in 15 school districts indicated a lack of systematic procedures for screening students and determining their eligibility for services. Typically, screening was synonymous with teacher referral, and relied upon teachers' anecdotal accounts of problematic student behaviors in the classroom. The determination of a student's eligibility for services was not consistent from district to district. Given any two districts in the state, it is possible that the same child could be found eligible for special education services in one district and not eligible in the other.

While all 15 districts use multi-disciplinary teams (MDTs), eligibility depends primarily upon the perspective of the school psychologist who undertakes a child's screening or assessment, using whatever instrument seems to be appropriate. This indicates that the school psychologist has a powerful influence on MDTs. Given that influence, school psychologists should utilize the highest standards in selecting instruments and procedures from those available. Based on the project's findings, there is sufficient information revealing inconsistencies in the overall assessment process and currently selected instruments to suggest that the Washington Association of School Psychologists should select this issue for further review and study.

There are several additional problems in regard to identification and screening. Most of the conventional assessment scales and procedures do not yield a quantification of behavior. Instruments in current use make quantification difficult. In the area of SBD, professionals must use frequency measures combined with descriptions of the behavior. Moreover, when professionals do not utilize systematic procedures for assessment, greater unreliability is likely to occur. This unreliability generates "false positives" and "false negatives" (i.e., students mistakenly identified as behaviorally disturbed, or behaviorally disturbed students not identified at all).

An analysis of the site interviews yielded seven categories representing the continuum of SBD students currently of age and possibly eligible for services in public schools in Washington. Anecdotal information gathered during the site interviews indicated that, in the interviewee's estimation, these categories account for a significant number of children and youth with behavior disabilities. The children and youth represented here are approximately 2-3% of the total K-12 population. This would put Washington at the conservative end of national prevalence estimates for this population. The seven categories are:

1. Students with problem behaviors who are not made a focus of concern, are not declared eligible, and are not served.

These school-age children exhibit inappropriate behavior to such a degree that their educational performance is affected. However, they are not referred, and thus not served, because of such variables as teacher tolerance level and teacher expertise in dealing with management problems.

2. Students with problem behaviors who may be a focus of concern, but are not declared eligible for services under the SBD category and are thus served outside of special education.

These children exhibit inappropriate behavior to such a degree that their educational performance is affected. They may be referred by their classroom teacher for outside assistance. In many districts, they may receive services (e.g., counselor, psychologist, local school child study team member) sufficient, in most cases, to remediate the problem.

3. Identified students who are declared eligible for services under the SBD category, and are receiving special education and/or related services in district.

This category includes students identified according to the criteria in WAC 392-171-386 who are currently receiving services.

4. Identified students who are declared eligible for services under the SBD category and are receiving services by district/agency or by agency.

These students exhibit behaviors which adversely affect their educational performance to such a degree that they require either a combination of district/outside agency support, or total outside agency support to meet their needs.

5. Identified students who are declared eligible for services but are served under other handicap categories.

These children exhibit inappropiate behavior to such a degree that they could be judged eligible for services for SBD children, but because of the presence of other conditions (e.g., learning disabilities, mild mental retardation, health impairments) may be placed in other special education categories. This occurs, in part, because of the difficulty of separating out singular etiologies for handicaps, and social pressure to classify children with more socially acceptable labels.

6. Identified students who may be declared eligible for services under the SBD category but are not served.

These students are usually found at the secondary level.

7. Adjudicated youth.

These youth exhibit inappropriate behaviors that adversely affect their educational performance. They are under the jurisdiction of the juvenile justice system and may not receive special education and/or related services.

2.   Comprehensive Assessment

Project staff examined a random selection of student files in order to discover what kinds of assessment instruments were in use. They found that the majority of such instruments were academic in nature (e.g., WRAT, Woodcock, Key Math, PIAT, etc.). When behavior assessments did occur, these were usually projective instruments such as the TAT, Sentence Completion, Rorschach, House-Tree-Person etc. Standardized behavior observation formats or behavior rating checklists were the exception, not the rule. School districts relied upon anecdotal reports of directly observed student behavior; there were very few standard observational formats utilized. The results of this investigation parallel the results of Smith, Frank, and Snider (1984), which indicated that academic and intellectual assessment data were readily available and judged by teachers and psychologists to be of highest quality. They also found that, while teachers and psychologists judged systematic, objective behavioral observations and rating scales to be of the highest value, such data were typically not available or of low quality.

A random selection of student files across districts revealed that over 80% of the students identified and assessed were of the externalizing type. Recent studies indicate that it is more likely that children with disruptive, externalizing types of behavior disabilities will have access to services via the referral process than students with internalizing problem behaviors. Students with internalizing behaviors frequently are not referred, even though their need for services is just as great (Achenbach & Edelbrock, 1978; Hersh & Walker, 1983; Ross, 1974; Walker & Rankin, 1983; Walker, Reavis, Rhode, & Jenson, 1985). This underscores the need for systematic screening procedures in order to give all children an equal chance to be screened and identified for special education services.

3.   Components of a Comprehensive Management Plan

The majority of districts reviewed by project staff gave little evidence of any kind of comprehensive management planning. An examination of a random selection of student files revealed that there was little consistency in determining the steps from initial screening through programming to evaluation. In many cases, programming for students seemed to depend upon the personal style of the teacher, or to be ad hoc in nature, subject to individual cases and shifts over time, or to emphasize crisis management at the expense of foresight and prevention. In addition, "least restrictive environment" (LRE) options varied from one district to the next. Thus, while some districts were fairly sophisticated in terms of determining and implementing various LREs, others had few options of this kind, and emphasized self-contained classrooms and resource room services.

4.   Inservice Training

The nature, content, and methods of disseminating inservice training also varied from one district to another. One district (which seemed to be the best in this regard) reported a consistent provision of inservice to staff through the ESD during the school year. This consisted of scheduled visits by itinerant ESD personnel who held "brainstorming" sessions with teachers. In addition, enough money was available district-wide to insure inservice throughout the school year. However, in the other districts, inservice needs were acknowledged but not always met. Typically, the ESD provided some inservice, but (because of lack of funds or staff) could not adequately meet the needs of the school districts it was supposed to serve. In addition, the delivery of inservice often took the form of responses to emergencies rather than as part of a careful systematically developed plan, reflecting a crisis management rather than preventive orientation.

5.   Pilot Study: Multiple Gating Screening Procedure

Project staff and task force members discussed the existing problems with screening procedures. They noted that there is a trend toward inclusion of the teacher's perspective in the screening process (Achenbach & Edelbrock, 1978, 1984; Ross, 1974; Smith, 1985). A pilot study to investigate the effectiveness of a multiple gating (also known as "multiphase") screening procedure was proposed.

The multiple gating screening procedure (Loeber, Dishion, & Patterson, 1984) uses teacher ratings and rankings, as well as observations of classroom and free play activities, to assess child behavior both qualitatively and quantitatively. Most importantly, child behavior is viewed along an externalizing/internalizing continuum. This gives the internalizing, withdrawn child an equal chance of being identified along with the externalizing, assertive child.

A multiple gating screening procedure involves several stages in distinguishing children with possible behavior disabilities from other children. Initially, the classroom teacher groups between 10 and 15 of the children in the class on an externalizing dimension. This dimension represents those problematic behaviors that are assertive and aggressive. The teacher also groups between 10 and 15 children in the class on an internalizing dimension. This dimension represents those problematic behaviors that are more "inward directed." The teacher then divides each group in two, placing the children for each dimension, into a "high" group and a "low" group. The "high" group includes those children who exemplify externalizing behaviors to the greatest degree, and the "low" group, those who display these behaviors to a lesser degree. Continuing the first phase, the teacher ranks the "high" and "low" groups for each dimension. This ranking results in a hierarchy of children within each dimension, with the child who most exemplifies that dimension at the top, and the child who least exemplifies it at the bottom. For each dimension, the top three students are selected to move into a subsequent phase.

In that phase, the teacher rates each child according to two indices. The first index is a record of the frequency with which a child exhibits maladaptive behaviors. The second index is an assessment of critical behaviors. The teacher notes, by means of a yes/no response, a child's maladaptive behaviors that, by their very serious nature, should they occur only once, require further assessment. If the child's scores on these two indices are high enough, he or she moves on to the next phase.

This phase involves observation of the child in classrooms and other environments to determine if the quantity and quality of the behaviors exhibited deviate enough, when compared to the behavior of peers, to warrant either a comprehensive assessment or intervention to remediate the problem behaviors.

Project staff initiated a field test of the multiple gating screening procedure in the spring of 1985. This field test was conducted in Highline School District #401. The intent of this pilot study was to establish preliminary data concerning the discriminative validity (i.e., the ability of the instrument to accurately discriminate behavior "normals" and those already identified as "SBD" through established procedures) and consumer (i.e., teacher or other service provider) satisfaction regarding the procedure.

The procedure was completed by 9 elementary school teachers, grades 1-5, representing 320 children. These teachers were selected because of the presence of at least one student with SBD mainstreamed into their classes, with a total of 10 students with SBD mainstreamed in the classes of the 9 teachers. The teachers were asked to complete the multiple gating screening procedure, however they were not told that the purpose of the procedure was to identify students with SBD.

Stage 1 of the multiple gating procedure correctly identified 9 of the 10 as being problematic to the degree that they were ranked among the top three students as exhibiting externalizing behaviors. The tenth student was ranked fifth by his teacher. The field test population included no children with internalizing behaviors. Nine of the 10 identified children were boys; however the multiple gating procedure successfully identified the one girl among the sample population.

Teachers reported that the procedure was "straightforward," "easy," and "fairly quick" to complete. Teachers took from 20 to 40 minutes to complete the procedure.

These preliminary data indicate that further study of the multiple gating screening procedure is warranted. The procedure, at Stage 1, discriminated children with SBD from their normal peers with 90% accuracy. Teachers also indicated satisfaction with the procedure. Total time to complete the procedure was only 20-40 minutes, a relatively short time considering the extent of the data gathered and analyzed.

One of the next steps in researching the validity of the multiple gating screening procedure should be to test the procedure's success in identifying children whose behavior disabilities are of an internalizing nature.

Summary

The responses to the questionnaires summarized the opinions and perspectives of administrators, assessment personnel, and teachers throughout Washington regarding services to children and youth with SBD. These responses indicate the following four areas of need:

1. A need for agreement in regard to identification and eligibility criteria for students with SBD.

2. A need to develop and implement a statewide comprehensive assessment procedure.

3. A need to identify the components of a comprehensive management plan.

4. A need to identify the nature, content, and dissemination methods of training for school staff.

A need for more resources was also frequently cited by respondents and is related, to some degree, to each of the four needs listed above.

The data from the on-site interviews and random checks of student files supported the findings from the questionnaires.

Discussion

The analysis of the responses to all questionnaires (Administrators, Assessment Personnel, Special Education Teachers, and Regular Education Teachers), the site interviews, and the sample programs in Washington resulted in the identification of the four areas of need that relate to the original objectives of the project task force. In this chapter, we discuss each of these areas with reference to the results from all task force activities, and include recommendations for future action by the working committees.

Identification, Eligibility, and Assessment

Screening and Eligibility Criteria

One of the objectives of the study was to estimate the number of children and youth with SBD in the state who are not being served or are being served inadequately or inappropriately.

During the 1983-84 school year, Washington provided special education services to about one half of one percent (or 3,400 students) of the total K-12 student population (730,736) under the SBD category (as reported in OSPI State Summary Report 1735: Special Education Average Student Enrollment, Form P223H 3). Nationally it is estimated that 2-12% of children and youth ages 3 to 21 should receive special education and related services because of their emotional disturbance (Grosenick & Huntze, 1980). However, the national percentage of these students actually being served as handicapped during 1983 was only 0.88% (Kauffman, 1986, p. 27). Given these estimates, seriously behaviorally disturbed students appear to be an underserved population both nationally and in this state.

When compared to national averages, the discrepancy in Washington appears significant. Although the percentage of students actually served nationally is far lower than estimates of need, that figure is still nearly 50% higher than the percentage served here. Furthermore, the number of SBD students receiving special education services in the state has steadily declined (by 33%) since 1976, while the number of students served nationally increased by approximately 25% during the same period. The surveys asked respondents to estimate the number of students who needed special services but were not eligible for them. Their estimates totaled over 14,000 students. In other words, survey respondents felt that actually about 2.5% of the student population is in need of services.

Project staff conducted on-site interviews with administrators in order to validate this estimate. These interviews resulted in the identification of the seven categories of students listed above. These seven categories include students whose problematic behaviors are significant enough in the view of school personnel to require various services to remediate them.   The students in all seven categories represent the population of SBD children and youth currently of age and possibly eligible for services in the state's public schools. Project staff and the persons interviewed estimated that these students represented 2-3% of the total K-12 population, a figure that would still put Washington on the conservative side of national prevalence estimates for these children and youth. However, only the students in Categories 3 and 4 (Identified-Declared eligible-Receiving special education services in district, Identified-Declared eligible-Receiving services by district/agency) are receiving services that are specifically intended for the SBD population. Students in the remaining categories are either receiving services intended for students with other handicapping conditions, benefiting from services only in certain cities or counties, or not being served at all.

The difficulties in determining exactly which students are unserved or underserved seem to be caused by a lack of clarity and consistency in the eligibility criteria for this population. For example, in response to the needs assessment questionnaire, administrators identified the same five types of behavior as characteristic of both the students receiving special education services and those who were not eligible for them. This may point to inconsistent means of deciding which students are referred for special education and which are not.

In addition, at the secondary level, confusion can result from students who either drop out of school or, in some cases, exit special education programs in the public schools in order to enter other special programs (e.g., alternative schools). In either case, it seems obvious that the student with actual or potential SBD presents special programmatic problems. Finally, during the site visits by project staff, a random selection of student files indicated that teacher referrals to MDT personnel resulted in a greater number of externalizing rather than internalizing students coming to the attention of the team.

A recent study commissioned by the US Department of Education to investigate the merits of changing the federal terminology from "seriously emotionally disturbed" to "behaviorally disordered" concluded that such a change would not affect the size or nature of the population served nationwide unless "the definition were made so detailed and explicit that it would take away much of the local autonomy that currently exists for operationalizing Federal intent" in regard to special education services (*Education for the Handicapped Law Report*, Suppl. 149, August 2, 1985, p. 191). Thus, we believe that it is appropriate to retain the current WAC definition for "serious behavior disabilities." Washington should concentrate its efforts on establishing reliable statewide eligibility criteria for students to be served.

Recommendations. In working toward this goal, the appropriate agencies and individuals in Washington should proceed according to the following recommendations submitted to the task force by the Identification and Assessment Working Committee:

1. OSPI, with the cooperation of ESDs/school districts, should determine the feasibility and appropriateness of a use of a valid reliable screening and comprehensive assessment procedure and if appropriate support its application.

    In pursuing an investigation of appropriate procedures, special attention should be directed to the following issues: (a) a comparison of the previously investigated multiple gating procedure with other established screening instruments or approaches in terms of validity, reliability, cost effectiveness, and time effectiveness; (b) the extent to which the misidentification of SBD children and youth has occurred because of these other instruments or approaches; (c) the degree to which the multiple gating screening procedure succeeds in identifying both externalizing and internalizing students, as compared to other instruments and approaches; (d) an investigation of the variables that may influence the outcome of the screening process (e.g., secondary school disciplinary policies that may cause students to be expelled/removed from school before screening and assessment can even begin); and (e) an investigation of those factors that may influence screening reliability and validity.

2. OSPI and ESDs/school districts should continue to investigate the reasons for the low identification rates of SBD students on a local and statewide basis, and complete this investigation by the end of the 1985-86 school year.

In addition, the Parent Advocacy Working Committee recommended that its members meet with attorneys employed by school districts to examine the legal implications of adopting the multiple gating screening procedure. OSPI and ESDs/school districts should also consider means of training school staffs to use it effectively.

In observing these guidelines for future action, Washington will be moving in the direction of establishing consistent, comprehensive statewide eligibility criteria for the SBD population.

Assessment Procedures

Assessments and their application are often closely related to the screening and eligibility issues discussed above. The data obtained from the assessment personnel questionnaire, and the results of the administrators' questionnaire revealed that the criteria used to determine eligibility for special services varied from one school district, MDT, and school psychologist to the next because of the variety of assessment instruments and procedures in use. Specifically, the study's review of randomly selected student files revealed that MDTs rely on intellectual and academic assessments and projective measurements, which meet the minimum eligibility requirements of Washington law, but most MDTs did not use other valid and reliable assessment strategies (i.e., those concerned with obtaining relevant information about medical status, cognitive functioning, and behavioral adaptation) which would have value in program planning by teachers and other service providers. In addition, there was very litle evidence of the use of systematic observational formats.

Similarly, the program presentations made to the task force, as well as the sites visited by project staff, indicated that teachers emphasized behavioral strategies in the classroom that relied upon measurable behavioral outcomes, and MDT activities indicated a continued reliance upon assessments and measurements whose results were not immediately applicable for classroom interventions.

Accordingly, MDTs are not using the full range of reliable and valid assessment strategies that exist (McGinnis, Kiraly, & Smith, 1984; Smith, 1985; Smith, Frank, & Snider, 1984; Walker, Reavis, Rhode, & Jenson, 1985) and therefore may not be obtaining all of the relevant data (e.g., medical, cognitive, etc.) that teachers consider useful for purposes of programming. Moreover, in the programs discussed above, the results of assessment that are being used are not being systematically converted into measurable behavioral outcomes that can be used by teachers and other service providers.

Recommendations. In sum, the data clearly pointed out the need to develop and implement statewide guidelines for comprehensive assessment procedures. In meeting this need, the Identification and Assessment Working Committee and the Comprehensive Management Working Committee submitted the following recommendations to the task force:

1. Washington should assist ESDs/school districts in developing a technical assistance manual with annotated samples of current practices for assessment personnel throughout the state. This resource would include those assessment instruments and procedures that are most reliable and valid, both for purposes of educational programming and as guidelines for consultations that involve psychiatric/medical and other related services.

2. Using this technical assistance manual, Washington and all relevant personnel should assist ESDs/school districts in developing guidelines for assessment that emphasize measurable behavioral outcomes to be readily converted by teachers and other service providers into educational practices.

3.   Washington should ensure that (a) assessment procedures are
     consistent across and within school districts; (b) these assessment
     procedures relate directly to the establishment of goals and
     objectives for each individual student, and (c) the
     instruments/procedures used in the assessment process
     appropriately differentiate students with SBD and similarly "hard
     to place" students from other children and youth.

Comprehensive Management and Interagency Coordination

A third area of need with regard to current Washington practices for
educating SBD students has to do with the lack of an organizing
framework, model, or plan for the delivery of services. Such a scheme
would include (a) initial screening and assessment, (b) placement selection,
(c) development of individualized behavior strategies, and (d) provision for
appropriate training and resources.

We have already shown that there are substantial problems with
screening in Washington. Screening is accomplished through the traditional
teacher referral process. This has resulted in students with "acting out" or
externalizing behaviors more frequently referred, assessed, and served than
those exhibiting more internalized behavior problems. Even within the
former group, there are discrepancies among districts in the determination
of which students receive services and which do not.

Placement Options

The setting in which to provide services to SBD students has long been a
controversial issue. Prevailing attitudes have changed over time. They have
included the belief that behavioral disabilities were the responsibility of
mental health professionals rather than educators, and that the best and most
efficient settings for these students were self-contained classes and separate
schools. Today, PL 94-142 clearly places responsibility with the public
schools, and the law's "least restrictive environment" demands put certain
pressure on schools to integrate these students into regular class settings
whenever possible. Problems continue because of uncertainties about what
to do with those "hard to place" students (and others such as troubled deaf
youth) who do not easily fit into the regular classroom (or exceed teacher
tolerance levels or competency to deal with their presence), but do need a
planned program of progressive inclusion. Behavior disabilities of the most
severe kind tend to be chronic and require continuous assessment and

comprehensive management throughout a child's school career and well into adulthood. Nevertheless, students whose behavior problems may never be successfully "remediated" have a right to the full range of special services available for ages 3-21, regardless of the financial burden placed on school districts.

Furthermore, there is a scarcity of research on the topic of program setting as it contributes to the improved management of "hard to place" students and others with SBD.

The results from the assessment personnel questionnaire echoed the findings from administrators by indicating a variety of program options, including resource, self-contained, and mainstream classes. However, there was little consensus on the ways to determine the "least restrictive environment," which seemed to be defined in terms that varied between schools or teachers. The data also indicated a continuing emphasis on services in more restrictive settings.

The on-site interviews confirmed that placement options tend to be restrictive, in either self-contained or resource classrooms. Informants frequently cited funding restrictions as the major obstacle to providing more comprehensive management and placement options.

Thus, in Washington as in other states, the data indicate that students tend to be served in restrictive settings. Walker, Reavis, Rhode, & Jenson (1985) and other authors have pointed to the negative effects of segregated placement, including: (a) depriving regular teachers of both the incentive and opportunity to develop the competencies needed to accommodate students in the regular classroom, and (b) reducing rather than increasing the student's ability to function effectively within and to cope with the demands of other environments.

The Sixth Annual Report to Congress on Implementation of PL 94-142 (US Department of Education, 1984) reports that progress has been made in serving students in less restrictive settings. The instructional and behavioral technologies do exist to effectively accommodate the needs of the great majority of behavior disabled children of school age in integrated placements, though for various reasons they have not been used effectively in the public schools (Becker, in press; Engelmann & Colvin, 1983; Joyce, Hersh, & McKibben, 1983; McDowell, Adamson, & Wood, 1982; Morra, 1978; Paine, Bellamy, & Wilcox, 1984; Rehmann & Riggen, 1977; Reid & Hresko, 1981; Reynolds, 1983; Walker, in press).

The literature attests that it is both desirable and possible to serve these students in settings less restrictive than their current placements. Schools should be able to provide full service delivery to these students in a continuum of educational settings.

In addition, the lack of enough adequate placement options in Washington has resulted in students being placed out of state at great cost to local school districts. However, Colorado has developed a system for returning students home again to receive all necessary services. Within the last five years, over 200 students initially receiving services out of state have returned, and (as of September 1985) only four students are being served outside the state (see Exhibit 7).

Recommendations.   In regard to placement options, the working committees submitted the following recommendations to the task force:

1. Washington should investigate and disseminate methods for developing and making use of less restrictive settings in the public schools.

2. There should be an emphasis upon selecting the least restrictive placement option during the screening and assessment of each student, including students that are considered "hard to place."

3. Following the lead of Colorado, Washington should reduce and ultimately eliminate the need for costly out-of-state placements by encouraging the development of programs so that traditionally "hard-to-place," "high-cost," students can be served as near to their homes as possible.

Curricula and Instructional Practices

The surveys of both special education and regular education teachers elicited information about the variety of curricula and instructional practices currently in use. Most of the responses indicated a preference for direct instruction and behavioral curricula, with an emphasis upon strengthening academic concepts, social skills, and student self-esteem. Similarly, both groups of teachers reported a variety of intervention strategies that they used in programming for behavior changes. Most of these highly preferred strategies could be called "behavioral;" they included "self-monitoring" and "modeling," the latter of which is emerging as a very important strategy for teaching appropriate social skills and adaptations to natural settings (Gaylord-Ross & Pitts-Conway, 1984).

In general, the survey indicated that many of the respondents were using curricula and instructional practices considered to be typical for effective model programs. However, there was no evidence that the curricula and strategies were being systematically used by teachers throughout the state. The results of the on-site interviews indicated a similar lack of systematic application. The programs in Washington that were reviewed by the task force revealed both strengths and weaknesses in their programming. On the one hand, the majority of these programs (92%) used student data on progress toward behavioral goals and objectives as the basis for decisions about programming and instruction, while over half (58%) used specialized curricula for teaching students appropriate social behaviors (e.g., Stephens Social Skills Curriculum, Walker Social Skills Curriculum). On the other hand, only 33% of the programs addressed the issue of the generalization of skills (a concern of the task force reviewers), and then only on an informal basis.

Recommendations. In light of these results from surveys, interviews, and review of sample programs, the Comprehensive Management Working Committee submitted to the task force the following recommendations in regard to programming (which covers both curricula and instructional practices):

1. Programming for the generalization of skills must occur in all of the program options for students with SBD.

2. Programming for each individual student must be aimed at returning the student to the regular education environment with the ability to perform satisfactorily in that environment.

3. Individual student programs should be comprehensive: they must address the environments in which a child or adolescent functions, and treat them as an integrated whole.

4. Individual student programs should be based on goals and objectives that result from the identification of student strengths and weaknesses (medical, cognitive, behavioral) by means of the assessment procedures.

5. There should be an emphasis on the use of observable and measurable events as a basis for programming decisions and changes; these events, as the major component of student data, should be continuously monitored and evaluated by the MDT.

6. The curricula and teaching strategies used for each individual student should cover each of the following six areas, which are emphasized in exemplary service delivery systems/models such as Colorado and Vermont:

    a. Environmental management (i.e., the internal environment of the classroom, the external environment of the mainstream setting, home, community).

    b.   Behavior management (e.g., self-control, task completion, etc.).

    c.   Academics.

    d.   Career/vocational education.

    e.   Affective education (e.g., social skills instruction, personality development, etc.).

    f.   Counseling (i.e., both individual and group).

Interagency Coordination

Another of the task force objectives was an examination of the relationship between schools and other agencies in order to identify those practices most likely to promote successful cooperative management. The lack of communication and coordination between schools and nonschool agencies has caused many problems for districts around the country. Most district administrators in Washington who responded to the questionnaire did report the use of outside agencies in serving SBD students. Some respondents, however, noted certain problems such as bargaining, funding, or lack of available support services. On the other hand, 83% of the programs in Washington reviewed by the task force entered into interagency working agreements and partnerships. Specifically, social service agencies and the schools worked together to provide comprehensive intervention for these students. In sum, it appears that while interagency cooperation of an exemplary kind exists in many localities (e.g., a network that involves school districts, the DSHS, and mental health agencies exists in some areas of the state), there is no overall, comprehensive scheme that would clarify and delegate the responsibilities of different agencies in regard to SBD and other "hard to place" students, as well as govern the relationships among these agencies.

Another problem that calls for some sort of interagency deliberation and cooperation is the uncoordinated, localized provision of services to adjudicated youth. The on-site interviews identified these youth as possibly eligible for services but not receiving them on a consistent basis.

By "adjudicated" youth, we mean those whose activities and behaviors bring them into contact with juvenile courts, detention centers, and correctional facilities. A 1979 nationwide survey of 204 juvenile corrections centers concluded that 41.1% of incarcerated youth were identified as handicapped (Morgan, 1979). Approximately 16% of these handicapped offenders were identified as "emotionally handicapped" (the highest percentage among the handicapping conditions), while only 2% of the general student population have been so labeled. During an oversight hearing on the provision of special education to handicapped juvenile delinquents (US Congress, District of Columbia Fiscal Affairs and Health Subcommittee), the General Accounting Office stated that 46% of incarcerated youth have been identified as handicapped (*Education Daily*, September 11, 1985). Recent national estimates indicated that 8% of the handicapped juvenile offender population were identified as "seriously behavior disabled," while approximately 60% were identified as "severe learning disabled." In addition, a joint survey by Al Lynch (Coordinator of Institutional Education, Division of Special Services and Professional Programs, OSPI) and Bob Thorton (Program Administrator, Program Services, Division of Juvenile Rehabilitation, DSHS) revealed that 40% of the state's incarcerated youth were found to be handicapped, and that one third of these were considered to be seriously behaviorally disabled. While there are many problems in determining the prevalence of handicapped juvenile offenders among the general student population, there seems to be a consensus among educators and legal experts that these youth are woefully unserved or underserved as far as special education services are concerned (Keilitz, 1984).

In Washington, a recent DSHS report (1983) recommended that coordination and referral procedures be developed to facilitate the transition of juvenile offenders between state institutions and public schools. In some localities, programs exist to provide educational services to offenders with behavior disabilities.

One example of such a program is the Whatcom County Juvenile Court Services Offender Education Unit (EU) (Freeberg, 1984). This program was designed to help youthful offenders (youth with "demonstrated educational difficulties" and "problem behaviors") with prescriptive educational services, on the theory that rehabilitation is necessarily prescriptive and educational, thus reducing the likelihood of repeated encounters with the criminal justice system.

Whereas the Morgan (1979) nationwide survey concluded that 41% of incarcerated youth were identified as handicapped, the EU study revealed 84% were certifiably handicapped. While Morgan found approximately 16% were "emotionally handicapped," the EU study found the incidence to be closer to 30%. Finally, while more recent 1984 demographics suggest 8% of handicapped youth are behaviorally disabled and 60% are "seriously learning disabled," the EU sample found the incidence of the latter to be 22%.

Operation of the EU program entailed collaboration among an educational psychologist, a facilities coordinator (facilitator), public school and juvenile court personnel, and (whenever possible) parents. The program has been successful to date because the majority of participating youth have been provided special education services by schools, whereas previously the majority were excluded from such services. Another success indicator is the close liaison between the EU and schools: The EU facilitator is currently regarded as extramural faculty instead of an occasionally visiting agent of the juvenile court. (For a detailed description of this program, see Freeberg, 1984.)

Members of the Interagency Services Working Committee indicated that such collaboration is needed for students whose involvement in the juvenile court system arises under state Families in Conflict statutes (RCW Chapter 13.32A). The Division of Child and Family Services' social workers are frequently unaware of the rights which disabled children have under state and federal law, and are often not cognizant of the educational and related services available through the local school districts. Better coordination between this agency and local school districts could result in the identification of children and youth with SBD who are currently not being properly served.

Thus, any comprehnsive plan for interagency cooperation should tartget this category of youth, and take into account the arrangements that already exist for implementing programs to meet the educational needs of this relatively underserved population.

Exemplary programs in other state. Project staff investigated nationwide model practices to determine their applicability in regard to students with SBD in Washington. From among the states that responded to an initial letter of inquiry, project staff selected six (Colorado, Georgia, Idaho, Iowa, Utah, and Vermont) whose programs met five standards established by Grosenick and Huntze (1983) for exemplary programs. First, each state provided a continuum of services (with a variety of placement options, from least to most restrictive) for this population. Second, each state had a set of comprehensive, formal, legal agreements that defined the responsibilities of the agencies that provided services (at both state and local levels). Third, each state had tackled the problem of funding by creating a special fund that was activated whenever parents, school districts, or community agencies were unable to pay for the costs of certain services to special needs students who were initially placed out of state to receive services. Fifth, each state provided educational services to adjudicated youth on a statewide basis.

Utah has developed an intriguing "behavioral cascading" model while Iowa has published (1985) an extensive training manual for assessment of behavioral disorders. Their approach is particularly appealing as it systematically outlines procedures in three major areas: analysis of the setting, analysis of pupil behavioral data, and analysis of individual traits.

Project staff determined that Colorado was the most exemplary state in regard to the features essential for the delivery of comprehensive services. For example, in Colorado there is a system of joint interagency programming that enables a student to receive all services over a period of time without gaps occurring in regard to meeting the student's total program needs. This system is based upon an excellent set of comprehensive interagency agreements that govern relationships among all agencies providing services[4]. In addition, the Colorado legislature has provided a special state revenue fund to be used as a supplementary source of funding by all state agencies serving handicapped students. Finally, Colorado has recently instituted a successful system for bringing students back into the state from out-of-state placements in order to receive all services as close to home as possible. Project staff and the task force agreed that these practices would have a positive impact in Washington and used them as standards or models when formulating the following recommendations.

Recommendations. After reviewing the results of the statewide study and descriptions of the samples of current practices in other states, the Interagency Services Working Committee submitted to the task force the following list of recommendations:

1. There should be a comprehensive, statewide programming, funding and management network that calls for the active participation of the three categories of agencies that provide services to children and youth with SBD:

    a. Educational (OSPI, ESDs, local level).

    b. Social/psychological DSHS and its divisions: Child & Family Services, Developmental Disabilities, Mental Health, Juvenile Rehabilitation.

2. OSPI and DSHS should create an interagency services data base that will list all agencies in these three categories and the kinds of services they offer, the listings to be groups according to ESD and/or DSHS service regions throughout the state.

3. There should be a model for interagency service delivery within each ESD and/or DSHS region that will treat students requiring comprehensive services as an "interagency focus of concern" and the subject of an "interagency cooperative agreement" (i.e., an interagency-level Individual Education Program). This model need not be identical in all regions, and should make use of or build

upon already existing arrangements and relationships. However, the Division of Child and Family Services regional case manager (or equivalent social services representative) and the ESD and/or school district representative(s) should act as joint "brokers" for services in regard to each student.

4. It is recommended that there should be a set of comprehensive, formal, legal agreements among all agencies at all levels (with a "super-agency agreement" at the state level) that clearly specifies responsibilities for delivering services (e.g., assessment, mainstreaming, etc.), and establishes funding mechanisms that ensure the efficient delivery of services. The major objective of these agreements should be the provision of services to all students with SBD (including those labeled "hard-to-place") within the boundaries of Washington, and to eliminate the need for expensive out-of-state placements. The set of agreements that exists in Colorado provides a model which can be adapted to meet the needs in Washington.

5. It is recommended that DSHS should develop means for an effective early identification of SBD children and youth in order to clearly assign service delivery responsibilities among its constituent divisions (i.e., Child & Family Services, Developmental Disabilities, Mental Health, etc.) as specified in the interagency cooperative agreements.

6. Services to adjudicated youth who are also identified as "SBD" should be consistently implemented on a statewide basis.

Parents and Other Family Members

In general, parents of children with SBD have not found participation in advocacy as rewarding as parents of children with other handicapping conditions (Bricker & Caruso, 1979; Marion, 1980). This is frequently due to the lack of communication between schools/agencies and these parents. Marion feels that parents need more information support and advocacy from educators and other professionals, who should also become more actively involved in increasing parents' awareness of their rights and responsibilities in regard to their children's education. This is especially important because such parent involvement is mandated in PL 94-142, the Education for All Handicapped Children Act. On the other hand, the knowledge that parents and other family members have obtained through daily experience with a behaviorally disturbed youngster needs to be shared with the professionals who are providing services to that child.

During visits to program in other states, project staff found that successful programs (especially those in Vermont) included parent participation as an important part of their comprehensive program management plan. In addition, successful programs provided a full service delivery system of family support that included advocacy, social services, counseling, and general parent training. Finally, in these programs, parents were actively involved as decision-makers on MDTs in regard to assessment, program planning, curriculum, placement options, and service options. Project staff felt that these exemplary program features to ensure successful parent advocacy and involvement should be systematically replicated in Washington.

Recommendations. After reviewing the results of the statewide study and descriptions of current practices in other states, the Parent Advocacy Working Committee submitted to the task force the following list of recommendations:

1. Washington should develop guidelines and procedures for implementing a system of support to parents (e.g., information support and advocacy from educators and professionals), as well as guidelines to assure parents equal participation in their children's educational planning.

2. Members of the Parent Advocacy Working Committee should meet meet with attorneys employed by school districts during the 1985-86 school year in order to examine the legal implications of the above recommendations.

Inservice Training

The results of the questionnaires indicated that inservice training for professionals working with SBD populations is a priority at both the state and national levels. Teachers and administrators both placed the highest priority on training in direct intervention strategies, tactics, and program options such as behavior management, social skills, counseling, and mainstreaming. Administrators also identified a need for inservice training related to comprehensive management (i.e., service delivery options).

During the on-site interviews and visits to programs in Colorado and Vermont, project staff discovered that the most successful school programs tended to have principals who performed a strong leadership role. Project staff also found that the administrators viewed this role not only in terms of organizing and administering a variety of services to students with SBD, but also in terms of providing assistance to the regular education teachers in their buildings (e.g., inservice training). These administrators also felt that they and their colleagues would benefit from comprehensive training in these areas.

Recommendations. After reviewing the findings of the study in regard to the topic of inservice training, the Comprehensive Management working Committee and the Interagency Services Working Committee submitted the following recommendations to the task force:

1. There should be a statewide system of both preservice and inservice training for special education personnel who work with children and youth with SBD. The content of this training should address the topics of prereferral screening, assessment, programming, curriculum development, and appropriate generalization strategies for these students.

2. There should be an ongoing, comprehensive, systematic inservice training program for regular education teachers. The content of this training should focus upon (a) the means to recognize "high risk" students, (b) encouraging tolerance toward these students, (c) how to distinguish between typical classroom behavior problems and the serious, chronic disabilities of SBD students, and (d) the skills and competencies to deal with these students in the regular classroom.

3. There should be an ongoing, comprehensive, systematic inservice training program for regular education principals and building administrators in order to enable them to implement and manage (a) the inservice training of personnel within their building, (b) a plan for the comprehensive delivery of services, and (c) effective means of prereferral screening, assessment, programming, and curriculum development.

4. Washington should determine whether adequate numbers of support personnel exist to provide intervention services to SBD and other "high risk" students, and take appropriate steps to develop preservice and inservice training programs to prepare such personnel if their numbers are found to be insufficient.

Task Force Recommendations

The task force appointed four working committees (Comprehensive Management, Identification and Assessment, Interagency Services, Parent Advocacy) to review the findings of the study. Each committee submitted recommendations to the task force for consideration. The task force reviewed these recommendations and reformulated them into the following list of recommendations that represent a consensus on the major issues:

Identification, Eligibility, and Assessment

1. The Office of the Superintendent of Public Instruction (OSPI), education service districts (ESDs), and local school districts should at least initiate the following by the end of the 1985-86 school year:

   1.1 Determine the feasibility and appropriateness of a screening procedure and, if appropriate, support its application throughout the state.

   1.2 Support this procedure for use with secondary-level students, if appropriate.

   1.3 Develop a technical manual that includes a sample of current practices for use in determining the eligibility of students for special services according to the category of "serious behavior disabilities."

   1.4 Give attention to early intervention as a consequence of identification, as well as other remediating prereferral conditions.

2. OSPI, ESDs, and local school districts should develop and implement statewide comprehensive assessment procedures by accomplishing the following tasks:

   2.1 Compile an annotated technical assistance manual to assist multidisciplinary team personnel statewide in making programming/placement decisions.

   2.2 Develop guidelines for assessment that emphasize the collection of pertinent data (e.g., medical, cognitive, behavioral) in the form

of measurable assessment outcomes that can be converted by teachers and other service providers into effective educational practices, regardless of the particular assessment strategy selected for use.

Comprehensive Management and Interagency Coordination

3. OSPI, ESDs, and school districts should develop guidelines to ensure an adequate number of program options and related services for all students with serious behavior disabilities. It is further recommended that:

    3.1 Individual students should be placed in the least restrictive setting(s) and as close to their homes as possible when able to perform satisfactorily in those environments, even though the need for a full range of placement options must be recognized.

    3.2 Individual student programs should be based upon goals and objectives identified by assessment procedures, with an emphasis upon measurable behavioral outcomes.

    3.3. Individual student programs should be holistic in nature and should cover the areas of environmental management, behavior management, academics, effective education, counseling, and continuous assessment of student progress.

4. OSPI should establish a joint committee with the Department of Social and Health Services (DSHS) in order to develop and implement the following:

    4.1 A set of comprehensive, formal, and legal agreements among all agencies that serve students with serious behavioral disabilities.

    4.2 A model of interagency service delivery within each ESD or DSHS service region such as that used in other states (e.g., Colorado) that will also eliminate the need for out-of-state placement by the development of programs that serve "high cost," "hard-to-place" students as near to their homes as possible.

    4.3 A statewide interagency data base that would include information about services available through each agency.

5. WAC 392-171 provides for assistance to parents of students with serious behavior disabilities. While this provision is available through state law, it is not always implemented. There should be a plan for such implementation.

    5.1 OSPI should assure implementation by developing procedures for a full-service delivery system of support for parents and other family members.

    5.2 OSPI should develop guidelines that assure parents equal participation in their children's educational planning.

Inservice Training

6. OSPI should develop a statewide system of both preservice and inservice training for all personnel who provide services to students with serious behavior disabilities.

    6.1 There should be training for special education personnel in the areas of screening, assessment, programming, intervention strategies, curriculum development, and generalization strategies.

    6.2 There should be training for regular education teachers (identification, tolerance, teacher competencies).

    6.3 There should be training for regular education principals and building administrators (management of in-house inservice training, comprehensive service delivery plans).

    6.4 There should be training to provide sufficient numbers of support personnel.

Implementation and Monitoring

The task force and its working committees include 76 persons who have devoted nearly two years of effort to this project. Thus, members of the task force feel that the results of the study warrant the establishment of a committee made up of representatives of the task force itself. This special committee will be responsible for seeing that the above recommendations are implemented. At least one person from each working committee will be represented to ensure that the special committee's membership reflect the broad spectrum of individuals concerned with the well-being of children and youth with serious behavior disabilities. In addition, the task force recommends that a full-time, interagency staff person be charged with the responsibility of monitoring the implementation of the recommendations.

References

Achenbach, T. M., & Edelbrock, C. S. (1978). The classification of child psychology: A review and analysis of empirical efforts. *Psychological Bulletin, 85*, 1275-1301.

Achenbach, T. M., & Edelbrock, C. S. (1984). The teacher report form of the CBCL, current advances with the CBCL, University of Vermont.

Becker, W. (in press). Direct instruction. In *Proceedings of the XVI Banff Conference on Education*. New York: Brunner/Mazel.

Bricker, D., & Caruso, V. (1979). Family involvement: A critical component of early intervention. *Exceptional Children, 46*(23), 108-116.

Edgar, E., & Hart, L. (1984). Determining inservice training needs in the state of Washington. Olympia, WA: Office of the Superintendent of Public Instruction.

Engelmann, S., & Colvin, G. (1983). *Generalized compliance training*. Austin, TX: PRO-ED.

Freeberg, C. H. (1984). *Evaluation report for the Offender Educational Unit (Third year evaluation)*. Bellingham, WA: Whatcom County Juvenile Probation Department.

Gaylord-Ross, R. J., & Pitts-Conway, V. (1984). Social behavior development in integrated secondary autistic programs. In N. Certo, N. Haring, & R. York (Eds.), *Public schools integration of severely handicapped students: Rational issues and progressive alternatives*. Baltimore: Paul H. Brookes.

Grosenick, J. K., & Huntze, S. L. (1980). *National needs analysis in behavior disorders*. Columbia, MO: Department of Special Education, University of Missouri.

Grosenick, J. K., & Huntze, S. L. (1983). *More questions than answers: Review and analysis of programs for behaviorally disordered children and youth*. Columbia, MO: Department of Special Education, University of Missouri.

Haring, N. G., & Phillips, E. L. (1962). *Educating emotionally disturbed children*. New York: McGraw-Hill.

Hersh, R. H., & Walker, H. M. (1983). Great expectations: Making schools effective for all students. *Policy Studies Review, 2*(1), 147-188.

Joyce, B. R., Hersh, R. H., & McKibbin, M. (1983). *The structure of school improvement*. New York: Longman.

Kauffman, J. (1980). Where special education for disturbed children is going: A personal view. *Exceptional Children, 46*, 522-527.

Kauffman, J. (1982). Social policy issues in special education and related services for emotionally disturbed children and youth. In M. Noel & N. Haring (Eds.), *Progress or change: Issues in educating the emotionally disturbed*. Seattle: University of Washington. (ERIC Document Reproduction Service No. ED 229 948)

Kauffman, J. M. (1986). *Characteristics of children's behavior disorders* (3rd ed.). Columbus, OH: Charles E. Merrill.

Keilitz, I. (1984). *The handicapped youthful offender: Prevalence and current practices*. Unpublished manuscript.

Loeber, R., Dishion, T. J., & Patterson, G. R. (1984). Multiple gating: A multi-stage assessment procedure for identifying youths at risk for delinquency. *Journal of Research in Crime and Delinquency, 21*(1), 7-32.

Marion, R. L. (1980). Communicating with parents of culturally diverse exceptional children. *Exceptional Children, 46*(8), 616-623.

McDowell, R., Adamson, G., & Wood, F. (1982). *Teaching emotionally disturbed children*. Boston: Little, Brown & Company.

McGinnis, E., Kiraly, J. Jr., & Smith, C. R. (1984). The types of data used in identifying public school students as behaviorally disordered. *Behavioral Disorders, 4*, 239-246.

Morgan, D. (1979). Prevalence and types of handicapping conditions found in juvenile correctional institutions: A national survey. *Journal of Special Education, 13*, 283-295.

Morra, L. (1978). *The individualized education program* (Monograph Series on PL 94-142 implementation). Washington, D.C.: US Office of Education, Bureau of Education for the Handicapped.

Noel, M. (1982). Public school programs for the emotionally disturbed: An overview. In M. Noel & N. Haring (Eds.), *Progress or change: Issues in educating the emotionally disturbed*. Seattle: University of Washington. (ERIC Document Reproduction Service No. ED 229 949)

Office of Superintendent of Public Instruction (OSPI), State of Washington (1984). State summary report 1735: Special education average student enrollment, Form P223H, for the school year ending 1984. Olympia, WA: Author.

Paine, S., Bellamy, T., & Wilcox, B. (Eds.). (1984). *Human services that work*. Baltimore: Paul H. Brookes.

Paul, J., & Warnock, H. (1980). Special education: A changing field. *The Exceptional Child, 27*, 3-28.

Rehmann, A., & Riggen, T. (Eds.). (1977). *The least restrictive alternative.* Minneapolis: The Minneapolis Public Schools.

Reid, D. & Hresko, W. (1981). *A cognitive approach to learning disabilities.* New York: McGraw-Hill.

Reynolds, M. (Ed.). (1983). Symposium on public policy and educating handicapped persons. *Policy Studies Review.* Lawrence: University of Kansas.

Ross, A. O. (1974). *Psychological disorders of children.* New York: McGraw-Hill.

Smith, C. R. (1985). Identification of handicapped children and youth: A state agency perspective on behavioral disorders. *RASE, 6*(4), 34-41.

Smith, C. R., Frank, A. R., & Snider, B. C. F. (1984). School psychologists' and teachers' perceptions of data used in the identification of behaviorally disabled students. *Behavioral Disorders, 10*, 27-32.

Stainback, W., & Stainback, S. (1984). Facilitating integration through personnel preparation. In N. Certo, N. Haring, & R. York (Eds.) *Public schools integration of severely handicapped students: Rational issues and progressive alternatives.* Baltimore: Paul H. Brookes.

U. S. Department of Education (1984). *Sixth annual report to Congress on implementation of the Education of All Handicapped Act, PL 94-142.* Washington, DC: US Government Printing Office.

Walker, H. M. (in press). *The anti-social child in school: Strategies for remediating aggressive and disruptive child behavior.* Austin, TX: Pro-Ed.

Walker, H. M., & Rankin, R. (1983). Assessing the behavioral expectations and demands of less restrictive settings. *School Psychology Review, 12*, 274-284.

Walker, H. M., Reavis, H. K., Rhode, G., & Jenson, W. R. (1985). A conceptual model for delivery of behavioral services to behavior disordered children in a continuum of educational settings. In P. Bornstein & A. Kazdin (Eds.), *Handbook of clinical behavior therapy with children.* Homewood, IL: Dorsey Press.

Warfield, G. J. (1975). Mothers of retarded children review a parent education program. *Exceptional Children, 41*(8), 559-562.

Notes

[1]This chapter is based on the authors' *Final Report* (January 1986) to the Division of Special Services and Professional Programs, Special Education Section, Office of the Superintendent of Public Instruction, Olympia, WA.

[2]For the sake of readability and convenience, we will sometimes use "SBD" as an adjective signifying "with serious behavior disabilities." We certainly do not endorse the adoption of this abbreviation as an official label, because of the risk of stigmatizing these individuals.

[3]The most recently available figures, for school year 1985-86, indicate very little change: 3,498 students were served as SBD out of a total enrollment of 743,172 (i.e., 0.47%).

[4]Readers interested in the Colorado Interagency Agreements should contact Calvin M. Frazier, Commissioner, Colorado Department of Education.

Exhibits

Exhibit 1

Needs Assessment Questionnaire

NEEDS ASSESSMENT QUESTIONNAIRE

SERVICE DELIVERY TO CHILDREN WITH SERIOUS

BEHAVIOR DISABILITIES (SBD)

Name:_____ Position:_____
         (person completing survey)

District:_____ ESD: _____

Directions: Indicate your response to each of the items below by writing the letter of your response in the blank at the left. For questions follow the specific directions of the item.

1. Do you have an identified SBD students in your district?

         a. yes
1.) _____ b. no

         If your answer to question number 1 is no, you do not need to continue with the questionnaire. Please return the questionnaire as directed on the cover letter.

         If your answer is yes, complete the following grid using the numbers of students served in the given categories. Please use 12/83 headcount.

	SBD STUDENTS SERVED			
In Dist	Other Sch Dist	ESD or Co-ops	Non-Public Sch Agency	
_____	_____	_____	_____	a. Total students placed in program
_____	_____	_____	_____	b. Elementary
_____	_____	_____	_____	c. Middle School
_____	_____	_____	_____	d. Junior High
_____	_____	_____	_____	e. High School
_____	_____	_____	_____	f. Regular Education Classes
_____	_____	_____	_____	g. Resource Room
_____	_____	_____	_____	h. Self-contained with regular education contact
_____	_____	_____	_____	i. Self-contained without regular education contact
_____	_____	_____	_____	j. Home and hospital
_____	_____	_____	_____	k. Other (specify) _____
_____	_____	_____	_____	_____

Needs Assessment Questionnaire
-2-

2. Does your district utilize formal cooperative agreements with non-public school agencies who provide services?

2.) _____
    a. yes
    b. no

If yes, check (✓) all that apply.

_____ a. Contract
_____ b. Letter or agreement
_____ c. Verbal agreement
_____ d. Other (please specify) _____

_____

3. Do you provide related/support services to SBD students in your district SBD program?

3.) _____
    a. Yes
    b. No (If no, go on to question Number 4)

If yes, who provides the related/support services to SBD students? Check (✓) all that apply.

_____ a. Aide
_____ b. Counselor
_____ c. Social Worker
_____ d. Psychologist (other than assessment)
_____ e. Other (please specify) _____

_____

Indicate your response to each of the items below by writing the number of students (headcount) in the blank to the left.

_____ a. Regular (student or teacher receives no related/support services.
_____ b. Regular with support (student or teacher receives related/support services as necessary.)
_____ c. Resource (student or teacher receives no related/support services.)
_____ d. Resource with support (student or teacher receives related/support services as necessary.)
_____ e. Self-contained (student or teacher receives no related or support services.)
_____ f. Self-contained with support (student or teacher receives related/ support services.)
_____ g. Other (please specify) _____

_____

4. Is funding for your SBD program sufficient?

    a. Yes
4.) _____   b. No

    Please check (✓) revenue sources that your district uses for funding
    your SBD program.

    _____   a. State and federal special education funds
    _____   b. Levy funds (outside handicapped formula)
    _____   c. Local funds
    _____   d. State remedial funds (Chapter I funds)
    _____   e. Other (please specify) _____

    _____

5. Are all students with serious behavior disabilities seen as the
    responsibility of special education?

    a. Yes
5.) _____   b. No

    If no, please indicate the following:

    a. Who is responsible for them? _____

    _____

    b. How are they served? _____

    _____

    c. What other services are provided? _____

    _____

    What are the major behaviors SBD students exhibit to qualify for your
    program? Please prioritize in order of highest occurance.

    a. _____

    b. _____

    c. _____

    d. _____

    etc._____

    By what means is change in student behavior measured? _____

    _____

Needs Assessment Questionnaire
-4-

5.) Continued

List intervention strategies used in your program (i.e.) time-out, in-house suspensions, counseling).

a. _____

b. _____

c. _____

d. _____

6. Are there SBD students in your program who need additional services?

    a. Yes
6.) _____   b. No (If no, go on to question Number 7)

If yes, indicate the additional services needed. _____

_____

_____

_____

7. Are there additional students with behavior problems who could be served given expanded resources?

    a. Yes
7.) _____   b. No (If no, go on to question Number 8)

If yes, what behaviors do these students exhibit? Prioritize in order of highest occurance.

a. _____

b. _____

c. _____

d. _____

etc. _____

8. Does your SBD program have measurable goals and objectives?

             a. Yes
8.) _____ b. No (If no, go on to question Number 9)

If yes, describe the method by which your goals and objectives are measured.

_____

_____

9. Does your program have a theoretical/philosophical model as its foundation?

             a. Yes
9.) _____ b. No (If no, go on to question Number 10)

If yes, check (✔) the model which best describes your program in the blank to the left.

_____ a. Psychoeducational
_____ b. Behavioral
_____ c. Cognitive behavioral
_____ d. Ecological
_____ e. Psychodynamic
_____ f. Psychoneurological
_____ g. Other (please specify) _____

10. Do you have a specific person to administer your SBD program?

             a. Yes
10.) _____ b. No (If no, go on to question Number 11)

If yes, check (✔) the appropriate blank to the left.

_____ a. Teacher
_____ b. Principal
_____ c. Consultant
_____ d. Coordinator
_____ e. Director
_____ f. Other (please specify) _____

Needs Assessment Questionnaire
-6-

11. Does your program utilize staffing ratio or guidelines?

a. Yes
11.)_____ b. No (If no, go on to question number 12)

If yes, indicate your response to the items below by writing the ratio or guideline in the spaces provided.

1. Student/teacher:

Resource Room _____

Self-contained _____

2. Student/support staff (please specify)

_____

_____

_____

3. Other (Please specify)

_____

_____

12. Do you have inservice training for staff serving SBD students?

a. Yes
12.)_____ b. No (If no, go on to question Number 13)

If yes, please describe _____

_____

13. Does your district need inservice training for staff serving SBD students?

a. Yes
13.)_____ b. No (If no, go on to question Number 14)

If yes, describe inservice training needs. _____

_____

_____

Needs Assessment Questionnaire
-7-

14. Given additional resources, would you make changes in your program?

14.)_____   a. Yes
             b. No

If yes, please describe the changes. _____

_____

_____

_____

Please use the space below for any further comments you would like to
make regarding the services/needs of SBD students.

_____

_____

_____

_____

IN ORDER TO VALIDATE THE QUESTIONNAIRE, IT MUST BE POSTMARKED NO LAT

THAN MARCH 9, 1984.

PLEASE FOLD, STAPLE, AND DROP IN THE MAIL. THANK YOU FOR YOUR HELP!

Exhibit 2

Administrators' Questionnaire

A STUDY OF STATEWIDE IDENTIFICATION AND SERVICE DELIVERY
TO CHILDREN WITH SERIOUS BEHAVIOR DISABILITIES (SBD)

ADMINISTRATORS' QUESTIONNAIRE

Questions 1 - 6 relate to the definition and eligibility criteria of
SBD students.

Present state rules and regulations require that a student be seriously
behaviorally disabled before being eligible for Special Education services. Questions 1 - 3 relate to WAC 392-171-386, definition and eligibility criteria for seriously behaviorally disabled.

1. Please determine whether or not each of the following items are
    sufficiently delineated in the WAC. Rate each according to the
    scale below.

                        Degree   Letter

                    Sufficient   = S
                    Insufficient = I

    Please indicate your response to each item by writing the appropri-
    ate letter in the blank at the left.

    a. Defines SBD population   ___ (001)
    b. Determines eligibility criteria   ___ (002)
    c. Defines assessment procedures   ___ (003)
    d. Prescribes services   ___ (004)
    e. Addresses policy issues   ___ (005)
        (re: right to an appropriate education)
    f. Other (please specify)_____   ___ (006)

    _____

2. Please indicate any changes that would improve WAC 392-171-386.

    _____   (007)

    _____

    _____

    _____

3. For the purpose of classification and eligibility for Special Education services, how does you district differentiate between moderate and severely behaviorally disabled students?

_____   (008)

_____

_____

Federal Rules and Regulations require that a student be <u>seriously emotionally disturbed</u> before being eligible for Special Education services. The next question relates to PL 94-142.

4. The PL 94-142 definition for serious emotionally disturbed students continues to be an issue. The following are summary statements of themes being discussed at the Federal level. Please rate each of the following according to the scale below.

Degree		Letter
Strongly Agree	=	A
Agree	=	B
Neither Agree or Disagree	=	C
Disagree	=	D
Strongly Disagree	=	E

a. PL 94-142 is an education law. Public education is ____ (009) not charged with placing students in Special Education in order to cure them, but rather in order to give them access to public education. Only those students who otherwise would be virtually deprived of an education are eligible for Special Education services.

b. As well as an education law, 94-142 guarantees the ____ (010) rights of handicapped students to Special Education and related services when the handicapped condition adversely affects educational performance.

c. States that find students eligible as "seriously ____ (011) emotionally disturbed" by terming them "behavior disordered" are influenced by a different conceptual frame of reference. Criteria utilized for definition and assessment procedures do not always correspond precisely to the Federal definition or intent.

d. The terms "behavior disorder" and "emotionally disturbed" are used interchangeably and refer to the ____ (012) full range of disorders, problems, and disturbances of child behavior encountered in school settings.

(Continued on next page.)

3

4. (Continued from previous page.)

    e. For the purpose of eligibility and assessment, the ___ (013)
        focus of attention must be on direct observation of
        overt student behavior over time and assessed with-
        in those settings where it is perceived to be
        disordered.

    f. For the purpose of eligibility and assessment, the ___ (014)
        focus of attention must be on both direct observa-
        tion of overt student behavior over time and emo-
        tional antecedents to the behaviors, such as the
        specific causal factors.

    g. The definition is adequate and we simply need addi- ___ (015)
        tional funds to be allocated to cover the costs of
        serving each student with SBD.

    h. The present level of funding is adequate, but the ___ (016)
        definition should be modified to focus on more spe-
        cific segments of the SBD population.

Responses to the first SBD Study questionnaire indicated that both
State and Federal Rules and Regulations have problems in clarification
of definition and criteria for determining eligibility. Questions 5
and 6 will provide information for possible recommendations for clarifying eligibility definitions.

5. Please write your own best definition of SBD.

    _____ (017)

    _____

    _____

    _____

    _____

6. Please write your own best eligibility criteria for SBD.

    _____ (018)

    _____

    _____

    _____

    _____

The following question relates to the formal assessment of SBD students. Respondents to the first SBD Study questionnaire reported that all of the following assessment strategies are being used in the assessment of students with SBD. However, the specific strategies vary from district to district.

---

7. Please rate each of the following assessment strategies according to how appropriate you feel they are to the assessment of students with SBD. Rate each item according to the scale below.

Degree	Letter
Highly Appropriate	= A
Somewhat Appropriate	= B
Neither	= C
Somewhat Inappropriate	= D
Inappropriate	= E

a. Assessment of academic achievement   ___ (019)

b. Assessment of intellectual functioning   ___ (020)

c. Analysis of personality traits ·   ___ (021)

d. Medical examination and history   ___ (022)

e. Neurological examination   ___ (023)

f. Documentation of long term behavior that   ___ (024)
    is counterproductive to learning

g. Analysis of behavioral deficits or excesses   ___ (025)

h. Social and development history, sociometric   ___ (026)
    procedure

i. Analysis of family interactions   ___ (027)

j. Measurement of the degree to which the   ___ (028)
    behavior is discrepant from the standards for
    the classroom

k. Other (specify)_____ ___ (029)

l. Other (specify)_____. ___ (030)

m. Other (specify)_____ ___ (031)

The following section relates to program setting options for students
with SBD. The objective of questions 8 and 9 is to obtain information
about program settings in which students with SBD are currently served. The nature and extent of your contributions to these questions
will be used by the study in comparing established program settings
across districts. The study will find common elements and make suggestions from exemplary settings for statewide application.
----

8. Respondents to the first SBD Study questionnaire reported that the
   following program settings were most often used for serving students with SBD. Please rate each of the following settings which
   your district uses according to how appropriate you feel they are
   for serving students with SBD. Rate each by circling the appropriate letter according to the following scale.

Degree		Letter
Highly Appropriate	=	A
Somewhat Appropriate	=	B
Neither	=	C
Somewhat Inappropriate	=	D
Inappropriate	=	E

A B C D E (032) a. Support services and training are provided
to the classroom teacher, who in turn is
reponsible for delivering services directly to students exhibiting inappropriate
behavior.

A B C D E (033) b. The special education teacher provides
some direct instruction to students in a
Special Education classroom setting and
other assistance (e.g., assessment, evaluation, and teacher consultation) takes
place in the regular classroom.

A B C D E (034) c. Special education services provided within
a public school setting with other profes-
sionals (e.g., mental health) providing
direct services to students.

A B C D E (035) d. Special education programs are provided
within a public school setting coordinated
with various services outside the public
school setting (i.e., off campus program,
community mental health facility, home-
based program).

A B C D E (036) e. A program operated in a special facility
away from the regular school setting.

9. Please describe any other program setting options that you believe are appropriate for serving students with SBD. Please check those presently being used in your district.)

_____ ___ (037)

_____ ___ (038)

_____ ___ (039)

The following questions relate to service delivery to students with SBD by agencies other than public schools. Many respondents to the first SBD Study questionnaire indicated that their districts have agreements with non-public school agencies for some service delivery to students with SBD. Your answers to questions 10 - 12 will provide information on the roles and relationships between these agencies and school districts in delivering services to students with SBD.

----

10. If your district has SBD students who are receiving agency services, please provide the following information for each student: Name of agency, location of service delivery setting, and description of service provided.

_____ (040)

_____

_____

_____

_____

_____

11. Please describe the students' behavior problems and the difficulties your district had providing appropriate services that prompted you to contract with an outside agency.

_____ (041)

_____

_____

_____

_____

_____

Respondents also indicated a need for greater planned inter-agency collaboration in providing full service delivery to students with SBD.

12. Please describe any collaboration plan or arrangement that your district has devloped in cooperation with non-school agencies.

_____ (042)

_____

_____

_____

_____

_____

_____

The following questions relate to education and intervention approaches that are used in serving students with SBD. Your answers to question 13 will be used to produce a profile of current approaches.

---

13. Please rate each of the following approaches according to your opinion as to the level of appropriateness as it applies to students with SBD. Rate each by circling the appropriate letter according to the scale below.

Degree		Letter
Highly Appropriate	=	A
Somewhat Appropriate	=	B
Neither	=	C
Somewhat Inappropriate	=	D
Inappropriate	=	E

A B C D E (043) a. The Special Education teacher is an interactionist, who is part of a comprehensive intervention or treatment plan, including participation of families, schools, and/or various child services agencies. The major goals are positive behavior changes in the student's environment. Intervention strategies are focused on the learned behaviors of the student as well as the behavior of others who interact with the student.

(Continued on next page.)

(Continued from previous page.)

A B C D E (044) b.   The Special Education teacher's role is
                          that of a technician, with classroom adap-
                          tation directed by clinical professionals
                          as an extension of a specific treatment
                          plan. Intervention strategies focus heav-
                          ily on motor, perceptual, and attentional
                          disorders. Management of behavior is
                          through use of a structural or stimulus
                          controlled environment.

A B C D E (045) c.   The major responsibility for services for
                          the student with SBD is the Special Educa-
                          tion teacher whose role is that of a lear-
                          ning specialist. Individual assessment
                          consists of direct observation of behav-
                          iors. Individual instruction consists of
                          learning sequences derived from the prin-
                          ciples of behavior shaping.

A B C D E (046) d.   The Special Education teacher's role is
                          that of a technician, with classroom adap-
                          tations directed by clinical professionals
                          as an extension of the therapy process.
                          Intervention strategies are focused on the
                          individual's treatment therapy. Learning
                          activities are oriented toward achieving
                          self-awareness and building relationships
                          with others. The atmosphere of the class-
                          room should be somewhat permissive.

A B C D E (047) e.   The Special Education teacher is a team
                          member who works with other profes-
                          sionals. The teacher is a combination of
                          a Special Education classroom teacher, a
                          resource to the regular classroom teacher,
                          a tutor, and facilitator of the teaming
                          effort. Intervention strategies are plan-
                          ned to occur in a variety of settings.

Respondents to the first SBD Study questionnaire identified a need for services for students with behavioral disabilities who do not meet eligibility criteria for Special Education programs/services. The following questions relate to these unserved and underserved behavior disabled students. Your responses to questions 14 - 17 will enable us to describe the service needs for these students and to summarize the attempts that have been made to fulfill those needs.

---

14. Estimate the number of students in your district with mild or moderate behaviors that adversely affect their educational performance to the degree that they have special service needs but are not eligible for Special Education programs/services.

	Total number of Students in Dist.	Number in Need of BD Services
Preschool	_____	_____ (048)
Elementary	_____	_____ (049)
Middle School	_____	_____ (050)
Junior High School	_____	_____ (051)
Senior High School	_____	_____ (052)
TOTAL	_____	_____ (053)

15. In Column 1, please check the services your district currently offers mild or moderate BD students from non-Special Education funds. (Services listed were identified from the first questionnaire.)

16. In Column 2, please check the services your district would offer mild or moderate BD students if state funds were provided.

Column 1 Currently Offered	Column 2 Would be Offered	Identified Services	
____ (054)	____ (070)	a.	Agency Services
____ (055)	____ (071)	b.	Counseling
____ (056)	____ (072)	c.	Family Assistance
____ (057)	____ (073)	d.	Social Worker Services
____ (058)	____ (074)	e.	Placement Options
____ (059)	____ (075)	f.	Smaller Class Ratios
____ (060)	____ (076)	g.	Medical Evaluations
____ (061)	____ (077)	h.	Special Curricula
____ (062)	____ (078)	i.	Adaptive Materials
____ (063)	____ (079)	j.	Residential Care
____ (064)	____ (080)	k.	Career Planning
____ (065)	____ (081)	l.	Variable Length Day Options
____ (066)	____ (082)	m.	Special Vocational Training
____ (067)	____ (083)	n.	Other (specify) _____
____ (068)	____ (084)	o.	_____
____ (069)	____ (085)	p.	_____

17. What factors prevent school districts from adequately serving students with <u>serious</u> behavioral disabilities?

_____ (086)

_____

_____

The following questions relate to inservice needs of Special Education personnel serving students with SBD.
----

18. Please list the four areas which you feel are the highest priorities of inservice training in your district in the area of SBD.

a. _____ (087)

b. _____ (088)

c. _____ (089)

d. _____ (090)

19. What specific SBD training do you feel you personally need as an administrator?

_____ (091)

_____

20. Please rate the effectiveness of the following delivery methods for inservice training for your district personnel serving SBD students. Rate each according to the scale below.

Degree		Letter
Highly Effective	=	A
Somewhat Effective	=	B
Neither	=	C
Somewhat Ineffective	=	D
Ineffective	=	E

a. Workshops in district ____ (092)
b. Workshops in ESD ____ (093)
c. Workshops at state level ____ (094)
d. College/University Courses ____ (095)
e. Speakers ____ (096)
f. Consultants working with staff ____ (097)
g. Visiting other classrooms/programs ____ (098)
h. Info.mal meetings with other teachers and ____ (099)
   support professionals for problem-solving
i. Other (specify) _____ ____ (100)
j. Other _____ ____ (101)

11

We are looking for innovative practices which have been introduced by
districts for students with SBD.   Questions 21 - 24 deal with these
innovations.
----

21. What means do you use to bring SBD students back into "regular"
    classrooms or less restrictive settings?

                                                            (102)
    _____

    _____

    _____

    _____

    _____

    _____

    _____

    _____

    _____

    _____

    _____

22. What kinds of interactions do you arrange between SBD classrooms
    and other classrooms?

                                                            (103)
    _____

    _____

    _____

    _____

    _____

    _____

    _____

    _____

    _____

    _____

23. Please describe some examples of model practices that you use in the following categories:

    a.   Behavior management:_____(104)

_____

_____

_____

    b.   Educational programming:_____(105)

_____

_____

_____

    c.   Team teaching:_____(106)

_____

_____

_____

    d.   Program settings:_____(107)

_____

_____

_____

    e.   Other:_____(108)

_____

_____

_____

24. If the resources could be provided, what are the most crucial changes and/or additions you feel could be made to improve the quality and effectiveness of your SBD program?   (109)

_____

_____

_____

_____

Thank you for your assistance!

Exhibit 3

Special Education Teachers' Questionnaire

A STUDY OF STATEWIDE IDENTIFICATION AND SERVICE DELIVERY
TO CHILDREN WITH SERIOUS BEHAVIOR DISABILITIES

TEACHER'S QUESTIONNAIRE

We are conducting a statewide study designed to identify the number of
children and youth with serious behavior disabilities (SBD) currently being
served. This section of the questionnaire (Questions 1- 6) addresses services
reaching the target population. Your response will provide a descriptive
profile of students currently being served and programs serving them.

---

1. How many years have you taught?   ___(001)

2. How many years have you worked with special education students?   ___(002)

3. With SBD students?   ___(003)

4. How many students with SBD do you currently teach in each of the following
    grade level categories:

    a. K thru 6   ___(004)
    b. Middle School   ___(005)
    c. High School   ___(006)
    d. Other (Please be specific):_____   ___(007)

5. Please indicate the number of SBD students you serve per day for each of
    the following time periods.

    a. Two hours or less   ___(008)
    b. Between two and four hours   ___(009)
    c. More than four hours   ___(010)

6. Please indicate the total number of SBD students you serve per day who
   exhibit the following behaviors with frequency and severity, adversely
   impacting academic performance.

   a. <u>Disruptive Behavior</u>: Includes talking out, out-of-seat,   ___(011)
      grabbing others' materials, running in the halls, making
      obscene noises, throwing spitwads, persistent talking to
      classmates, complaining, arguing with teachers or others.
   b. <u>Socially Inadequate and Immature Behavior</u>: Includes temper   ___(012)
      tantrums and crying, oppositional behavior and negativism,
      depression, developmental regression, dependency and help-
      lessness, obsessive-compulsive behaviors, phobias, eating
      disorders.
   c. <u>Social Withdrawal Behavior</u>: Includes social isolation,   ___(013)
      elective mutism.
   d. <u>Self-Stimulatory and Self-Injurious Behavior</u>: Includes   ___(014)
      hair-pulling, hand-biting, eye-gouging, self-hitting, or
      skin tearing. Also, repetitive arm flapping and rocking
      are examples.
   e. <u>Aggressive Behavior</u>: Inflicting harm, injury, or discomfort   ___(015)
      on persons, or damage to property. Includes verbal or
      physical aggression, "naughty finger."
   f. <u>Other</u> (please specify):_____   ___(016)

   _____

   _____

Question 7 refers to support/assistance services for teachers. Your responses
will provide us with your preferences and priorities according to how important you feel the service is to you.

---

7. In the listing below, please rate the support/assistance service <u>you</u> pres-
   <u>ently utilize</u> in your work with SBD students as to its importance to you.
   Rate each service by circling the appropriate letter, according to the the
   following scale:

Degree		Letter
Highly important	=	A
Somewhat important	=	B
Neither	=	C
Somewhat unimportant	=	D
Unimportant	=	E

   a. Instructional Assistants/Aides   A B C D E (017)
   b. Professional Consultation   A B C D E (018)
   c. Curriculum Specialists   A B C D E (019)
   d. Counseling   A B C D E (020)
   e. Social Worker   A B C D E (021)
   f. Specially Designed Curriculum/Materials   A B C D E (022)
   h. Other (please specify)_____   A B C D E (023)
   i. Other _____   A B C D E (024)

The purpose of questions 8 and 9 is to provide a description of the current curriculum for service delivery to SBD students. The study will find common elements and make suggestions from exemplary curricula for statewide applications.

---

8. Please check any of the special designated curricula listed below that you utilize in work with SBD students.

    a. Adaptive behavior (social skills)   ___(025)
    b. Career/vocational education   ___(026)
    c. Academic   ___(027)
    d. "Pre" Academic   ___(028)
    e. Daily Living "Survival Skills"   ___(029)
    f. Building Self-Concept and Self-Esteem   ___(030)
    g. Compliance Skills_____   ___(031)
    h. Other (please specify)_____   ___(032)
    i. Other_____   ___(033)

9. Please list any special materials/equipment you use to support your curriculum with your SBD students.

    _____(034)

    _____

    _____

    _____   _____

The purpose of questions 10-14 is to provide a clear description of instructional practices currently serving the SBD students. The study will compare established instructional methods and make recommendations for a resource guide for SBD teachers. The resource guide for programming for SBD students will include identification of best practices for meeting the needs of the SBD students.

---

10. Please check any of the following assessment tools and/or procedures that you use to identify student behavior for intervention.

    a. Daily observation   ___(035)
    b. Referral information   ___(036)
    c. Teacher made tests   ___(037)
    d. Commercial test   ___(038)
    e. Other (please specify)_____   ___(039)
    f. Other_____   ___(040)

11. Please check any of the following intervention strategies that you use in programming for behavior changes.

    a. Self-monitoring   ___(041)
    b. Reinforcement   ___(042)
    c. Differential reinforcement of other behavior   ___(043)
    d. Reminders/antecedent cues   ___(044)
    e. Contingency contracting   ___(045)
    f. Compliance training   ___(046)
    g. Peer modeling   ___(047)
    h. Restitution/overcorrection   ___(048)
    i. Group goal setting and feedback   ___(049)
    j. Verbal instruction   ___(050)
    k. Modeling   ___(051)
    l. Rehearsal   ___(052)
    m. Prompting   ___(053)
    n. Other (please specify) _____   ___(054)
    o. Other _____ ___(055)

12. Once you have begun a program of interventions to change the behaviors of an SBD student, how do you measure the targeted behavior changes (e.g. weekly behavior check-list, daily counts of the behavior, daily self-monitoring by the student, etc.)?

    _____ (056)

    _____

    _____

    _____

13. What is the average number of academic and/or social behavior change objectives per SBD student (on a typical day)?   ___(057)

14. What is the average number of minutes spent daily in direct teacher/student instruction per objective (on a typical day)?   ___(058)

Questions 15, 16, and 17 refer to the inservice needs of teachers serving SBD students. The responses will be compared across local districts for the purpose of making recommendations for inservice considerations to the OSPI.

---

15. Please list the four areas which you feel are the highest priorities for inservice training in your district in the areas of SBD.

    a. _____ (059)

    b. _____ (060)

    c. _____ (061)

    d. _____ (062)

16. What specific SBD inservice training do you feel you need as a teacher? (This need not be the same as the priorities you listed for the district.)

    _____ (063)

    _____

17. Please rate the effectiveness of the delivery methods you have used and/or the inservice sessions you have attended. Rate each by circling the appropriate letter according to the scale below.

Degree of Effectiveness	Letter
Highly Effective	A
Somewhat Effective	B
Neither	C
Somewhat ineffective	D
Ineffective	E

a.	Workshops in district	A	B	C	D	E	(064)
b.	Workshops in ESD	A	B	C	D	E	(065)
c.	College/University courses	A	B	C	D	E	(066)
d.	Speakers	A	B	C	D	E	(067)
e.	Classroom based training	A	B	C	D	E	(068)
f.	Consultants working with staff	A	B	C	D	E	(069)
g.	Visiting other classrooms/programs	A	B	C	D	E	(070)
h.	Informal meetings with other teachers and support professionals for problem sharing/solving	A	B	C	D	E	(071)
i.	Other (Specify):_____	A	B	C	D	E	(072)

We are looking for innovative practices which have been introduced by teachers of SBD students. The following questions (18 - 22) deal with these innovations.

---

18. What means do you use to bring SBD students back into "regular" classrooms or less restrictive settings?

(073)

_____

_____

_____

19. What kinds of interaction do you arrange between SBD classrooms and other classrooms?

(074)

_____

20. Please describe some examples of model practices that you use in the following categories:

a. Behavior management: _____(075)

_____

_____

b. Educational programming: _____(076)

_____

_____

c. Team teaching: _____(077)

_____

_____

d. Other: _____(078)

_____

_____

_____

21. Please describe some examples of communication systems between Special
    Education teachers, parents, and regular education teachers?   (079)

    _____

    _____

    _____

    _____

22. If the resources could be provided, what are the most crucial changes
    and/or additions you feel could be made to improve the quality and
    effectiveness of your SBD program?   (080)

    _____

    _____

    _____

    _____

    Thank you for your assistance!

Exhibit 4

Additional Questions for Assessment Personnel

13

The following questions were requested by the assessment personnel
members of the SBD Task Force. They relate to the role and function of
the school psychologist and school social worker (WACs 180-79-195,
180-79-210, 180-84-015, and 392-171-386).
---

25. In Column 1, please rate each of the following functions according
    to your opinion as to the level of importance as it applies to your
    current role/job description. Please fill in the blanks with the
    appropriate number according to the scale below.

Degree	Number
Highly Important	= 5
Somewhat Important	= 4
Neither	= 3
Somewhat Unimportant	= 2
Unimportant	= 1
No involvement	= 0

26. In Column 2, please estimate the percentage of time you currently
    spend on each function.

Before you complete Columns 3 and 4, please consider any changes in the
importance of functions and the percentages of time spent on functions
that would enable you to more effectively meet the needs of SBD
students.

27. In column 3, please rate each of the following functions according
    to your opinion as to the level of importance as it would apply to
    an ideal role/job description for meeting the needs of SBD students
    (Please use the same scale above).

28. In Column 4, please estimate the percentage of time you would
    ideally spend on each function as it relates to SBD students.

14

(Continued from previous page.)

Function	Column 1	Column 2	Column 3	Column 4	
a. Assessment	____	____	____	____	(110)
b. Behavioral Observation	____	____	____	____	(111)
c. Consultation	____	____	____	____	(112)
d. Coordination Community Resources	____	____	____	____	(113)
e. Counseling/ Interviewing	____	____	____	____	(114)
f. Home/Community Environments	____	____	____	____	(115)
g. Interpreting Analysis	____	____	____	____	(116)
h. Program Development	____	____	____	____	(117)
i. Program Evaluation	____	____	____	____	(118)
j. Provide Training Staff Parents	____ ____	____ ____	____ ____	____ ____	(119) (120)
k. Research/ Evaluation	____	____	____	____	(121)
l. Other	____	____	____	____	(122)

29. Please indicate the number of students in your building/s eligible for special education and classified SBD who receive only related services (e.g., counseling). Please describe the service and who provides the service.

_____ (123)

_____

_____

_____

15

30. Do you provide related services to students with behaviors that
adversely affect their educational performance but are not eligible
for special education? If so, please describe the services you
provide.

_____   (124)

_____

_____

_____

Exhibit 5

Regular Education Teachers' Questionnaire

A STUDY OF STATEWIDE IDENTIFICATION AND SERVICE DELIVERY
TO CHILDREN WITH SERIOUS BEHAVIOR DISABILITIES

Regular Education Teacher's Questionnaire

1. How many years have you taught?   _____

2. How many years have you worked with special education
   students?   _____

3. With students labeled as SBD students?   _____

4. Which grade(s) do you currently teach?

   a. Elementary
   b. Middle School/Junior High School   _____
   c. High School   _____
                                                                _____

5. Please indicate the number of SBD students you serve per
   day for each of the following time periods.

   a. Two hours or less
   b. Between two and four hours   _____
   c. More than four hours   _____
                                                                _____

6. Please indicate the total number of SBD students you serve
   per day who exhibit the following behaviors with frequency
   and severity, adversely impacting academic performance.

   a. Disruptive Behavior: includes talking out, out-of-seat,
      grabbing others' materials, running in the halls, making
      obscene noises, throwing spitwads, persistent talking to
      classmates, complaining, arguing with teachers or others.   _____
   b. Socially Inadequate and Immature Behavior: includes
      temper tantrums and crying, oppositional behavior and
      negativism, depression, developmental regression,
      dependency and helplessness, obsessive-compulsive
      behaviors, phobias, eating disorders.
   c. Social Withdrawal Behavior: includes social isolation,   _____
      elective mutism.
   d. Self-Stimulatory and Self-Injurious Behavior: includes   _____
      hair-pulling, hand-biting, eye-gouging, self-hitting, or
      skin tearing. Also, repetitive arm flapping and rocking
      are examples.
   e. Aggressive Behavior: inflicting harm, injury, or   _____
      discomfort on persons or damage to property. Includes
      verbal or physical aggression, "naughty finger."
   f. Other: (please specify) _____   _____

   _____

   _____   _____

SBD
Regular Education Teacher's Questionnaire
Page 2

The purpose of the following questions is to provide a description of instructional practices currently serving the SBD students. The study will compare established instructional methods and make recommendations for a resource guide for teachers.

7. Please describe some examples of instructional practices that you utilize in your work with SBD student(s).

    _____

    _____

    _____

8. Please list any special designated curricula that you utilize in your work with SBD student(s) (e.g., social skills, etc.).

    _____

    _____

    _____

9. Please list any special materials/equipment you use to support your curriculum with your SBD student(s).

    _____

    _____

    _____

The following questions refer to support/assistance services for teachers. Your responses hopefully will provide us with your needs, preferences, and priorities.

10. Do you receive sufficient support from Special Education in maintaining your SBD student(s) in your class?   _____yes   _____no

Please use the space below for comments that you would like to make regarding the services provided by Special Education.

SBD
Regular Education Teacher's Questionnaire
Page 3

11. In the listing below, please rate the support/assistance service you
presently utilize in your work with SBD students as to its importance
to you. Rate each service by circling the appropriate letter, according
to the following scale:

Degree	Letter
Highly important	A
Somewhat important	B
Neither	C
Somewhat unimportant	D
Unimportant	E

a. Instructional assistants/aides   A   B   C   D   E
b. Professional consultation   A   B   C   D   E
c. Curriculum specialists   A   B   C   D   E
d. Counseling   A   B   C   D   E
e. Social worker   A   B   C   D   E
f. Specially designed curriculum/
   materials   A   B   C   D   E
g. Special education teacher   A   B   C   D   E
h. Other _____   A   B   C   D   E

12. What means do you need to successfully bring SBD student(s) back into
your "regular" classroom?

_____

_____

_____

13. Please describe some examples of communication systems between Special
Education teachers, parents, and regular education teachers.

_____

_____

_____

14. If the resources could be provided, what are the most crucial changes
and/or additions you feel could be made to improve the quality and
effectiveness of the SBD program?

_____

_____

_____

SBD
Regular Education Teacher's Questionnaire
Page 4

The following questions refer to the inservice needs of teachers serving
SBD students. The responses will be compared across local districts for
the purpose of making recommendations for inservice considerations to the
OSPI.

15. Please list the four areas which you feel are the highest priorities
    for inservice training in your district in the area of SBD.

    a. _____

    b. _____

    c. _____

    d. _____

16. What specific SBD inservice training do you feel you need as a teacher?
    (This need not be the same as the priorities you listed for the district.)

    _____

    _____

17. Please rate the effectiveness of the delivery methods you have used
    and/or the inservice sessions you have attended. Rate each by circling
    the appropriate letter according to the scale below.

Degree	Letter
Highly effective	A
Somewhat effective	B
Neither	C
Somewhat ineffective	D
Ineffective	E

a.	Workshops in district	A	B	C	D	E
b.	Workshops in ESD	A	B	C	D	E
c.	College/university courses	A	B	C	D	E
d.	Speakers	A	B	C	D	E
e.	Classroom based training	A	B	C	D	E
f.	Consultants working with staff	A	B	C	D	E
g.	Visiting other classrooms/programs	A	B	C	D	E
h.	Informal meetings with other teachers and support professionals for problem sharing/solving	A	B	C	D	E
i.	Other (specify) _____					
	_____	A	B	C	D	E

Thank you for your assistance.

Exhibit 6

Sample Programs in Washington

1. Spokane Public Schools
    Behavior Intervention and Resource Room Combination--An Approach That Works

TARGET POPULATION

SBD children and youth.

PROGRAM DESCRIPTION

This elementary school program combines a resource room with a behavior intervention room. The resource room uses a combination of assertive discipline, a point system for appropriate/inappropriate behaviors with points given each half hour, a quiet room area for crisis management, and natural consequences to manage behavior and academic learning. Teaching strategies in this resource room range from individual work to large group activities and instruction. Some cross-age tutoring is also utilized. Social skills instruction and home-based reinforcement are also emphasized in this program.

The behavior intervention room focuses on remediation of problematic behaviors. Criteria for appropriate behavior(s) may differ according to the special needs of each child: the delivery of reinforcers such as school privileges, computer time, stickers, lunch with the teacher, etc., is contingent upon meeting these individual criteria.

CONTACT

Celia Chally Dodd
Principal, Logan Elementary School
Spokane Public Schools No. 81
Spokane, WA

2. Tacoma School District
    The Off-Campus Therapeutic Learning Center Program

TARGET POPULATION

This program is a Therapeutic Learning Center for secondary students with severe behavioral disabilities. It serves both junior and senior high school students throughout the Tacoma School District. It is designed for those students whose extreme behaviors prevent successful school attendance; those with a history of unpredictably violent, abusive, or bizarre behavior, and those who are severely depressed, withdrawn, self-destructive or exhibiting mild schizophrenic symptoms.

PROGRAM DESCRIPTION

The program focuses on positive behavior change, growth in self-esteem, and social skills. The primary program goal is to prepare each student for successful return to a less restrictive educational environment or vocational setting. The low student-staff ratio allows for a highly individualized behavioral and academic program which is, at the same time, tightly structured.

The behavior management program has three facets: 1) the classroom points and check system, 2) individual target behavior contracts, and 3) consistent staff modeling of behavior.

1.   The point system is the day-to-day framework of the behavior
management program. Students earn positive points for on-task and appropriate
behavior during classes and for positive interactions during breaks and
lunch.   The check system is used when a student chooses to persist in
disruptive behavior. It outlines a series of consequences for such behavior.

2.   The target behavior contracts are used to pinpoint specific
behavioral goals.   Student and teacher together determine target behaviors,
behavioral objectives, and reinforcers.   Contracts may include specific steps
to be taken in the event of extreme occurrences; i.e., an aggressive student
may contract to leave the building for a specified length of time when about
to "lose it."

3.   Positive modeling by staff is an ongoing and important component in
the program for behavior change.   Program staff consciously develop a give and
take style of communication with students and one another, striving to express
feelings clearly and constructively in a non-threatening manner. Students are
encouraged to do the same--to talk out rather than act out.

The academic program can serve both junior and senior high school students
with reading levels from third grade to college. It can meet the needs of a
student on either a short-term (one semester) or a longer term basis. Classes
are scheduled in three curriculum areas: basic skills, life/career skills,
and communication skills.

Basic skills are those required for high school entry or graduation: English
and language arts, math, and social studies.

The life skills classes are essential to the program because behaviorally
disabled students often feel they have no control over their environments. By
learning to take control over situations such as budgeting money or applying
for a job they are in some measure learning to take control of themselves.
Life skills classes emphasize jobs, health, and "living on your own," a
budgeting and consumer unit.

The communication skills module consists of a minimum of three weekly group
sessions and regular social work services both one-on-one and with the group.
Group activities cover skills such as accepting responsibility, building
self-confidence, anger management, and decision-making.

To maximize the probability of effecting positive change in student behavior,
the off-campus staff works in concert with whatever support services the
students and their families consult--counselors, psychiatrists, or juvenile
authorities. Those who are not involved with mental health services are made
aware of the resources available to them in the community. Supportive
communications between school, family, and service systems are given high
priority by off-campus staff.

Procedures for leaving the program are developed in a step-by-step fashion.
As individual students meet their behavioral goals off-campus they are
included part-time in on-campus classes. The amount of time spent on-campus
increases as behavioral goals are met at each step. Individual student
progress determines the length of time necessary before a student is returned
full-time to a school building or community/vocational placement.   By

carefully planning and monitoring each exiting step, the program staff strive to avoid the failures that too often result when a student who has been successful in a self-contained program is mainstreamed too abruptly into less structured classes.

CONTACT

Chris Hinds
Off-Campus Therapeutic Learning Center
3113 S. Pine
Tacoma, WA 98402

3. Issaquah School District
   The Integrated Classroom

TARGET POPULATION

SBD children.

PROGRAM DESCRIPTION

The integrated classroom acknowledges the right of the special child to develop social and academic skills while performing at his/her developmental level. It is a recognition that all children have special needs.

An integrated classroom serves the developmental needs of a variety of children in a heterogeneous mix which includes 1/3 above average, 1/3 average, and 1/3 below average (including special education students). Developmental needs are met by instruction in communication skills, social skills, classroom survival skills, and group interaction, all of which facilitate academic growth.

Regular district and supplemental programs are used and modified to meet the needs of heterogeneous grouping. Teachers use direct instruction, focusing on group work rather than independent study, in a highly structured environment where expectations are clearly stated. Group instruction is followed by individualized responsibilities contingent upon individual abilities. Aides are used for general teacher support and small group direct instruction.

CONTACT

Abby Adams, Director
22211 SE 72nd Street
Special Education
Issaquah School District
Issaquah, WA 98027
206/392-0746

4. Kennewick School District
    Developmental Therapy Program

TARGET POPULATION

SBD children in the district.

PROGRAM DESCRIPTION

Developmental Therapy is a psychoeducational curriculum for social and emotional growth. It is organized around the sequences of normal developmental milestones all children experience. Because of this emphasis on mastery of normal milestones, Developmental Therapy is a "growth model" rather than a "deficit model." Kennewick School District addresses the elementary SBD population through this developmental therapy model. This model was originally developed at the Rutland Center in Georgia. In this model, there are four basic curriculum areas: behavior, communication, socialization, and academic. The curriculum requires the monitoring of measurable objectives and the use of specifically designed materials and activities. The program is nationally validated and is generally accepted as a model that is effective in changing behavior.

CONTACT

Lannie Smith
Director of Special Services
200 S. Dayton
Kennewick, WA 99336
509/582-1250

Othene H. Bell
Special Services Program Manager
200 S. Dayton
Kennewick, WA 99336
509/582-1250

5. Evergreen School District
    Behavior Disorder Program

TARGET POPULATION

SBD students.

PROGRAM DESCRIPTION

The Evergreen School District strives to provide SBD students with the learning experiences and assistance to acquire the basic social and academic skills needed to benefit from access to public education.

The following components of the program are viewed as important:

1. Vocational awareness and work experience
2. Training in the rights and responsibilities of citizenship
3. Social skills, awareness training, communication training, and problem solving
4. The opportunity to participate in a regular classroom (mainstreaming)
5. Training assistance on the long-term effects of substance use and abuse as it relates to ability to function in the school setting
6. Academic assistance in reading, math, language, and study skills.

CONTACT

Sue Ballard
Director of Special Services
7000 NE 117th Avenue
Evergreen School District
Vancouver, WA
206/256-6022

6. Clarkston School District
    Primary Intervention Project

TARGET POPULATION

Students in the K-3 age range who are identified by their classroom teacher through observation or group screening as experiencing learning and/or behavioral difficulties.

PROGRAM DESCRIPTION

Clarkston School District is one of ten school districts in the state operating a pilot program in elementary counseling known as the Primary Intervention Project (PIP). Operating in two elementary schools, paraprofessionals known as counselor-aides do individual and group interventions with children from K-5 with emphasis on the K-3 group.

Screening activities in the beginning of the school year include individual teacher staffings and brief behavior rating scales. More detailed behavioral and academic assessment is used for pre-/post-evaluation purposes and to determine more exact student behavioral needs for the program. Goals are determined with parental and teacher input and parental permission is required for participation.

Intervention strategies include the development of a trusting relationship between child and counselor-aide leading to sharing of feelings and goal directed work on specific behavioral needs. Behavioral interventions are also carried out between counselor-aide and classroom teachers. Students sometimes meet in group sessions to work on specific social skills and to develop more appropriate behavioral modeling to transfer back to the classroom.

One of the key elements of PIP is the close relationship with the mental health profession. Clarkston School District works closely with the Asotin County Mental Health Center; two of its staff members serve as trainers, supervisors, and consultants to the project.

PIP in Clarkston is more school-based than home or family-based; however, attempts are made to involve the family in home visits and parent training classes. Parent involvement is also sought in setting the goals for children's participation in PIP.

The most distinctive features of PIP are the use of counselor-aides with initial and ongoing training from mental health consultants as well as the close relationship between the school district and the mental health center, working to the advantage of both organizations.

CONTACT

Mr. Lloyd Walles
Clarkston No. 250, ESD 123
P.O. Box 72
Clarkston, WA 99403
509/758-2532

7. Tacoma School District
    District Placement Procedures

TARGET POPULATION

The placement procedures described are for the SBD students served by Tacoma schools.

PROGRAM DESCRIPTION

Tacoma School District exemplifies the multiple approach to service delivery. It is the overriding philosophy of Tacoma School District that SBD students should participate in natural environments and that coping skills should be taught. Focus is on learning about oneself, through a developmental approach. Tacoma School District attempts to bring home, school, and community together in a holistic approach to meeting student needs.

Assessment of individual students is accomplished by a Multi-Disciplinary Team (MDT). Once declared eligible for special services the student has available a wide range of options, from full-time mainstreaming to a self-contained placement with assistance from a social worker.

CONTACT

Mr. John Iverson
Central Administration Building
Tacoma School District
Tacoma, WA 98401
206/593-6973

8. Yakima School District
    Social Skills Training Project

TARGET POPULATION

Elementary level SBD students.

PROGRAM DESCRIPTION

Yakima's SBD Social Skills Training Project involves student placement in two
elementary classrooms at a single school.   Placement is in the afternoon;
students are in their home school during morning hours. The curriculum is
non-academic and includes instruction in appropriate social behavior,
interpreting body language, systematic relaxation techniques, and self-esteem
building.   Program staff teach social skills to target students in the
afternoon, but serve as liaison between home and school, as well as monitoring
student behavior on buses and other forms of transportation that students
might take to and from school. They also participate in MDT meetings and
observe target students in their home schools to ensure generalization
carryover of behaviors learned in the home and the classrooms.   Students are
in the program on a contract basis, and can earn their way out of the class by
learning and exhibiting targeted social behaviors.

CONTACT

G. Campbell
K. Campbell
Yakima School District
104 N. 4th Avenue
Yakima, WA 98902
509/575-3230

9. Children's Orthopedic Hospital and Medical Center, Seattle
    Inpatient Psychiatry Unit Diagnostic Classroom

TARGET POPULATION

The diagnostic and treatment services are available for preschool and
elementary-age children who are experiencing severe behavior problems.   The
range of psychiatric disorders represented by this population includes
depression, suicidal ideation, aggression, anorexia nervosa, oppositional and
anti-social disorders, developmental delays, etc. Many of these children have
experienced serious abuse and/or neglect, although organic problems are part
of the diagnosis for some patients.

PROGRAM DESCRIPTION

The Inpatient Psychiatry Unit and its Diagnostic Classroom serve approximately
100 patients per year who are referred by parents, physicians, schools,
community agencies, etc., from cities and towns throughout the state. These
patients are served by a multi-disciplinary team which consists of a medical
director, psychologist, social worker, educator, child care specialists, and
specialists in other disciplines such as speech, occupational therapy, etc.

In addition, the Unit functions as a training facility for the University of Washington and provides training opportunities for students in psychiatry, psychology, social work, education, etc.

The Inpatient Diagnostic classroom provides the following services:

1.   Diagnosis: All patients are assessed by means of formal academic testing procedures as well as by systematic observation of their social behavior with adults and with other children.

2.   Instruction: Patients attend school for three hours in the morning during which time they engage in traditional learning activities such as reading, math, spelling, social studies, etc. Instruction is provided in both individual and group settings.

3.   Consultation and placement: The staff makes contact with receiving schools or child care facilities at the time of discharge to design the most appropriate public school education for each patient. Typically, one or more on-site visits are made to each patient's school by members of the Unit's team.   This time-consuming activity is essential to obtaining the best possible program for each child.

4.   Follow-up: Regular post-discharge contact is made with school and community agencies so as to follow patient progress and to consult with these facilities as problems arise.

CONTACT

Paul Lichter, M.Ed.
Children's Orthopedic Hospital and Medical Center
Inpatient Psychiatry Unit Diagnostic Classroom
4800 Sand Point Way, NE
Seattle, WA 98105
206/634-5000

10. ESD #101
    Serious Behavioral Disabilities
    Regional Technical Assistance/Consultant Model

TARGET POPULATION

SBD students in school districts served by Educational Service District #101.

PROGRAM DESCRIPTION

The Regionally Based Technical Assistance/Consultant Model is designed to provide ongoing assistance, training, and direct consultative intervention to the 26 school districts and agencies that serve the behaviorally disabled. The project is designed as a process consultation model utilizing a total systems approach to diagnosing and solving the unique problems of managing the behaviorally disabled student in each school district and agency program. The regionally based behavioral consultant provides onsite technical assistance to expand the staff's specific assessment and intervention skills, conducts onsite demonstrations of behavioral management techniques, assists in program development and evaluation, develops and conducts topical workshops, and provides a brokerage service when needed to match specific outside resources with school district and agency needs.

CONTACT

Mr. Cliff Christiansen
Regional Behavioral Disabilities Consultant
W. 1025 Indiana
ESD 101
Spokane, WA   99205
509/456-7086

11. Lutheran Social Services of Washington and the Shoreline School District
    The Individual Achievement Program

TARGET POPULATION

This program serves middle school children (12-15) whose behaviors could no longer be tolerated in a regular classroom setting.

PROGRAM DESCRIPTION

The Individual Achievement Program is a cooperative program developed by Lutheran Social Services and Shoreline School District because both institutions felt the need to provide a program that would serve the target population. The mutual goal of both institutions is to work on the problem behaviors and then to mainstream the students to the most appropriate classroom setting. Therapeutic strategies include counseling, behavior management through a point system, group participation, individual attention, and family involvement.

CONTACT

Karen L. Stolfi
Lutheran Social Services of Washington

Paula H. Horn
Shoreline School District

12. Project Interface-A Cooperative Program of Educational Intervention

Project Interface is a cooperative effort between the Division of Juvenile Rehabilitation, Spokane County Juvenile Court, and Educational Service District 101.

TARGET POPULATION

To qualify for this project students must be:

1. junior/senior high age/level
2. involved with the juvenile court system
3. educationally "at risk"

PROGRAM DESCRIPTION

This project is designed to provide linkage between the educational community, student, family, juvenile justice system, and community in order to enhance the educational experience of juvenile offenders. The project has the following goals:

1.   to modify conditions in the existing educational and juvenile justice system which result in the appropriate identification of juvenile offenders with special education and support needs;

2.   to promote linkages beteen the two systems which will match the needs of juvenile offenders to appropriate educational programs/services;

3.   to decrease an offender's penetration into the juvenile court system by providing appropriate educational programs/services as well as ongoing follow-up and support;

4.   to reduce and prevent recidivism; and

5.   to collect valid and reliable data with which to measure the effectiveness of the identification procedures, the system for matching offenders to educational programs/services, and the programs/services themselves in terms of their ability to reduce delinquency.

CONTACT

Cliff Christiansen
ESD 101
W. 1025 Indiana
Spokane, WA   99205
509/456-7086

13. Spokane County Juvenile Detention Center
    Educational Program

TARGET POPULATION

Students who are sentenced to serve time in this detention facility are eligible for this program. It is, therefore, an adjudicated population.

PROGRAM DESCRIPTION

This school program is provided for all handicapping conditions at the Spokane County Juvenile Detention Center. This program provides educational programs for an average of 3-4 weeks. It is designed to insure that juveniles, even when incarcerated, can receive a free, appropriate public education.

14. Federal Way School District
    Service Delivery Programs

TARGET POPULATION

SBD students.

PROGRAM DESCRIPTION

The Federal Way School District provides services for SBD students at the elementary through secondary level. Remediation of problematic behaviors is accomplished through a variety of teaching procedures at a number of different schools.

Components of the programs include behavioral management strategies such as behavior contracts, home-based reinforcement systems, special materials (Walker Social Skills Curriculum), and specialized instructional methods (small group and 1:1 instruction).

Distinctive features of the program include low student-staff ratio, special services support, emphasis on mainstreaming, daily group sessions, and small group counseling by a psychologist.

CONTACT

Gretchen Caulfield
303 SW 308th
Federal Way, WA 98023

15. Spokane School District
    Placement Procedures

TARGET POPULATION

Students suspected of, or already classified as having severe behavioral disorders.

PROGRAM DESCRIPTION

Spokane School District, when considering a student for placement in the SBD program, implements a comprehensive assessment procedure to determine eligibility for inclusion in the program. Prior to assessment, documentation of prior interventions is required, and at the MDT staffings, all special education personnel are included to insure that all perspectives on the problem are represented. There is a focus on observable, measureable behaviors as the basis for classification.

For those students who are classified as SBD, a range of placement options are available. Intervention specialists are utilized to coordinate a districtwide program providing programming to SBD students. Extensive utilization of behavior management, social skills instruction, placement options, and parent involvement ensures a variety of instructional alternatives for the SBD child.

CONTACT

Dr. Robert Knox
Special Education Supervisor
N. 200 Bernard
Spokane Public Schools
Spokane, WA   99201
509/455-4514

16. Bellevue Public Schools
    Seriously Behaviorally Disabled Program
    Cascade Middle and High School

TARGET POPULATION

Cascade is a special education program for youth in the Bellevue School District who have been identified as having serious behavioral disabilities. These youths have been unable to function within a mainstream school setting. They may also have difficulties such as delinquency and drug abuse in home and community settings.

PROGRAM DESCRIPTION

The Cascade Program is self-contained and has both teaching and counseling components. There is a two and one-half hour morning session for high school students and a two-hour afternoon session for junior high school students. The shortened school day accommodates youths who have been unable to maintain behavior control for a full school day. Those able to endure a longer school day have an option for "contact classes" in mainstream schools in addition to the partial day at Cascade.

The goal of the Cascade Program is to help students make a successful transition into mainstream academic or vocational life in a relatively short period of time. In order to do this, emphasis is placed on affective education. This means teaching the students skills or behaviors they can use as positive alternatives to the ones which have been getting them into trouble. It also means helping students to learn about and develop the more positive aspects of their personalities and aptitudes. In addition to individualized academic instruction, the curriculum includes such topics as communication skills, decision making, anger management, impulse control, positive self-image building, and issues of drug abuse. To enhance learning and ease the transition back into a mainstream classroom, material is presented using a group learning model in which students learn study skills as they master the content of the material presented.

Individual counseling provides an opportunity for students to deal with personal issues in a confidential one-to-one setting. Family counseling is also available through the program.

Positive parent involvement is encouraged and maintained in a number of ways. Initially, parents are involved in the IEP process; parents are regularly informed of student progress toward goal attainment; parent conferences are held when there are behavior or attendance problems. Occasional parent group meetings are scheduled during the school year. These meetings serve several purposes: 1) parent support group; 2) exchange of information regarding school policies, transfers, etc.; 3) opportunity to teach parenting/communication skills to reinforce those learned by the students.

When appropriate, Cascade coordinates its services with those of other helping professionals and agencies outside the program such as probation officers, private therapists, Department of Social and Health Services, etc.

The transition back into a mainstream school begins when a student's behavioral goals are consistently met at Cascade. The behavioral goals for Cascade students are the acquisition and generalization of the behaviors they need at school and on the job. For this reason the students take responsibility for making and monitoring progress on their own behavioral goals. Initially, the students are involved in writing their own IEPs. Weekly contracting with students is used to measure step-by-step progress toward goal attainment.

17. Stevenson Elementary
    Bellevue, WA

TARGET POPULATION

The Seriously Behaviorally Disabled Special Education Program at Stevenson Elementary serves from six to fourteen students from first to fifth grades who have been identified as having severe behavioral and/or emotional disabilities which interfere with their educational performance and are unable to be served at their home school.

PROGRAM DESCRIPTION

This program includes the services of a full-time special education teacher, a part-time special education teacher who also serves other mildly handicapped students, a full-time Youth Eastside Services counselor, and a full-time classroom aide. The teachers plan, evaluate, and carry out the academic program for each student on an individual or small group basis. The aide assists the teacher in preparing and correcting academic materials, helps the students one to one as needed in special education and mainstream classes, and supervises the students on the playground. The counselor helps the teacher plan and carry out a classroom management system, sees the students for individual counseling 45 minutes per week, handles crisis situations as they arise, plans and teaches a social skills/self-esteem building curriculum, and meets with the parents of each student and their families in conjuction with the teacher. She also provides an early inservice for mainstreaming teachers regarding SBD programming and develops a careful monitoring system of student progress. The SBD staff works together as a team, constantly assessing the progress of each student and readjusting the program to better serve student needs.

18. Grand Coulee Dam School District 301J
    Motivation and Behavior
    Home/School Cooperative Approaches

TARGET POPULATION

Any students who are experiencing difficulty in school--either behavioral or academic.

PROGRAM DESCRIPTION

Three approaches are used in Grand Coulee Dam School District 301J. They are the "Note Home Program," the parent telephone call-in procedure, and contracting with parents, students, and teachers.

The Note Home Program establishes consistent communication between the teachers, parents, and student. A note home is sent daily describing the child's academic achievement, behavior, and any homework. Reinforcement, delivered by the parent, is contingent upon receipt of a note which indicates that the student met minimum criteria for "well done" on that day. The program improves communication between home and school, and facilitates improved behavior and increased learning at school.

Contracts between student and teacher also result in improved behavior at school. These contracts are written agreements guaranteeing that when a student behaves in a certain way s/he is reinforced appropriately.

CONTACT

Michael J. Cashion
Director, Special Services
Grand Coulee Dam School District
Stevens & Grant
Coulee Dam, WA 99116
509/633-2143

19. Cheney Public Schools
    Secondary Student Intervention Project (SSIP)

TARGET POPULATION

While primarily designed to meet the unique social and educational needs of group home and special education students, the project has been expanded to address the needs of other students as needed. Project staff has prioritized the population to be served as follows: 1) behaviorally disabled students, 2) other special education students, and 3) regular students who have become a focus of concern as a result of chronic school problems.

PROGRAM DESCRIPTION

The intent of SSIP, an alternative to suspension, is to provide a positive short term intervention/prevention plan coupled with a school survival course to increase the success of students experiencing difficulty in school. The SSIP Teacher/Facilitator helps students forecast consequences, explore alternatives, make decisions, and develop specific plans, which lead to more productive behaviors in the students' regular classes.

Three major components combine to provide alternatives to suspension: 1) time-out room, a crisis intervention setting where a student's stay is usually temporary, varying according to individual needs; a successful intervention followed by a return to the regular class is the desired goal; 2) a school survival course, a 12-hour structured class provided throughout the trimester; it is presented in small groups and designed to help the students acquire skills to cope more effectively at school; and 3) a multidisciplinary assessment team that meets at regularly scheduled times to consider appropriate prevention/intervention procedures for individual students.

CONTACT

Bill Moore
Coordinator, Pupil Services
520 4th Street
Cheney Public Schools
Cheney, WA
509/235-6205

20. Tacoma School District
    Mason Junior High School SBD Program

TARGET POPULATION

Children in this program must be severely behaviorally disordered in order to receive services.

PROGRAM DESCRIPTION

This program uses a Therapeutic Learning Center (see program description #2 above) to help the severely behaviorally disordered student both behaviorally and academically in order to promote the transfer of learning in school to the community as well as to outside, mainstream classes. The program emphasizes a structured environment for learning. Behavior modification intervention, through individualized programming, is the preferred mode of service delivery.

All student programs are individually oriented to meet specific needs. Daily reports to parents, adjusted curriculum, and use of outside resources are all available for implementation.

CONTACT

Dolores Keller
Tacoma School District
Mason Junior High School
Tacoma, WA

21. Lake Washington School District
    Social Skills and Study Skills Program

TARGET POPULATION

This program is effective with mild behavior disordered and learning disabled children.

PROGRAM DESCRIPTION

The Lake Washington Social Skills and Study Skills Program for secondary mild behavior disordered and learning disabled students is designed to teach youth how to cope and think in school. The social skills component has been piloted at the junior and senior high school levels. A class called "social skills" has been formed, and this class includes both special education and regular education students. The social skills component features material on how to deal with parents and teachers and how to interact appropriately with peers. There is an emphasis on study skills also. This is designed to assist the student in mastering curriculum areas such as social studies, science, and language arts. The classes are staffed by regular education teachers.

CONTACT

Ruth Hayes
Director, Special Education
Lake Washington School District
P.O. Box 2909
Kirkland, WA 98033
206/828-3201

22. Spokane Valley Cooperative for Special Education and
       Spokane Community Mental Health Center
    School Day Treatment Program

TARGET POPULATION

Children ages 6-14 who exhibit: physical and/or verbal aggressiveness toward others, defiance of authority, refusal to cooperate with school rules/tasks, low self-esteem, poor classroom skills, family problems, withdrawal, and depression.

PROGRAM DESCRIPTION

The School Day Treatment Program is an innovative program that combines community mental health services with the school agency services to elementary age SBD children. Mental health professionals work with children in the school setting to provide counseling--both individual and group--to remediate behavioral problems. Constant interaction between professionals (mental health professionals and teachers) help to provide a comprehensive program for these children.

The program is designed to develop additional communication skills in order to teach children to resolve conflicts with appropriate verbal abilities rather than physical aggressiveness, to express themselves in direct ways rather than use evasiveness or denial, to develop listening skills, to act rather than react, and to choose positively directed behavior rather than maladaptive and inappropriate behavior.

CONTACT

Sheila Bell
Spokane Valley Cooperative for Special Education
Spokane, WA

23. Mid-Columbia Psychiatric Hospital
    Child/Adolescent Day Hospital Program

TARGET POPULATION

Children and adolescents (ages 8-17) who are experiencing moderate to severe levels of emotional and behavioral disturbance.

PROGRAM DESCRIPTION

The Day Hospital Program offers crisis stabilization, liaison with the community, and carefully planned discharge and placement. The basic therapeutic program utilizes the Development Therapy Model. (See program description #4 above.) Objectives are used for program planning, grouping clients, and documenting each client's progress.

Emphasis is placed on applied behavioral analysis and contingency management techniques to increase the amount of appropriate and adaptive social behavior. The use of group process techniques is a part of the behavior change plan. Several types of group meetings are held on a regular basis with all the clients.

A primary focus in the therapeutic program is on client skills for interacting in peer groups through the use of group process techniques. These techniques, employed several times daily in group meetings, help the individual learn verbal problem-solving skills, and how to set realistic goals.

Milieu, individual, group, family, academic, recreational, and expressive therapies are all provided on a daily basis based upon individual needs. In addition, educational and psychological testing is provided to those clients deemed in need of those services. Consultation with referring agencies and schools is routine. At the time of each client's stay, a report is written which includes an educational and behavioral assessment, identification of treatment needs, and appropriate recommendations.

CONTACT

Jayne Gosnold
Coordinator
Child/Adolescent Day Hospital Program
Mid-Columbia Psychiatric Hospital and Community Mental Health Center
1175 Gribble
Richland, WA   99352
509/943-9104

24. Highline School District
P.A.C.T. (Parents, Adolescents, Counselors, and Teachers)

TARGET POPULATION

SBD adolescents.

PROGRAM DESCRIPTION

The PACT Program is a concerted effort of parents, adolescents, counselors, and teachers to change behaviors which prohibit placement in regular education classrooms. Interfering behaviors might include violent temper outbursts or disruptions or extremely withdrawn and fearful responses to the usual school environments.

PACT classrooms offer a highly structured, therapeutic environment in which students learn alternatives to inappropriate behavior. They learn ways to gain positive attention and are provided with many opportunities for success--which translate into increased self-esteem.

Parent involvement is a crucial part of PACT. Teachers communicate daily to parents on student progress. Parents attend a support group where they share ideas and concerns with each other, learn parenting skills, and get information on PACT curricula and activities. Families are involved in counseling to learn how to interact with their adolescent as he/she is trying to make changes.

Adolescents in PACT are expected to recognize the need for changed behavior and to work to learn new skills. Although they are discouraged and often angry, they are helped to appreciate their strengths and to set goals for themselves to acquire needed skills.

Support staff assists teachers, parents, and students in determining target behaviors, planning appropriate interventions and offering encouragement and support. PACT staff includes a psychologist, family counselors, and a classroom counselor. In addition, the staff works with other service providers in the community in an attempt to secure as much help for students and their families as possible.

PACT teachers are the primary facilitators of student behavior change. They provide opportunities for success throughout the school day by carefully planning lessons and activities to meet individual students' needs. Teachers and their aides provide frequent feedback to students on their progress toward identified academic and behavioral goals. They communicate daily to parents--offering support and suggestions where necessary.

CONTACT

Ms. Judy Burnett
PACT Program
Highline School District

25. North Thurston School District
    Chinook Middle School
    Behavior Exploration Tri-Level System

TARGET POPULATION

The North Thurston School District operates a tri-level program system to serve severe behavioral disabled and specific learning disabled students.

PROGRAM DESCRIPTION

The program is located at Chinook Middle School. The system's model is as follows:

Level I: Staffed by one teacher and one 7-hour instructional aide, this level is for students who demonstrate a severe behavioral problem and who require a high level of consistency in behavior management and structure. The majority of these students are assigned from 4 to 6 hours in this program.

Level II: Staffed by one teacher and one 5-hour instructional aide, this level is designed for students exhibiting specific behaviors and requiring no more than 4 hours of behavioral management and/or academic support.

Level III: Staffed by one teacher and one 3-hour instructional aide, this level targets students who may exhibit minor behavioral problems and who also require one to two hours of academic support in language arts and/or mathematics.

Additionally, the program is supported by a school social worker, the program psychologist, and other special education support personnel as required by individual student needs.

As student behavior improves, Level I students move up to Level II. Students who can handle more academic independence move from Level II to Level III or into a basic education class. Level II students make transition into basic education as they acquire a higher academic level in language arts and math.

Although Level I focuses on behavior, academic performance and growth are equally important. Levels II and III utilize a variety of materials. Some students who are in basic education, social studies, or science classes receive support during reading time. There is an Access Model component, teaching reading skills through the basic education classroom texts. For all students, the emphasis is on identifying academic needs and planning a program to meet these needs.

CONTACT

Carolyn Lint
Fritz Mondau
North Thurston School District
6202 Pacific Avenue S.E.
Lacey, WA 98503

Exhibit 7

Exemplary Programs in Other States

COLORADO: SPECIAL EDUCATION SERVICES UNIT

The Special Education Services Unit of the Colorado Department of Education is currently serving approximately 9,500 students identified as "SIEBD" (students with "significant identifiable emotional or behavioral disorders"). These students (ages 5-19) are receiving services in metropolitan, suburban, and rural school districts through a variety of delivery systems, including self-contained SIEBD programs, resource programs, consultative services, and multicategorical programs. Nevertheless, these various types of service delivery systems share (1) a common philosophy, (2) a model process for identification, assessment, and programming, and (3) a set of interagency agreements that govern the coordination of services.

The current special education philosophy is summed up in the statement, "it is more important to individualize than categorize." In other words, special education in Colorado is no longer a group of programs established according to categories of disabilities but a process for identifying and serving the unique needs of each individual student. Once educators and other service providers have identified a student's social and classroom management needs, they can begin to determine the nature, scope, and intensity of services to meet those needs.

There have also been recent changes in the assumptions underlying screening, assessment, programming, and service delivery. Thus, a student's needs, rather than disability or handicapping condition, assure that screening becomes a means of obtaining a holistic view of student functioning rather than assessing eligibility for a particular program. The purpose of assessment, therefore, is to provide information that is critical in determining programming, not to merely prove the existence of a handicap. Thus, assessment is changing from a predetermined battery of routinely administered psychometric tests to a multidisciplinary process of sampling student behaviors in order to make informed judgments about that student. In regard to programming, "individualized instruction" is no longer interpreted as one-on-one instruction, but is viewed as combining all school resources in unique ways dictated by an individual student's needs. The purpose of such programming is to teach students and help them reach their full potential, not to rehabilitate them and mold them to fit the "norm." Parents become equal partners in the educational decision-making process, not passive outsiders routinely informed of their child's progress. Finally, instead of being served by teachers who are certified in specific handicapping conditions, students are served by teachers who have the competencies to meet the students' identified needs. For teachers of SIEBD students, this has resulted in the creation of inservice programs and activities in order to develop the required competencies.

In addition to sharing this underlying philosophy, schools in Colorado rely upon a common set of procedures for identification, assessment, and placement, called the "Colorado Process Model." The process begins with the referral of a student (usually by a teacher) for the purpose of specifying the student's educational needs. While a rather precise definition of SIEBD exists in the state legal code (Administration of the Handicapped Children's Education Act, 1976), this definition is not a label for categorizing certain kinds of troublesome students but rather a source of criteria for pinpointing a student's behaviors and needs. These criteria focus upon the student's own behaviors (whose frequency and intensity are measured by means of a behavioral checklist) and upon the types of interventions that the school can provide (measured by another checklist that deals with teacher interactions, classroom structure, etc.). When the combined scores of both checklists reach the point where the student's behaviors are so frequent and intense that the student cannot be educated in the regular school program and the staff have exhausted all appropriate interventions, then the student may be identified as SIEBD and become eligible for some kind of special education services.

During both the screening and assessment stages of the process, professionals examine student behaviors and needs in five areas: Psychological, Educational, Social, Communicative, and Physical. The purpose of assessment is to yield data that are useful for determining needs and services. Screening and assessment are followed by "staffings" (multidisciplinary team conferences): participants try to determine whether the student is able to benefit from regular education. The emphasis is upon keeping a student in the regular education program if at all possible, even if this requires modifications or individual programming. If not, then the multidisciplinary team will need to determine what sort of placement the student requires.

There are a number of placement options, arranged into a continuum of services that provides for five levels or categories of placement, from least restrictive (a regular education setting with resource personnel) to more restrictive (a closed facility with intensive intervention). In each of these options, the programming for SIEBD students consists of six components: Environmental Management, Behavior Management, Academics, Career/Vocational Education, Affective Education, and Counseling. These components are individually adapted to each student according to that student's identified needs.

The legal and economic foundation for this continuum of services resides in a comprehensive set of formal, legal agreements between the Colorado Department of Education and five other agencies: the Division of Youth Services, Division of Mental Health, Division for Developmental Disabilities (all in the Department of Institutions), the Department of Health, and the Department of Social Services. A copy of these agreements is included in Appendix C of this report.

These agreements state the responsibilities of each agency in regard to providing specific services, especially for SIEBD and other "hard-to-place" students. The agreements also specify the mechanisms for funding these services. For example, the Colorado legislature has provided a special state revenue fund to be set aside as a supplement to be used by all state agencies serving handicapped students. Money from this fund is activated whenever parents, school districts, or community agencies are unable to pay for the costs of certain services. The agencies that jointly provide the services must request the money they need from a special commission that authorizes the issuance of funds.

· To summarize, the Colorado Department of Education's program for SIEBD children and youth is exemplary because of the continuum of services that it provides, its emphasis upon least restrictive environment in regard to placement, a comprehensive set of interagency agreements that define and clarify responsibilities, and provisions for a special fund that exists to meet all funding contingencies.

The ultimate goal is for all students to receive services as close to their homes as possible. Five years ago, over 200 of these students were sent out of state for their education, whereas in 1985 only 5 students left the state (and 1 of them returned). The exemplary features of this statewide program will ensure that Colorado schools continue to make progress in identifying, planning for, and serving SIEBD students.

CONTACT

Brian McNulty
Executive Director
Special Education Services
Colorado Department of Education
303 W. Colfax
Denver, CO
303/573-3233

GEORGIA: THE GEORGIA PSYCHOEDUCATIONAL CENTER NETWORK

The Georgia Psychoeducational Center Network is a statewide, comprehensive, educational, treatment program for severely emotionally disturbed, severely behaviorally disordered, and autistic children and youth from birth through 18 years old. Serving approximately 10,000 youngsters each year, the network consists of 24 nonresidential, community-based centers with numerous satellite facilities. Each center works with local school systems or Cooperative Educational Services Agencies (CESAs) within its assigned region, which consists of two or more counties.

The network is funded by the Georgia General Assembly through the Georgia Department of Education, Program for Exceptional Children, with local school systems and CESAs serving as fiscal agents for the program. Federal support through Chapter I 89-313 funds supplement state funded programming for infants and preschool children ages birth through 4 while adolescent services are partially supported by P.L. 94-142 VI-B funds. All services are provided without fees. A special fund exists for the purpose of paying for extra services students may need, especially students whose service costs cannot be covered by state or federal financial arrangements. School systems provide transportation for youngsters to attend psychoeducational classes and work cooperatively with the respective centers to meet housing needs.

The major admission requirement is the presence of an emotional disturbance or behavioral disorder severe enough to require a specialized treatment program. Children with secondary handicapping conditions are accepted if the primary disability is a severe emotional disturbance or severe behavioral disorder. Children who have mild to moderate behavior or discipline problems are not eligible.

Each center provides services for two general age groupings: birth through age 14 and ages 15-18. These comprehensive services include referral, treatment, periodic evaluation, and follow-up. Service delivery is a cooperative effort involving psychologists, psychiatrists, teachers, social workers, parents, and agency personnel. The emphasis is upon reducing the need for residential placement by enabling youngsters to remain in their homes while receiving services. The treatment approach for children and youth varies from center to center, depending upon diagnosis and individual needs; there is a continuum of service delivery models available which range from satellite programs in regular education schools and self-contained classrooms/resource rooms to consultative services in regular education classrooms. The IEP for each student is the responsibility of the center, not the school district, even though the center staff work to maintain the student's participation in the regular school program to the greatest extent possible.

A cooperative agreement exists between the Georgia Department of Education (Division of Special Programs and the Office of Vocational Education) and the Georgia Department of Human Resources (Division of Mental Health and Mental Retardation, Division of Rehabilitation Services, and Division of Youth Services). This agreement outlines the responsibilities of these agencies in the areas of evaluation and assessment, referral and admission, appeals procedures, the IEP, and release or termination. Similar cooperative agreements among agencies exist at the local level.

These unique elements lead to the success of the Georgia Psychoeducational Center Network and assures the provision of quality programming to meet the needs of severely emotionally disturbed, behaviorally disabled youth in Georgia.

CONTACT

Project T.A.P.S. (Teaching Adolescents Personal Success)
North DeKalb Psychoeducation Center
3601 Sexton Woods Drive
Chamblee, GA   30341
404/452-1165
404/455-3916

VERMONT: A SERVICE DELIVERY MODEL
FOR EMOTIONALLY DISTURBED STUDENTS

In June 1983, the Vermont State Department of Education's Steering Committee on Emotional Disturbance issued a report on the current service delivery options for the state's emotionally disturbed (ED) students (365 students were served in 1982-83). The Committee found that special education program development for ED youngsters was lagging behind the development of services for students with other handicapping conditions largely because of confusion over definition and identification procedures, a lack of readily available public school programs, and inadequate local and state advocacy for ED students. The Committee recommended that an effective state-wide service delivery system be planned and implemented, and that systematic attention be directed to the issues of ED definition and identification, teacher training, advocacy, and interagency collaboration.

In response, the Committee (augmented by educators, school administrators, and mental health service professionals) met during 1983-84 to develop a statewide service delivery model to meet the needs of ED students, especially in the traditionally underserved rural areas (which means most of the state). This delivery model is currently being implemented.

This model is based upon an ecological approach that promotes the improvement of interactions between the student and significant others in the student's total environment. The model emphasizes the following features: close working relationships between schools and community agencies; a multi-disciplinary team approach to student identification, referral, assessment, programming, and evaluation; providing a continuum of services in the least restrictive setting possible for ED students as close to home as possible; multidistrict pooling of resources and skilled personnel (a necessity in Vermont); program components that address family support and training needs.

The model consists of six program components (these are identical to the program components for SIEBD youths in Colorado). The environmental management component deals with ways to monitor student behavior in the "internal" environment of the ED classroom and the "external" environment of the mainstream education program, home, and community. The behavior management component focuses upon student behaviors necessary for learning and self-control (task completion, following directions, controlling impulses, cooperation with peers and adults, etc.). The academic skills component is concerned with promoting those functional skills that the student will most often use in both school and vocational environments; materials and teaching strategies are responsive to the particular needs of the individual learner. The career/vocational education component emphasizes the type of curriculum and out-of-school placements that promote social and other functional skills needed for future job success. The affective education component concentrates upon systematic instruction to help students acquire information, attitudes, and social skills that will result in appropriate behavior and positive personal growth. Finally, counseling provides support to students through individual, small group, or family oriented sessions that may be held in school or elsewhere.

These six program components are included at each of the five levels of the continuum of services for ED students, ranging from most restrictive (Level V) to least restrictive (Level I). The number of students requiring out-of-state residential placements (Level V: Residential Treatment Programs) are expected to decrease as other program options for ED students are developed. The Committee anticipates that up to 75% of ED students now in costly residential placements could benefit from programs at the next level (Level IV: Multidistrict Programs), developed for middle and high school students. Programs at the next level (Level III: Intensive Resource Room Programs) are to be developed in towns or regions where large numbers of ED students can be maintained in their home schools and receive a combination of regular and special education services or full-day special education services. Less severely involved ED students would continue to receive services at the next restrictive level (Level II: Mainstream Special Education Programs). At Level I: Regular Education Programs, mildly disabled students with emotional and/or behavioral problems will receive most of their services in school from regular educators and school guidance staff, with only limited consultation by the local special educator.

One example of the kinds of programs in Vermont is the Homecoming Project, which is operated under the auspices of the Center for Developmental Disabilities at the University of Vermont. As its name indicates, the project removes ED and "autistic" students from residential placements and returns them to regular education classrooms (with appropriate support systems) in their home communities. This project exemplifies one of the chief philosophical assumptions underlying the statewide service delivery model: that ED students be served close to their homes in the least restrictive environments possible.

Vermont's service delivery model is similar to those of Colorado and Georgia. Vermont not only offers a continuum of services for students defined as "ED" or "BD" but also supports this continuum by means of a set of comprehensive interagency agreements that specify responsibilities for the delivery of services. In addition, the state has tackled the problem of funding by establishing a special fund to pay for services to "high-cost" students. Finally, a parallel tracking system shared by the relevant agencies (education, social services) is being developed as a means to monitor student progress over time.

CONTACT

Karen Windels
Emotional Disturbance Consultant
Vermont Department of Education
Special Education Unit
Montpelier, VT 05602-2703
802/828-3141

IDAHO: EDUCATING STUDENTS WITH EMOTIONAL
OR BEHAVIORAL PROBLEMS IN THE PUBLIC SCHOOLS

The State of Idaho Department of Education has developed a statewide system for providing services to students identified as having emotional or behavioral problems. This system has provisions for more effective screening and assessment, placement, programming, interagency cooperation, and funding.

Screening consists of two phases. Preliminary screening (which takes the form of either community or classroom surveys) involves surveying a population to locate all students who appear to deviate from accepted emotional or behavioral standards in a school or district. Compared to teacher referral, this large group screening procedure is considered to be a more effective means of locating students with nondisruptive ("internalizing") emotional and behavioral problems. A Child Study Team (equivalent to a multidisciplinary team) is responsible for the systematic screening that occurs once students have been identified by means of the surveys. This systematic screening consists of behavioral rating scales, checklists, or direct observation; the particular approach used depends upon the size of the district, the number of students initially identified, and the resources and personnel available.

The objective of both systematic screening and assessment (which may occur after the completion of screening, or a direct referral) is to determine whether the student is eligible for special education services as "emotionally impaired" (according to the state of Idaho definition). There are a variety of placement options available once a student's eligibility has been determined (a Child Study Team first asks whether the student can succeed in the regular school environment without adaptations or modifications). These options range from a regular education classroom with limited special education consultation to residential treatment behind the walls of an institution. There is thus a continuum of services available for "emotionally impaired" students in Idaho. These services include both educational and social/psychological and other support services that a student may require. In regard to each individual student, there is an emphasis upon tracking student progress, conducting annual reviews, and providing opportunities for transitions into less restrictive settings.

The North Idaho Children's Home (NICH) is an example of one type of program available. NICH is a private, non-profit, residential center for children between the age of 6 and 18 years. Among the services that NICH offers are the Special Care Program, which provides intensive treatment for children with serious emotional disturbances, and the Home Education Center, which serves children in residence at NICH who are "emotionally impaired" and unable to attend public school. Educational programming at NICH is individualized and designed to meet specified criteria and instructional objectives rather than being referenced to general norms or grade levels. When the goal is to prepare the child to re-enter the public school system, the educational program stresses motivation, academic preparation, and appropriate school behavior. For other children, the NICH offers vocational assessments and training, a GED or high-school equivalency program, and arrangements for placing students in various job sites or job training programs.

Children and youth who reside at NICH are assigned to one of five levels, which are differentiated according to responsibilities expected of residents and the corresponding privileges they receive. Children at Level I exhibit the most severe behavior problems and require the most behavior management. As their behavior improves, they can move up to Level II, where there are fewer responsibilities and more privileges. As students move from one level to the next, their educational programming focuses less on behavior management and more on academic growth and performance. Level V is practically the stage for eventual departure from NICH. (For a similar "multilevel" model, see the description of the North Thurston School District Behavioral Exploration Tri-Level System in Appendix A.)

The statewide institutional framework for this particular program and others is based upon comprehensive legal agreements among service delivery agencies at all levels, which include provisions for special funding to meet all contingencies.

CONTACT

North Idaho Children's Home
P.O. Box 319
Lewiston, ID   83501
208/743-9404

IMPLICATIONS OF SBD RESEARCH TOWARD ACHIEVING EXCELLENCE IN CLASSROOM INSTRUCTION AND ADMINISTRATION

John P. Jewell

The purpose of this chapter is to share findings from the Washington Statewide Serious Behavior Disabilities Study that will be useful to administrators and policy makers in evaluating local district programs. School districts need a system that is simple, cost effective, and meaningful to the community and staff. The effective delivery of programs for the behaviorally disabled is dependent, to a great extent, on how carefully the program is planned, carried out, and modified to respond to changing conditions and needs. This chapter reviews findings from the Statewide SBD Study and looks at program planning and evaluation as a set of activities designed to assist the development and improvement of services for students with behavioral disabilities. It concludes with recommendations as to the characteristics of an outstanding program.

The study obtained information and data about the best practices occurring in districts that serve youth with serious behavioral disabilities (SBD). District representatives shared overviews of their programs. Their presentations to researchers included: (a) descriptions of the population served; (b) procedures for screening, referral, and assessment; (c) placement options and intervention strategies; (d) goals and objectives of the delivery model; (e) curricula, special materials, instructional methods, and descriptions of the assistance received from noneducational agencies; (f) provisions for family and community involvement; and (g) summaries of the programs' distinctive features. Twelve presentations were made from eastern Washington districts and twelve from western Washington. Researchers reviewed each of these programs by rating the following elements of excellence: systematic screening, multidisciplinary team assessment, continuum of behavioral objectives for students, monitoring, data-based decision making, special instructional procedures, parent community involvement, systematic transition, program for inservice, and program evaluation. These elements of excellence were based on a review of the literature. They correlated highly with achievement and positive behavior changes. Local districts that are in the process of improving their programs have found these elements very helpful for designing a program evaluation instrument.

Good planning and evaluation includes four major characteristics as outlined in *Standards for Evaluations of Education Programs, Projects, and Materials* (Joint Committee on Standards for Educational Evaluation, New York: McGraw-Hill, 1981). The first of these characteristics is *utility*, which relates to the extent to which planning and evaluation efforts serve the program development and improvement needs of the user. The second major characteristic is *feasibility*. This factor is intended to reflect the need for program planning and evaluation efforts to be realistic and cost effective. The third characteristic is *propriety*. This characteristic refers to the degree to which efforts are carried out in ethically and legally responsible ways. The last characteristic mentioned by the Joint Committee is *accuracy*. Planning and evaluation activities should be conducted in manners which are defensible and accurate. Taking these characteristics and the elements of excellence that were identified in the Statewide SBD Study into consideration, this chapter presents a model for local school district use. The model, including the elements of excellence, and related questions that can be asked in evaluating a program are shown in Table 1, along with a summary of the results and the consequent goals for a program.

The model meets the first characteristic of *utility* in that it focuses on the important characteristics of a program for SBD students as identified after a review of the literature. It may serve the user in setting direction for future program improvements. Special Education/Parent Advisory Committees might use the information to influence the school board or the state legislature to provide better programs. School district administrative staff might use the information for redistributing current resources to meet the needs of the community and behaviorally disabled students.

The model meets the second characteristic of *feasibility* in that it is simple, easy to understand and uncomplicated in data collection procedures. "Elements of Excellence" questions are asked of key administrators' staff, advisory committee members, parents, and other interested parties. The model may be used with one group or several groups depending on the purpose of the study. Because of its simplicity and uncomplicated data collection procedures, the model is cost effective, especially when you consider that most of the work of identifying elements of excellence and reviewing the literature has been done and reported in the Statewide SBD Study.

The third characteristic is *propriety*, meaning carrying out the study in an ethical and legal manner. Evaluations should be based on the premise of developing better programs for students using the basic characteristics of outstanding programs. Propriety also ties appropriateness to the purpose of the study. The evaluation efforts should be realistic and conducted in a manner that considers the rights and integrity of individuals and groups. We found that teachers are well organized in collecting data and making student program decisions: Our model also focuses on the positive

Table 1
Evaluation Model with Sample Results

Elements of Excellence	Questions Asked	Results	Goals for Program
Systematic Screening	Is there a systematic screening to identify students?	District only conducted Childfind and Extended School Year screening.	To develop a system (multiple gating) for systematically screening for behavioral disabilities.
Multidisciplinary Team Assessment	Are students given a multi-disciplinary assessment prior to program entry that provide pertinent data in the form of measurable assessment outcomes that are converted by teachers into effective educational practices?	Assessments were conducted on all students but were used primarily for eligibility identification.	To develop curriculum-based assessments that provide pertinent data in the form of measurable assessment outcomes.
Continuum of Options	Is there a continuum of district options for students related to degree of handicap?	Lacked resources for residential placements.	To develop a day care program similar to residential care.
Behavioral, Measurable Objectives	Are appropriate behavioral, measurable objectives written for each student?	Objectives were written in behavior terms but quality was not monitored.	To develop a system for quality control.
Continuous Monitoring	Are students' objectives monitored on a continuous basis?	Continuous monitoring was occurring in most classrooms. The district did not have a system for checking on monitoring procedures.	To develop a simple district evaluation system to inform staff of importance of monitoring.

Table 1, Continued

Elements of Excellence	Questions Asked	Results	Goals for Program
Student Program Data	Are decisions about student programs data-based?	Approximately 80% of the teachers were measuring behavior and basing program decisions on data.	To increase inservice training to staff on data-based decision making.
Special Instructional Procedure & Curricula	Are procedures in curricula specially designed for the student related to the handicapping conditions?	A systematic strategy for transferring students between levels was needed.	To develop strategies for transferring students.
Parent/Community Involvement	Are parents appropriately involved in assisting the school in addressing the student's handicapping condition (sign language, SBD counseling, family therapy, etc.)?	Parent advocacy is limited to a small program called PACT.	To develop a larger advocate constituency group.
Systematic Transition	Are student provided a systematic transition program?	63% of the students are employed two years after graduation.	To develop guidelines for systematic transition.
Inservice Training	Is inservice designed specifically on an individual basis for the staff?	Inservice is designed for groups rather than for individuals.	To design a system that provides inservice based on individual needs.
Program Evaluation	Is the program evaluated annually based on student data? student data-based.	District evaluation was subjective rather that system.	To design and implement a student data-based evaluation

characteristics of staff decision making rather than demonstrating improper or weak components. Our purpose was to enhance programs.

The reporting of the data must be *accurate* and defensible and that may be the weakest component of this model. The accuracy of descriptive data is always open to criticism. For example, the interpretation range of response may be quite high when the question is asked, "Is there systematic screening to identify at-risk students?" The reason for a wide variety of responses may be attributed to varying perceptions of the terms "systematic screening" and "at-risk." Unless terms are carefully defined, interpretations may significantly alter the findings. Considering the purpose of this study and the limited amount of time available to evaluate the program according to the criteria, it was felt that the descriptive data was defensible and accurate enough, as many decisions to be made about programs are basically political rather than data based. The limitations of descriptive studies are many but should not stop the researcher from gathering the most accurate information possible for policy decisions. For the remainder of this chapter, we will review some of the findings from the Statewide SBD Study that related to each of the "Elements of Excellence." Then we will discuss how the findings may apply to any district's attempts to fine tune programs for the behaviorally challenged student.

Systematic Screening

Findings from the Statewide SBD Study

In the Statewide SBD Study, one of the first questions asked of districts was, "Is there systematic screening to identify at-risk students?" There are many reasons for screening students, the most obvious rationale is to improve a student's instructional program. Screening assists school district personnel in (a) recognizing individuals who need specially designed instruction, (b) making decisions as to whether formal identification and assessment is necessary, (c) grouping students for better services within the regular education environment, (d) gathering information that will assist in writing better objectives for remedial strategies, and (e) avoiding spending taxpayers' monies inappropriately on assessments not needed. We found in the Statewide SBD Study that there were inconsistent approaches when deciding which students were referred for special education and which ones were not. We reported that the internalized, withdrawing child often was not given an equal chance of being identified along with externalizing assertive children. Surprisingly, many districts in Washington did not have a systematic process, but waited until a student was referred by a teacher to the psychologist. This often led to a costly assessment procedure which in many cases was unnecessary if systematic screening had occurred to assist the team in distinguishing children with possible behavioral disabilities from other children. It was felt that the process of screening also provides a greater awareness to the teacher of the importance of making decisions based on carefully collected data.

Application of the Statewide SBD Study to a Local District

When evaluating a local district program the same question can be asked, "Is there systematic screening to identify at-risk students?" Districts may find they are conducting childfind procedures birth to five as well as extended school year screening, but beyond that are not identifying at-risk students using systematic procedures. If we rely basically on the random initiative of regular education teachers, principals, counselors, and parents to refer students to special education, the students' rights to a program depends on the possibility of being selected for screening. A goal should be to conduct regularly scheduled screening which would encourage continued heterogeneous grouping of students with regular education peers but with supportive assistance to the student with behavioral disabilities. Systematic screening can provide the staff with a powerful decision-making tool that will provide better services to students in the regular education setting. Hill Walker and his colleagues (e.g., Walker, Severson, & Haring, 1985) have been developing a system that appears to be quite useful for screening (see the chapter by Walker and Fabre in this volume). The procedure relies on teacher judgment and normative criteria to identify elementary grade level children exhibiting behavior disorders.

Multidisciplinary Team Assessment

Findings from the Statewide SBD Study

The enactment of the Education For All Handicapped Children Act of 1975 (PL 94-142) required districts to conduct multidisciplinary team assessments. It is the intention of the law that a multidisciplinary team assessment for each child provides professional staff members with better information about a child than one would have if the assessment were conducted by just one or two individuals. The Statewide SBD Study found that districts were conducting assessments, but there was not careful application of that assessment data to the classroom environment. The professional skills of different team members were used to determine strengths and weaknesses of the student and to possibly identify a handicapping condition. But often knowledge from assessments was not used in the regular or special education classroom environments. Psychologists in most cases were charged with consolidating the reports written by other team members into one report. These reports should have indicated how the team might best function in providing services for the student. The assessment process should have helped all the team members understand the child and should have suggested instructional strategies and materials that the teacher and other staff can use. Multi-disciplinary team assessments should also provide the staff with feedback on using various strategies to achieve progress. The team should use the data and systematically report back on student progress that relates to the collected data.

The Statewide SBD Study found educational staff often uncoordinated in establishing meaningful assessment strategies. Teachers emphasized behavioral strategies in the classroom that relied on measurable behavioral outcomes. They primarily relied on assessments and measures that were seen by the classroom teacher as not applicable for classroom intervention. Psychologists were using basically projective instruments (e.g., TAT, Sentence Completion, Rorschach House-Tree-Person, etc.) to measure behavior. Standardized observational formats or even behavior rating checklists were the exception and not the rule for psychological observations. School district administrators relied primarily on anecdotal records and few had standard observational formats.

The field in Washington is moving toward curricular-based assessments in conjunction with normed referenced assessments. If multi-disciplinary team assessments are to be meaningful and useful, then the assessments must tie into the curriculum that has been adopted by the local education agency.

Application of the Statewide SBD Study to a Local District

In evaluating a local district the question needs to be asked, "Are students given multidisciplinary team assessments, prior to program entry, that provide pertinent data in the form of measurable assessment outcomes that are converted by teachers into effective educational practices?" The district needs to keep in mind the quality of assessments and how they are used. The data collected should go beyond identifying the student for eligibility. It should provide an action plan for them. Large amounts of taxpayers' money should not be spent for assesments that have minimal value to the classroom teacher and other team members. The assessment information must be used primarily to assist staff, parents, and others in conducting measurable behavior change activities. The field needs to move beyond simple identification of students to meaningful assessments that deliver a plan of action for all team members including the parent.

Continuum of Options

Findings of the Statewide SBD Study

The question asked of the statewide participants who shared exemplary programs was, "Is there a continuum of district options for students related to the degree of handicap?" The majority of districts in Washington were not able to offer the services that were considered necessary for students with behavior disabilities. In most cases districts would offer more services for students if possible. Some additional services they would like to offer are counseling, family assistance, social work, smaller class ratios, medical evaluations, special curricula, adaptive materials, residential care, career planning, varying the length of the day, and special vocational training. They would also like state agencies to coordinate services for the behaviorally disabled. It is surprising that districts don't have a full range of options for placing students. These are the most difficult students to handle. One would imagine that more effort would be expended to develop programs for these students.

When administrators were asked to list innovative practices, most of them mentioned resource rooms combined with mainstreaming as a means of bringing students back into the regular classroom. Model behavior management practices often consisted of behavior modification, modeling, natural consequences, as well as team teaching and providing various levels of program settings. The responses from the questionnaire showed no consistency to any one model or practice. It appeared that districts felt that the state did not provide financially for a continuum of options and students were not being successfully educated or showing change in positive directions, within the limited resources expended. These findings reflected a lack of local, state, and national leadership to provide for the behaviorally disabled.

Application of the Statewide SBD Study to a Local District

"Is there a continuum of options for students related to the degree of handicap?" In evaluating their programs, local districts might consider asking this question of staff, parents, and the community. In Washington, group homes are closing, forcing more disturbed youth into communities. These children are often without support groups and family assistance. Group home administrators, police departments, and social and health agencies many times see problems with educational delivery systems that are unrecognized by educators. They may feel that the district provides a continuum of options for a certain segment of students but lacks services for others. They may also be providing services to youth unserved by the educational system. It is important that the questions about the continuum of options be asked beyond the educational community.

There may also be a perception among some special education teachers that services generally are not being provided to students in the mainstream, when actually, some may be provided through counseling, social work services, as well as psychology and other related services. But the perception may have a relationship to the lack of usable assessment materials, communication, and the limited amount of services (e.g., counselors assigned to three buildings, psychologists to six buildings). It also may be perceived by the teachers that related service personnel do not measure outcomes. It is therefore important to explore the intensity and/or frequency of related services as they apply to the continuum. To say counseling services are provided is certainly misleading, if few children can receive services.

Administratively, we have a lot more to learn about the relationship of a continuum of options to administering programs. Many questions are still unanswered. Washington requires districts to provide a continuum of options but it doesn't define what the continuum should be. It leaves that definition to the local school districts. In reviewing district procedural handbooks, one should check to see if a continuum of options is identified. Some additional questions that relate to the continuum are: How do staff, parents, community, and administrators describe the term "options" as it relates to students with behavioral disabilities? Washington state requires districts to meet the requirements of individualized educational programs (IEPs) but doesn't fund programs based on IEPs. The state requires districts to provide individualized programs but provides inadequate revenues that encourage political competetion for funds between groups of parents of students with different handicaps. How can one provide a continuum of options when resources are extremely limited? The questions regarding continuum may need to be explored beyond the local district and include the state and nation.

Behavioral Objectives for Students

Findings from the Statewide SBD Study

The question, "Are appropriate behavioral measurable objectives written for each student?" relates back to the type of data that has been collected (e.g., medical, cognitive, behavioral, etc.). Since teachers, for the most part, were not using the data collected from multidisciplinary team assessments to set their objectives, one might make the assumption that the objectives being written would reflect the bias and educational background of the teacher. The collective thinking of the team was not being reflected in objectives for the student. The Education for All Handicapped Children Act requires districts to write objectives for students, but are those objectives appropriate? Are they based on collected assessment data? Do they address the whole child? Are they written so that team members know immediately what the objective is? In reviewing the research, we found that achievement correlated to the teacher knowing what they were doing in the classroom. Achievement seemed to be connected with the obsession to meet particular objectives for students. Good teachers had high expectations, coupled with sensible management solutions. Good teachers could immediately tell you what was expected of their students. Multidisciplinary teams can help techers know what to expect of their children if they develop measurable assessment outcomes that can be easily converted by the teacher or service provider into effective educational practices.

Application of the Statewide SBD Study to a Local District

In local districts, all special education students should have measurable objectives. But are those objectives appropriate? Do they relate back to the assessment? Are they written to fit the students' needs? Do the objectives fit a local curriculum designed for students with similar characteristics? Are the objectives written for the student in a manner that activates all team members, including parents? The district should collect data to answer these questions. Since the team and parents sign the IEP indicating approval, we often assume that the IEP objectives are appropriate. But we can't say with authority that the objectives are appropriate unless systematic procedures are enacted to review their appropriateness.

In one local district there was a strongly felt need by the administration for related services personnel to write objectives that were more in tune with classroom behaviors. The IEP process should tie related services into the classroom objectives, producing a common professional approach to the student with a behavior handicap. The Statewide SBD Study was especially beneficial to this local district in that it raised many questions regarding the appropriateness of student objectives. The district had worked hard to provide inservice training to its teachers and staff members on the mechanics of writing objectives. Now they want to look at the quality of those objectives as they relate to the individual student. They also need to look at the process that involves the team in selecting particular objectives that are clearly communicated to each other.

Monitoring

Findings from the Statewide SBD Study

The Statewide SBD Study researchers asked districts, "Are student objectives monitored on a continuous basis?" A review of the literature indicates that when students are on their own, they spend less time in academic learning compared to those students that teachers monitor. Without monitoring, there is a potential for much more wasted time. Coupled with monitoring, we also found pacing was quickened if the teacher monitored successfully. The quicker the pace, the more content was covered and the more learning occurred.

Teachers informally indicated to us that if they could keep the student in active learning, the disruptive behaviors diminished. Active students took on more positive feelings about their classroom and themselves. Monitoring also allowed the teacher to build in breathing time for the student. This breathing time was important but it needed to be carefully structured for students with behavioral challenges. It is important that output be measured and monitored, but output is not the only goal of teaching. It is important that students have some down time and breathing space, but without careful monitoring, that time can be excessively unproductive. Monitoring also relates closely to indications that test grades are positively related to academic achievement and behavioral management success. Grades do act as an outside catalyst for changing behaviors. They are also a simple system for the student to measure progress. When a student understands how to get a grade and what the parameters of the grade are, the classroom teacher has a grading system for changing behaviors that can be quite successful. But the teacher does need to be careful that the grading system does not discriminate against the student because of his/her handicapping condition. Monitoring needs to be looked at in a broader sense of pacing, content coverage, high expectations, grades on a regular basis, and data provided to the student, the teacher, and other support staff that indicate progress of the student toward a particular goal.

Application of the Statewide SBD Study to a Local District

In Washington, review of student objectives is accomplished to a degree through monitoring conducted by the Educational Service District. Monitors recently visited one district to see if continuous monitoring of students' objectives was occurring. Of the 24 classrooms reviewed, only one teacher was not keeping continuous data. This was a great concern to the local administrators because one teacher does affect the lives of many students. The Statewide SBD Study has pointed out the importance of monitoring objectives that teachers and related service personnel are using. Districts should be looking at ways to assure students of a better education by training personnel in monitoring objectives. Districts should go one step further and actually monitor, on a selective basis, the on-task behavior of the team.

Data-Based Decision Making

Findings from the Statewide SBD Study

"Are decisions that are made on student programs data-based?" Overwhelmingly, teachers in the study (81%) indicated they measured behavior changes by rating each student on change variables daily or weekly, based on counts of behaviors or a point system. The majority of respondents reported setting on average of between four and six academic and/or behavior change objectives per student per day. The average number of minutes spent daily in direct instruction per objective ranged from 2 minutes to over 4 hours, with 5 minutes most often reported. Overall, the state study indicated that many teachers are using instructional practices that are found in effective model programs. However, further analysis of the responses about model practices indicated no clear evidence that these practices were being systematically applied by teachers throughout the state. One could assume this is happening at the local district as well.

Application of the Statewide SBD Study to a Local District

When one local district evaluated its model for SBD students, it asked the question, "Are student programs based on decisions from data?" Montiors were hired to review the IEPs. The district's computer management system was also examined to see if it could answer that question. It was found that the extended school year decisions were made on data, but after that, it appeared curriculum decisions were uniformly based on student data. It was estimated that approximately 80% of the teachers were measuring behaviors and changing programs accordingly. About 20% of the teachers were not regularly measuring behavior and consequently were not making decisions based on data. The perception was that the 20% of the teachers were more concerned about group interaction than tracking individual student performance. There was also a feeling that they were the same teachers having difficulty managing group behaviors. Could this be because they were not focusing in on the individual child's performance? Or, do these teachers need skills in identifying appropriate objective behavior? Since building principals evaluate special education teachers, there might be a correlation between principals that measure behavior and teachers that measure behavior. The findings for the local districts indicate that the district may need to expend more resources in helping staff with data-based decision making processes.

Special Instructional Procedure and Curricula

Findings from the Statewide SBD Study

The Statewide SBD Study indicated that special education teachers preferred direct instruction in programming for behavior changes. Of the cognitive based approaches, those materials and activities which strengthened social skills and self concepts were most often used by the teachers. More important, perhaps, was the teacher's preference for strategies (i.e., social interaction, self-monitoring, modeling) that build and strengthen adaptive behaviors. When asked the question, "Are procedures and curricula specially designed for the student that relate to the handicapping condition of behavioral disability?", many of the respondents were found to be using instructional practices considered to be typical for effective model programs. However, there was no evidence that the curricula and strategies were being systematically used across the districts by teachers. The results of the site interviews indicated this lack of systematic application. From this data, one can assume that local districts probably reflect the same lack of direction in making decisions regarding specialized curricula for teaching students appropriate social skills behavior.

Application of the Statewide SBD Study to a Local District

A local district that used the statewide study to examine their situation found local teachers preferred direct instruction and behavioral curricula when programming for behavioral changes. Materials didn't necessarily make a strong program, but it was very difficult to have an effective program without appropriate support materials. In reviewing what was available in the district, it became quite evident that there was a noticeable lack of materials that had solid research track records. The district asked the same question as in the state study, "Are procedures in curricula specially designed for students that relate to the handicapping condition?" The results for the district seem to parallel that of the state. The district needed a more systematic approach for choosing curricula. Elementary counselors, psychologists, and other support personnel were using specialized materials, but each of them had a different system for choice. The teachers also were developing their own individualized programs for students. The management system for the classroom fell on the teacher's shoulders and in few cases, if any, were teachers addressing the issues of generalization. It became quite apparent that the district needed a more systematic management approach so duplication of effort would be minimized. General guidelines were developed for the program in the area of selecting specialized procedure and curricula, but no monitoring was occurring to see that those guidelines were being followed. Again, the Statewide SBD Study was very helpful in assisting this district in becoming aware of the necessity of asking questions about the selection of materials and curricula for behaviorally challenged students.

School districts have limited resources to deliver services to the handicapped child. In order to maximize these limited resources districts have grouped children into programs, so that strategies and materials applicable to the groups can be provided at minimum costs. For example, the teacher for the behaviorally disabled develops curriculum for the behaviorally challenged student. The teacher has been trained in that area and consequently buys material and equipment that would focus on this population. Districts have assumed that these trained staff members will make appropriate selections and provide strategies that will assist in overcoming or compensating for a handicapping condition. The state study found that many of the teachers were using instructional practices considered to be typical for effective model programs. However, curricula strategies were not being systematically developed across individual districts. The district, in programming for students from one level to another, needs a system that easily adapts to new students. Without a clear outline of the system, children lose learning time. The district has set a goal to clearly articulate the process of transferring from each level.

Parent/Community Involvement

Findings from the Statewide SBD Study

Project staff found that successful programs include parent participation as an important part of their comprehensive program management plan. In addition, successful programs provide a full service delivery system of family support that includes advocacy, social services, counseling, and general parent training. Successful programs include parents on the multidisciplinary teams as decision makers in program planning, curriculum, placement options, and other service options. The task force recommended that Washington develop guidelines and procedures for implementing a system of support to parents as well as guidelines to assure parents' equal participation in their child's educational planning.

In reviewing the literature, it was found that parents play an important role in the formation of emotional health even though there is a great deal of uncertainty that surrounds the relationship of the parent to mental illness of their children. It is widely accepted that parents play this important role in the formation of emotional health. We know that the cause of behavioral disorders is difficult to discover and is often unknown. Parent mishandling, inborn congenital problems, environmental conditions, and institutional barriers are just a few of the many causes for mental illness. Generally, parents of children with serious behavioral disorders have not participated in advocacy. This may be due to a variety of reasons such as the lack of communication between schools and agencies. We also know that most advocacy appears to come from mothers concerned about their children. Mothers have often been blamed for the poor emotional health of their children. Consequently, it is understandable that mothers would not be comfortable in the advocacy role if their child is experiencing emotional problems. It is seldom that you find a father volunteering at the local school building or serving on local school district committees. Parent advocacy for mental retardation, hearing impairment, and learning disabilities has been quite acceptable in the state, but it appears that advocacy for behaviorally challenged students is not yet widely accepted. More study needs to be conducted in this area to understand why advocacy is not occurring at a level that would provide for these students' appropriate programs.

Application of the Statewide SBD Study to a Local District

Districts should ask the question, "Are parents appropriately involved in assisting schools in addressing the students' handicapping condition?" We should be looking for more than just involvement in the multidisciplinary team process. We should be looking for parents serving on special education advisory committees advocating for behaviorally disabled and parent groups that meet on a regular basis to discuss child-rearing techniques that apply to children who have behavioral disabilities. For students that are identified as behaviorally disabled to attend the PACT (Parents, Adolescents, Counselors, and Teachers) program in Highline School District, their parents must participate in the program: admittance to the program requires their participation. The PACT program is a concerted effort of parents, adolescents, counselors, and teachers to change behaviors which prohibit placement in a regular education classroom. It offers a highly structured therapeutic environment in which students learn alternatives to inappropriate behaviors. They learn ways to gain positive attention and are provided with many opportunities for success, which translates into increased self esteem. Parent involvement is a crucial part. Teachers communicate daily to parents on student progress. Parents attend the support group where they share ideas and concerns with each other, learning parenting skills, and getting information on PACT curricula and activities. Families are involved in counseling to learn how to interact with their adolescent as he/she is trying to make changes. This highly structured program for parents works for the small number of secondary students that are eligible for the PACT program. However, due to limited resources, districts are unable to provide this kind of service for all behaviorally disabled students.

Systematic Transition

Findings from the Statewide SBD Study

"Are students provided a systematic transition program?" For purposes of this section, "systematic transition" refers to preparing the student for the world of work by assisting him/her in finding an appropriate job before graduation. When the 24 districts that appeared before the task force subcommittee shared their programs for behaviorally disabled, few had transition guidelines. Despite Dr. Gene Edgar's (1986) popular study, which indicates large numbers of handicapped students are not employed in Washington three years out of school, the state has done little to address the problem of transition. There have been a few small state projects and some inservice training initiated through federal funds, but no general progress has been made by school districts in the area of providing systematic transition programs.

Application of Statewide SBD Study to a Local District

Dr. Gene Edgar (University of Washington) has been participating with school districts in the state examining the employment rate of students that are graduating from special education. He found that, statewide, 58% of students with handicaps that had graduated two years ago were currently employed (Edgar, 1986). Dr. Jim Affleck and Dr. Greg Weisenstein (also from the University of Washington) have assisted school districts in developing a transition project to assist students and increase success rates (Affleck & Weisenstein, 1986). These districts have employed individual teachers to assist in transition of students. Administratively, they feel they are doing a better job in transition and are now developing guidelines. Systematic transition is an element of excellence that should be monitored carefully by districts.

Program for Inservice Training

Findings from the Statewide SBD Study

In conducting the state study, we were interested in examining the nature, content, and method of disseminating inservice training in Washington. Our findings indicated that districts, including educational service districts, seemed to vary a great deal from one another in their commitment to providing inservice to teachers and staff members in the area of behavioral disabilities. In addition, the delivery of inservice often took on the form of responding to emergencies rather than being part of a systematically developed plan. The development of inservice appeared to reflect a crisis management rather than a preventive operation. Outstanding local district programs had the opposite approach. They carefully designed programs with prevention as the primary goal. From our interviews with district administrative staff, it appears that those districts with the most comprehensive programs had inservice training to meet individual teachers' needs. Inservice programs were offered specifically to assist the teacher, psychologist, and other support staff members in designing effective programs for identified students within their buildings.

Application of the Statewide SBD Study to a Local District

One district took the question regarding inservice one step further and asked, "Is inservice designed specifically on an individual basis for each staff member?" They found that inservice training was provided in significant amounts for teachers of certain populations of students but was very limited for the behaviorally disabled. The more severely disabled the student or grouping of students, the more often the teams met to discuss, plan, and provide internal inservice. They also found that, in those programs that were dealing with the most severely behaviorally disabled students, the teams were meeting on a weekly basis and also designing much of their own inservice training.

When behaviorally disabled students are placed in regular education classrooms or resources rooms, intensive involvement in training often diminishes. Districts should examine both how much training is happening and what kind of training in terms of each handicapping condition. The strength of the inservice program depends largely on the involvement of the special education administrator and the commitment that adminsitrators have for inservice training. In practically all situations, inservice is not being provided on an individual evaluation basis but rather on a general feeling that inservice is needed and should be provided. Many of the teachers in the special education program are receiving inservice on direct instruction techniques but often this inservice does not relate directly to behavioral disabilities.

Program Evaluation

Findings from the Statewide SBD Study

When the 24 school districts were sharing their programs with the task force, most of them indicated that they did evaluate their programs at least on an annual basis. But few of the programs evaluated on the basis of student behavioral data. While informal planning and evaluation is often helpful to school districts, it has serious limitations. Evaluation efforts of this kind are usually subject to criticisms due to lack of documentation. Lack of documentation increases the chances of developing a plan that may not be the best guide for service delivery efforts. It also raises questions of propriety since program modifications cannot be traced back to a source nor the procedures for evalution inspected and critique by others.

Application of the Statewide SBD Study to a Local District

Most districts have not conducted in depth evaluations of their special education programs for behaviorally disabled students based on student growth data. Often on an annual basis, they ask special education teachers to review and submit a document on progress made on particular goals set for either students or programs, which in a sense is program evaluation. But the basis of change of programs should be on student outcomes. In response to this, districts should develop a clear evaluation component for each handicapping condition.

A Model for the Future

If the author could forecast an exemplary model for the near future, it would include each of the elements of excellence as a foundation for the program.

1. Screening would be conducted through a multiple gating or multiphase procedure. The purpose of the procedure would be to reduce referrals based on prejudice; inability to teach; unwillingness to accept differences; lack of information, materials, and curriculum; and other factors that result in inappropriate referrals. A regular education teacher assistance team would be used to assist in the screening process and to design programs for students having difficulty. Students would be referred for special education services only after the intervention of a teacher assistance team and a screening process that examines the student in terms of the classroom environment and school climate, including teacher/pupil/class interaction.

2. Assessment would be conducted by a multi-disciplinary team in the natural setting (i.e., regular education). The assessment would be formative for each team member and reflect strategies that not only identified abnormal behaviors, but also strategies used to realign behaviors. One of the team functions would be to assess the overall team approach to the student. The team would evaluate the teaching process, as well as medical, social, and counseling processes, so that assessment and eligibility for specially designed programs or special education would be based on more than teacher/pupil/class interaction.

3. Interagency cooperation would automatically occur when a student is referred. Through interagency agreements personnel would be committed to be part of a working team. These governmental agencies would be under one funding umbrella which would promote a holistic, ecological, and behavioral approach to solve the puzzle of emotional disturbance. Medical, psychological, psychiatric, health, counseling, and social work assistance as well as university inservice, parent training, and other professional assistance would be organized under this funding system to allow easy access to needed services by students and parents.

4. Parent involvement would be a requirement. If society is going to spend the tax dollars and resources necessary for changing a student's behavior, then the primary care givers should have the responsibility to be part of the team. Our government should expect parental commitment to child care and training. Parent involvement should be on a daily basis. A behavioral disability is a societal problem and is directly linked to the home. The home must be involved with the community to increase the chances of changing behaviors. To establish and maintain parental involvement, the criminal justice system should be included in community/interagency agreements.

5. Curricula and instructional practices would reflect the latest technology and research. Modeling and self-monitoring behavioral strategies would be taught to the students and parents. The primary emphasis of all team members would be on changing, modifying, and correcting destructive behavior patterns.

Presently, special education teachers tend to take on three distinct roles. They use behavioral techniques in their own special classrooms; use ecological models while working with psychologists, counselors, and other specialists; and play a consultant role while working with other teachers. Since the primary emphasis would not be on academics but on behavior changes, under this model, students would be required to achieve like other students but would receive additional assistance in the regular education classroom. The special education teacher would be a consultant and team teacher with the regular education teacher. Aide time and additional time for planning and consultation would be built into the teaching schedule. Materials and curricula would be based on the work of Dr. Hill Walker and his colleagues (Walker, Hops, & Greenwood, 1984).

6. A continuum of options would be provided. The primary delivery system would be in regular education programs. Behaviorally disabled students would be with normal peer models. Presently, research indicates that placing a student in a restrictive environment may reduce the student's ability to function effectively in regular environments. Instead of serving the majority of behaviorally disabled students in resource rooms and self-

contained classes, the behaviorally disabled students would be in regular education classrooms.

7. An extended school year would be provided for all behaviorally disabled students. Students with serious emotional disturbance should not be dropped from programs because the regular school year ends. The disability goes on, and so do the problems that the disability generates to society. Therapy, medical and psychiatric assistance, counseling, parent involvement should continue through the summer months with the intent and resolution to solve the problems.

8. An evaluation system would be stipulated by law and specifically funded so a meaningful process would be developed. So often districts and states require an evaluation process but do not fund one. Consequently, evaluation is an add-on to other responsibilities for staff and it becomes a low priority. Evaluation often ends up being highly subjective and usually in the form of a cursory end-of-the-year report. Funding should be based on the successful completion of an evaluation.

Regional, state, and local personnel should have specific, interrelated duties to evaluate programs for behaviorally disabled students. The process should identify the number of youth being served appropriately or inappropriately, the number of students involved or not involved, parental involvement, relationships of agencies, criminal statistics, therapies and current practices. Teams should be rated on the long-term success of students. Evaluation efforts should be extended into a long-term study–possibly over a 25-50 year period of time.

9. An Interagency Individual Educational Plan (IIEP) would be required to reflect involvement of related services and each agency. This IIEP would also include all requirements of present IEPs with the addition of agency participation. It would outline the involvement of medical personnel, psychiatric assistance, family interventionists, nutritional experts, educators, counselors, administrators, parents, and other necessary persons. These Interagency IEPs would reflect what each team member would provide for the student, family, and team.

10. The model would include a funding system that would place all involved agencies under one funding umbrella. Funds would be disbursed as services are provided based on individual plans for each student. Multi-agency participation and responsibility would occur through statewide agreements to Interagency IEPs. Services between agencies would occur automatically when a student entered the system. Recommended ratios for at least 210 program days are:

Pupil/Teacher and Pupil/Aide Ratio
  6:1   Regular classroom ratio (For every 6 identified SBD
        students, one teacher and one aide would be provided)
  8:1   Self Contained classroom ratio
  12:1 Resource room ratio

Medical Ratios
  50:1   Nurse
  50:1   Psychiatrist
  100:1   Nutritionist

Counseling and Family Interventionist Ratios
  50:1   Family Interventionist
  50:1   Counselor/Psychologist

 # Behaviorist/Curriculum Specialist and Evaluators
  3000:1   State Agency Researcher and Evaluator
  500:1   Regional Specialist
  500:1   University Inservice Specialist and team member with
           the state agency

Criminal Justice System
  50:1   Specialist/Coordinator

In conclusion, an exemplary model would reflect each of the elements of excellence with a funding system that ties agencies together so services would be coordinated. Curricula would be based on establishing measurable behavior changes. The regular education classroom would be the primary place for academic instruction with the regular classroom teacher as part of the team. Exclusion of students from the regular education classroom would be infrequent; instead, specialists would be employed to work with the regular education teacher and students. Students would learn appropriate behaviors through a behavioral, holistic, ecological approach involving a full component of team members. Evaluation would be based on individual student progress. Also, it would include the evaluation of team processes and regional and state effectiveness. Evaluation would be performed by an outside team on at least a yearly basis. Evaluations would be shared with boards of education, legislators, and congress.

References

Affleck, J. Q., & Weisenstein, G. R. (1986). *A realistic transition model for secondary school handicapped students*. Seattle: University of

Washington, Experimental Education Unit.

Edgar, E. B. (1986). *Washington state follow-up data of post-secondary special education students.* Seattle: University of Washington, Experimental Education Unit.

Walker, H. M., Hops, H., & Greenwood, C. R. (1984). The CORBEH research and development model: Programmatic issues and strategies. In S. Paine, G. T. Bellamy, and B. Wilcox (Eds.), *Human services that work.* Baltimore: Paul H. Brookes.

Walker, H. M., Severson, H., & Haring, N. G. (1985). *Standardized screening and identification of behavior disordered (SSBD) pupils in the elementary age range: Rationale, procedures and guidelines.* Eugene, OR: University of Oregon, Center on Human Development.

ASSESSMENT OF BEHAVIOR DISORDERS IN THE SCHOOL SETTING: ISSUES, PROBLEMS, AND STRATEGIES REVISITED

Hill M. Walker and Ted R. Fabre

Assessment of behavior disorders in the school setting has become an increasingly controversial topic within the past decade and presents a myriad of intractable and complex issues. Controversies surrounding such practices as the definition of emotional/behavioral disorders in school; the referral, screening, and identification of children who are at risk for these disorders; and the certification and placement procedures used in serving them have generated strong and sometimes acrimonious debates in the professional literature with little resolution or consensus achieved on the basic questions involved (Forness, 1985; Galagan, 1985; Kauffman, 1982; Smith, 1985; Ysseldyke, Algozzine, & Epps, 1982; Ysseldyke, Christenson, Pianta, & Algozzine, 1983; Ysseldyke, Thurlow, et al., 1983). Professionals in the field of behavior disorders are often polarized by these debates, thereby preventing adoption of standardized, effective practices which have the potential to ameliorate many of the barriers that have historically constrained effective services to this handicapped population.

The purpose of this chapter is to review current and historical practices in the assessment of mild behavior disorders within the school setting. The general content areas and specific issues selected for treatment by the authors have direct implications for the assessment of behavior disorders in the school setting; possess some degree of professional salience within the educational or psychological literature; influence, constrain, and/or mediate actual assessment practice; and are controversial in that there seems to be divergent professional opinion regarding their definition and/or resolution. Following a review of the current state of assessment and service delivery practices for the BD population in regular and special education, the chapter will address issues, problems, and strategies in two major sections. These will focus respectively on conceptual and procedural topics.

The content of these sections will not be presented in an unbiased or objective fashion. The authors will question many of the assumptions that guide current practices in relation to the measurement of behavior disorders in the school setting. In the authors' view, some of these assumptions obstruct the adoption of assessment practices which will more functionally serve the needs of behavior disordered children in the school setting. Although clear-cut solutions will not be provided to the complex problems of definition, classification, and measurement that continue to plague the behavior disorders field, the authors will advocate for specific perspectives and practices that, in their opinion, have potential to constructively influence contemporary practice in the assessment of mild behavior disorders. The Current State of Assessment and Service Delivery Practices for Behavior Disordered Pupils in School

Historically, public schools have underserved and excluded behavior disordered students from appropriate services. For example, a national survey by Grosenick and Huntze (1980a) found that 741,000 pupils or approximately three fourths of the school age SED population were not provided any special education services. The situation was equally grim for a substantially larger number of pupils with less severe behavior disorders. During the past five years, pupil behavior disorders that span the full range of severity have emerged as a critically important priority for school districts, providers of related services, policy makers, and state/federal agencies (US Department of Education, 1986). Nevertheless, current school practices fall far short of minimally acceptable standards for the great majority of behavior disordered pupils (Noel, 1982; Walker, Reavis, Rhode, & Jenson, 1985). For example, Grosenick and Huntze (1980a) estimated that three fourths of all BD pupils in school are currently served in either self-contained or more restrictive settings (i.e. separate day schools, alternative schools, residential placements). Another estimate, reported by the US Department of Education (1985, Table 6C1), is that only 42.72% of children 3-21 years old that are provided services for emotional disturbance are served in a regular classroom environment. Referral processes for BD pupils are often unstructured and highly subjective and idiosyncratic to specific teachers (Grosenick & Huntze, 1980a; 1980b; Noel, 1982). This predicament persists in spite of significant technological advances in assessment and intervention that have been achieved for behavior disordered pupils in the past decade (Cullinan, Epstein & Lloyd, 1983; Jones & Jones, 1986; Reitz, 1985; Walker, Reavis, Rhode, & Jenson, 1985). Our collective response, as educators, to the needs of this population has been characterized by comparatively low quality professional practices and an extreme reluctance to either formally identify or to assume program responsibility for school age pupils with serious behavior disorders (Lentz, 1985; Neel & Rutherford, 1981; Reitz, 1985; Walker, Severson, Haring, & Williams, 1986).

Why do school districts persistently deny appropriate services to the BD student population in the face of consistently high priority ratings and the strong perceived need for these services? There is voluminous speculation on this question in the professional literature centering on the following potential causes: (a) the pejorative and stigmatizing effects of the labels used to designate SED or SBD pupils as handicapped in order for them to qualify for specialized services (Huntze, 1985; Jenson, 1984; and Kauffman, 1982), (b) the absence of parent/professional advocacy groups for this population (similar to those that exist for learning disabled, mentally retarded, or autistic children) because of the implication that parents of BD pupils are responsible for their children's school related behavior problems (Wood, 1985), (c) the relative unavailability of adequately trained personnel (resource teachers, school psychologists, counselors) to serve the BD pupil population in school settings (Grosenick & Huntze, 1980b), (d) the absence of an agreed upon conceptualization, program orientation and theoretical perspective relating to behavior disorders that can serve as a basis for effective program development (Noel, 1982), (e) concerns over the possible escalating costs of serving this population along with the related concern of over identification, and (f) educators' inability to agree upon objective criteria relating to what constitutes disordered pupil behavior in the school setting. The constraints that this last issue places upon screening and identification practices and the inability of the behavior disorders field to rationally define its subject matter content are, in the authors' view, among the most significant factors in explaining the public schools' inadequate response to this handicapping condition.

There seems to be general agreement within the educational community that using current ED/BD definitions, along with eligibility criteria and screening/assessment procedures based upon them, we are not capable of reliably separating behavior disordered from non-behavior disordered pupils or deciding which identified pupils are most in need of existing services (Gerber & Semmel, 1984; Gresham, in press). In commenting on federal and state definitions/eligibility criteria, Kauffman (1980, 1982) notes that, using existing approaches and criteria, the construct of emotional disturbance: (a) has no objective reality, (b) does not unambiguously distinguish between populations of normal and behavior disordered pupils, and (c) becomes whatever professionals choose to make it.

This approach has allowed regular classroom teachers to assume the role of gatekeeper for determining access of BD pupils to existing services via the referral and certification process (Gerber & Semmel, 1984). Thus, regular teachers are usually in a position to solely determine which pupils and how many pupils from their classes are able to access services through referral for evaluation, certification, service, and/or placement. Following a teacher referral, multi-disciplinary child study teams characteristically engage in a process which confirms the child's eligibility as handicapped. An impressive body of research suggests: (a) that once referred, teacher nominated pupils are extremely likely to be certified as handicapped, (b) there is a high degree of overlap in the behavioral characteristics and performance deficits of referred and non-referred pupils, and (c) the actual data collected regarding the referred pupil's deficits and/or behavioral excesses have little impact on the certification decision (Ysseldyke, Algozzine, & Epps, 1982; Ysseldyke, Algozzine, Shinn, & McGue, 1982; Ysseldyke, Christenson, Pianta, & Algozzine, 1983). In fact, children are often certified, even if performance data are contraindicative and disconfirming, suggesting that referral and certification decisions are in part political ones (Gerber & Semmel, 1984). Analysis of existing practices indicate that pupils with externalizing behavior disorders or problems are far more likely to be referred than those with other, less aversive behavior problems (i.e. social withdrawal, depression, phobias, and so forth). It is clear that service delivery practices relating to the assessment of behavior disordered pupils, as well as other types of handicapped pupils in school settings, are often arbitrary, subjective, and not grounded in empirically based procedures and instrumentation.

Ironically, technologies exist to screen, identify, measure, and remediate the broad range of behavior disorders encountered in the school setting. However, because of competing models of human behavior, psychological assessment, and therapy, and a reliance upon medically based, clinically oriented definition and classification systems that often have only limited applicability to the school setting, the field of behavior disorders has exhibited both paralysis and ambivalence regarding its legitimate domains of activity. Children in general, and especially behavior disordered children, have not been well served by this dilemma. The tragic result of this professional immobility is that many children with legitimate behavior disorders are frequently denied access to services that could significantly affect their educational adjustment and social development because they do not fit vaguely defined eligibility criteria and categories of emotional/behavioral disability (Forness, 1985; Galagan, 1985; Smith, 1985).

What is an "emotionally disturbed" or "behavior disordered" child? Unfortunately, professionals have been unable to agree on a precise use of these terms (Balow, 1979; Huntze, 1985; and Jenson, 1984). Thus, in part, the answer depends upon who is asked, and his/her particular philosophical orientation regarding human behavior and psychopathology. The results of a recently commissioned study by the US Special Education Programs Office concluded that while there was probably justification for changing the ED label for pupils with behavior disorders, it was judged too inconvenient to do so. For reasons relating to matters of substance and philosophy, as well as clarity, the term "behavior disorders" will be used whenever possible in the remainder of this paper to refer to the full range of disorders, problems, and disturbances of child behavior commonly encountered in the school setting.

The educational system continues to have problems in deciding its proper role in relation to child behavior disorders. This problem has been compounded by definitional vagueness, conflicting support service demands from school professionals, and territorial imperatives concerning professional legitimacy and competence relating to serving the full range of needs of this population. There is, however, an increasing trend for school systems to provide for the full range of needs and service demands of this population of children (Noel, 1982). This is probably a function of at least three developments: (a) the passage of PL 94-142, (b) an improving technology for the delivery of high quality intervention services in the school setting, and (c) the publication of efficacy studies of non-school-based mental health services for children which tend to show weak effects on child behavior in the school setting (Achenbach, 1974; Levitt, 1971; Noel, 1982; Shepard, Oppenheim, & Mitchell, 1971).

Schools have also experienced great difficulty in distinguishing discipline problems from behavior disorders and subsequently, in deciding how to deal with them in a programmatic sense. At present, we do not have classification taxonomies or measurement strategies that will allow us to make these discriminations with precision and reliability. If a child is perceived as having a behavior disorder or as being emotionally disturbed, a therapeutic regimen of some type is the most likely response to the problem; however, if it is perceived as being a discipline problem or representing social maladjustment, the pupil is usually exposed to a control, containment, or punishment strategy (Neel & Rutherford, 1981). It is apparent that definitional criteria and assessment procedures play an important role in determining a school system's response to dysfunctional child behavior, with equally powerful implications for the children involved.

Another factor that contributes to our imprecision in assessing and remediating behavior disorders in the school setting is the failure to discriminate between dysfunctional child behavior in school and non-school settings and to program for it accordingly. Traditionally, schools have adopted a medically based, clinical perspective in the definition, assessment, diagnosis, and treatment of behavior disorders in children. Dysfunctional or pathological behavior is seen as specific to, and originating within, the child. Thus, behavioral and emotional difficulties are viewed as "steady state" traits or stable phenomena that are relatively invariant across settings (Ullmann & Krasner, 1965). However, it should be noted that the most recent edition of the American Psychiatric Association's Diagnostic and Statistical Manual (1980) does acknowledge that symptoms of such phenomena in childhood disorders are differentially displayed across settings.

Advocates of this trait approach suggest that a diagnosis of behavioral/emotional difficulty in one specific setting (e.g., school) has no validity unless manifestations of it are also observed in a variety of other settings (e.g., home, community, clinician's office). Rarely are disorders considered setting-specific when viewed from either a "states and traits" model of personality (Allport, 1966, 1974), or from a medical "disease" model of psychopathology (Ullmann & Krasner, 1965, 1969). An increasing amount of evidence, however, supports the position that human behavior (in both pathological and nonpathological forms) is, to a significant degree, situation-specific (Johnson, Boldstad, & Lobitz, 1976; Mischel, 1968, 1969; Wahler, 1969; Walker, Hops, & Johnson, 1975). However, Patterson and his associates (Patterson, 1982) have noted that although approximately only 50% of pupils who are outside the normal range of adaptive behavior in school are also deviant in the home setting, those who display such deviance across both settings are more likely to have severe disorders. There are at least four broad interactions between type of setting and the presence or absence of disordered child behavior: (a) the child is disordered at school only, (b) the child is disordered in nonschool settings only, (c) the child is disordered in both school and nonschool settings, or (d) the child is not disordered in either the school or nonschool setting.

Schools and the behavior disordered children they serve could potentially benefit from the development of definitional, classification, and assessment models whose content is focused on child behavior in the school setting, as opposed to a continued reliance on generic, setting-nonspecific systems whose content is frequently determined by a mixture of parent, teacher, and clinician's ratings. Such a system could facilitate decision-making relating to identification, service delivery, and remediation within the school setting, as well as the referral of children to clinical facilities and resources external to the school setting when such referrals are indicated.

In the authors' opinion, the factors discussed above account for many of our problems in serving behavior disordered children in school. Further, these factors are largely contextual in nature. That is, they are a function of attitudes, assumptions, expectations, and beliefs relating to human behavior and its causes that we have learned to view as valid, true, and appropriate. In the authors' view, these contextual variables are at the core of our problems in serving behavior disordered children because they so directly influence the assessment, classification, and service delivery decisions we make as professionals. Unfortunately, variables of this type often control the assessment process in ways that do not serve the best interests of behavior disordered children.

Conceptual Issues

Divergent conceptualizations of human behavior, the etiology of emotional/behavioral disorders, and behavior classification systems have exercised a powerful influence upon the assessment of behavior disorders in the school setting. The types of assessment procedures chosen (e.g., projective tests, teacher or parent ratings, sociometrics, behavioral role play tests, clinical interviews, or direct observations in the natural setting and the interpretation of results) are all directly influenced by these conceptualizations. At present, there appears to be little hope of achieving a conceptual consensus among professionals regarding these issues. As a result, the prospect of achieving uniformity in the decision-making process is bleak. The only consensus seems to be that everyone is dissatisfied with traditional efforts at defining, classifying, and identifying emotional/behavioral disorders in children (Wood & Lakin, 1979).

Major conceptual issues that impinge upon the assessment of school behavior disorders include: (a) the influence of models of personality upon conceptualizations of child behavior; (b) the use of vague constructs such as emotional disturbance to refer to disordered child behavior; (c) the influence of classification systems upon conceptualizations of disordered behavior in the school setting; (d) the reliance upon conceptualizations of disordered child behavior in school which are not specific to that setting; (e) the influence of setting and behavioral expectations upon child behavior; (f) the role of social agents' tolerance levels in defining disordered child behavior; and (g) the criteria used for determining disordered behavior in the school setting. These issues and their implications for the assessment process are elaborated in the present section.

The Influence of Models of Personality Upon Conceptualizations of Child Behavior

There are numerous theories of personality which purport to account for both normal and abnormal behavior. Conceptualizations of psychopathology and psychotherapy have traditionally developed from theories of personality (Hyman et al., 1979). Ultimately these theories have a powerful influence upon one's view of child behavior disorders; for example, how they are defined, acquired, measured, and remediated. Further, they describe personality development processes in broad, generic terms, with the home setting viewed as having the greatest influence in the social and personal development of the child.

Many explanations have been promulgated to account for the instructional process, and impressive efforts have been mounted to develop a unified theory of instruction (Bruner, 1968). In the area of child behavior and social development in the school setting, however, we have relied upon psychology and psychiatry to provide explanations via personality theory. Hyman et al. (1979) describe five models of personality which have most influenced educators' conceptualizations of disordered behavior. These are: (a) psychodynamic-interpersonal, (b) behavioral, (c) sociological, (d) eclectic-ecological, and (e) humanistic. These theories provide "windows on the world" for school professionals serving children with behavior disorders. The same behavioral phenomena can be described, analyzed, and interpreted using each of these different models, and it is likely that radically different explanations of the problem will result from each.

In some respects these theories have done more harm than good in terms of our efforts to develop effective interventions and services for behavior disordered children in the school setting. Some of their more deleterious functional effects have been to: (a) focus our attention on alleged causal variables that are either specific to the child or external to the school setting; (b) cause us to seek explanations of disordered child behavior within the realm of intrapsychic, nonobservable phenomena, rather than to analyze child performance within the context in which it is judged to be problematic; (c) cause us to give up on problem amelioration as a function of the discovery of causal variables that are viewed as too deeply imbedded in the personality to be responsive to change procedures; (d) influence us, as educators, to apply indirect methods of treatment (e.g., verbal psychotherapies) to produce changes in overt behavior patterns (aggression, social withdrawal, conduct problems); (e) provide support and encouragement for the continued use of projective assessment methods with behavior disordered children as a vehicle for explaining why the behavior problem exists and for deciding upon appropriate therapies (the validity of these methods for both purposes is extremely limited); and (f) influence us to view problematic child behavior in terms of trait labels (e.g., devious, manipulative, aggressive, obsessive) which suggest stable manifestations of the trait label or attribute across settings and time.

School systems are in need of a model of child behavior and school psychopathology which is both experientially and empirically based. It should focus on overt, observable child behavior in the school setting, that is, on what children say and do, not what they think and feel. The content of this model should include variables such as: (a) the interactions that occur between children and school social agents (peers and teachers); (b) the characteristics of the school setting and opportunities it provides for social and educational development; (c) the performance demands and behavioral expectations of school personnel; (d) the tolerance levels of classroom teachers in defining and labeling deviance; (e) the role of the home and school settings in either producing and/or maintaining disordered child behavior; (f) constraints of the school system in serving behavior disordered children; (g) effective therapies and interventions for different types of behavior disorders common to the school setting, and (h) taxonomies and classification systems that describe school-related behavior disorders. With such a model, we would be in a far better position to deliver cohesive, relevant, and cost-effective services to behavior disordered children which would have some likelihood of directly affecting their social and educational development in the school setting.

Emotional Disturbance Versus Behavior Disorders

The educational system's adoption of the term "emotional disturbance" to describe children who experience disorders of behavioral functioning is unfortunate. Use of this term focuses the attention of educators upon emotional antecedents to disordered behavior and leads to a search for child-specific etiological factors to account for behavioral problems. In those cases in which potential causal agents are identified via assessment or clinical judgment, their programmatic implications for educators are often extremely limited and sometimes function to absolve responsibility for any remediation.

Both Huntze (1985) and Jenson (1984) have recently called for replacing the label of emotional disturbance with the term behavior disorders. They have made a persuasive case for advantages that would accrue from such a change. The present authors strongly endorse this proposal and believe that it would be an important first step in improving professional practices in this area.

A number of investigators have urged that conceptualization of disordered child behavior be based upon direct assessments of overt behavior rather than upon systems that rely on clinical inference (Clarizio & McCoy, 1976; Freemont & Wallbrown, 1979; Quay, 1972; Ross, 1971; Walker, 1979). Schools would substantially benefit from restricting their assessment efforts to overt, observable dimensions of child behavior within those settings where it is perceived to be disordered. A measurement strategy of this type focuses our attention upon alterable variables (i.e., the child's competency or skill level, situational demands and expectations, and environmental contingencies as possible causal agents).

Unless criteria can be developed which will reliably distinguish emotionally disturbed from behavior disordered children, which is clearly not the case at present, the authors recommend that we discontinue use of the term emotional disturbance. Further, the term behavior disorders should be reserved for describing disordered child behavior that can be observed and assessed reliably in those settings where it is judged to be a problematic or maladaptive.

The Influence of Classification Systems Upon Conceptualizations of Child Behavior in School Settings

Classification systems for describing psychopathology and disordered functioning abound in the clinical literature. In 1966, the Committee on Child Psychiatry of the Group for the Advancement of Psychiatry noted that at least 24 different systems had been proposed for classifying the behavior disorders of childhood (Freemont & Wallbrown, 1979). The most current edition of the American Psychiatric Association's *Diagnostic and Statistical Manual of Mental Disorders* (DSM) (1980) devotes an entire section to the disorders of infancy, childhood, and adolescence. Clearly our problem is not unavailability of systems for classifying child behavior disorders. Rather, our classification difficulties using these systems have centered on (a) lack of relevance to the school situation; (b) diagnostic imprecision based on the behavioral criteria contained in these systems; (c) the relative inability of these systems to identify homogeneous groupings of children with specific behavior disorders who may or may not share common etiologies; (d) the lack of utility of these systems as a basis for comparing different interventions for the same behavior disorder, and (e) the inability of these systems to prescribe measurement strategies, other than clinical judgment, for assessing child status on specific disorders.

Traditional classification systems have generally failed in each of the aforementioned areas. Other criticisms include a lack of specificity, a failure to include developmental perspectives, a failure to distinguish child from adult disorders, a failure to specify sex- and age-related behavior disorders, and a lack of consistency in classification criteria (Achenbach, 1978, 1979; Achenbach & Edelbrock, 1978; Freemont & Wallbrown, 1979; Reichler & Schopler, 1976).

Reichler and Schopler (1976) suggest that classification should provide a basis for prevention, prescription, and prognosis (i.e., the functions of diagnosis). No classification or diagnostic system currently available provides for these functions in relation to childhood behavior disorders in the school setting. This goal is not likely to be attained until systems are developed that are based upon the ratings or judgments of key social agents in the school setting (e.g., teachers, psychologists, peers, professionally trained observers) in relation to behavioral descriptions of what children say and do in that setting.

The primary content sources for the development of traditional classification systems are: (a) the clinical judgment(s) of mental health professionals, (b) the cataloguing of presenting symptoms of children seen in child guidance clinics and other mental health settings, and (c) parent and teacher ratings. Parent and teacher ratings have been sampled to a substantially lesser degree in traditional systems than have clinical judgment and cataloguing of symptoms.

The DSM classification system is perhaps most representative of the types of childhood disorders identified when clinical judgment is the primary content source. The system contains five major groupings distinguished from each other by predominant area of disturbance (see Table 1). With the exception of the categories under "Behavior (Overt)," the disorders represented by these major groupings have only limited reference to the kinds of behavior disorders and adjustment problems children exhibit at school and which disrupt educational or social development; yet this system is used extensively by school professionals in diagnosing and classifying child behavior disorders in the school setting. The authors are not denying the generalized validity of these disorders--just their relevance for the task of identifying and prescribing for behavior disorders at school.

Numerous studies in the published literature, over the past two decades, have reported attempts to develop empirically based classification systems for child behavior disorders (Becker & Krug, 1964; Kulik, Stein, & Sarbin, 1968; Patterson, 1964; Phillips, 1968; Quay, 1964, 1972; Ross, Lacey, & Parton, 1965; Walker, 1970). As a rule, these studies have factor-analyzed ratings of child behavior by teachers, parents, and clinicians in an attempt to isolate homogeneous behavioral groupings for diagnostic and treatment prescription purposes. The number of factors identified in these studies has varied from two to as many as thirteen (Peterson, 1965; Spivack & Swift, 1966) and have been classified into broad and narrow band syndromes. Replication of broad band syndromes are achieved more easily than are narrow band ones (Carlson & Lahey, 1983). Nevertheless, empirically derived systems of this type generally have much greater relevance for school behavior disorders than do traditional models based largely upon clinical judgment.

Few studies have been reported in which standardized intervention procedures have been developed explicitly for use with homogenous groupings of children representative of factor-analytically derived, broad band syndromes or behavior disorders. The work of the senior author and his colleagues at the Center at Oregon for Research in the Behavioral

Table 1

(1980) DSM Childhood Disorders

1. Intellectual
    -Mental Retardation
2. Behavior (Overt)
    -Attention Deficit Disorder
    -Conduct Disorder
3. Emotional
    -Anxiety Disorders of Childhood or Adolescence
    -Other Disorders of Infancy, Childhood, or
    Adolescence
4. Physical
    -Eating Disorders
    -Stereotyped Movement Disorders
    -Other Disorders with Physical Manifestations
5. Developmental
    -Pervasive Developmental Disorders
    -Specific Developmental Disorders

Note: From *Diagnostic and Statistical Manual of Mental Disorders* (3rd ed.) by the American Psychiatric Association, 1980. Copyright 1980 by American Psychiatric Association. Reprinted by permission.

Education of the Handicapped (CORBEH) (1971-79) is a case in point (Walker, 1977; Walker & Hops, 1979; Walker, Hops, & Greenwood, 1976, 1984). Over an eight-year period, they developed, tested, and validated four comprehensive behavior management packages for use with commonly encountered school behavior disorders. Each package contains specific identification criteria and measurement instruments/procedures for use in screening, assessment, and program evaluation. These packages are designed respectively for use with acting out, low academic survival skills, socially withdrawn, and socially agressive pupils in grade K-4. More work of this type needs to be conducted so that an array of standardized intervention procedures/programs will be available to school professionals in providing for the full range of behavior disorders in school age children.

In the last few years, some positive and potentially very useful work has occurred in the development of empirically based classification systems that are applicable to school-related behavior disorders (Achenbach, 1978, 1979; Achenbach & Edelbrock, 1978; Freemont & Wallbrown, 1979; Ross, 1980; Schaefer, 1982). In some instances, this work has been directed toward specific school behavior problems (Freemont & Wallbrown, 1979). Other investigators have distinguished behavioral content, rating instruments, and empirically derived clusters for school versus home settings (Edelbrock, 1979). Further, Achenbach and Edelbrock (1979) and Edelbrock (1979) have identified behavioral clusters and classification systems that are specific to sex and age levels. This work recognizes that the content of specific behavior disorders is often quite different for males and females and that the behavior problems children experience show some change across age levels.

Freemont and Wallbrown (1979) reviewed different systems for categorizing learning and behavioral content that can be directly observed in the classroom or that are based upon psychological constructs which can be inferred from same by mental health specialists. These authors suggest a school-specific classification system for use in diagnosis, assessment, and treatment prescription that consists of seven behavior patterns. Quay's (1972) system of four behavioral clusters is subsumed by Freemont and Wallbrown because they view them as representative of stable behavior patterns that are observable and that can be rated reliably in the classroom. The seven patterns are: (a) personality problems, (b) conduct problems, (c) immature, inadequate behavior, (d) socialized delinquency, (e) severe emotional disturbances, (f) social misperception, and (g) learning disabilities. The latter three categories were included to provide coverage of major areas of problematic functioning not addressed by the Quay system. One very positive feature of this work is the attempt to produce a classification system based upon observable, overt classroom behavior that is specific to the school setting.

Several investigators have argued for the validity of bipolar classifications of disordered child behavior (Achenbach & Edelbrock, 1978; Edelbrock, 1979; Ross, 1980; Schaefer, 1982). Ross (1980), after reviewing available evidence on classification of child psychopathology, suggests that a strong case can be made for reducing existing behavioral clusters, factors, or patterns to a broad band, bipolar dimension that characterizes the direction of disordered behavior, that is, either toward or away from the social environment. This dimension has been variously conceptualized as: (a) excessive approach behavior (aggression) versus excessive avoidance behavior (withdrawal), (b) conduct problems versus personality problems, and (c) internalizing (problems with self) versus externalizing (problems with the environment). Achenbach and Edelbrock (1978) and Edelbrock (1979) note that in spite of the diversity of rating instruments, raters, settings, and studies reported in the literature, there is strong evidence for the existence of such a bipolar conceptualization of child behavior disorders. This bipolar conceptualization has a great deal of relevance for the treatment of school-based child behavior disorders.

Ross (1980) suggests that behavior which our society defines as disordered or problematic falls into two major classes, depending on whether the behavior deviates from the norm by occurring too rarely or too frequently. For example, behavior disordered children are usually either deficient in appropriate adaptive skills and competencies that contribute to satisfactory educational and social development and/or they engage excessively in maladaptive, inappropriate behavior that competes with such development and is outside the referring agent's range of tolerance. On the one hand, we are dealing with insufficient levels of behavior which call for an acceleration intervention to build in the desired skills, competencies, or behavioral responses. In contrast, excessive levels of maladaptive behavior usually require a deceleration procedure designed to reduce or eliminate specific pinpoints. The CORBEH behavior management packages referred to previously are divided equally into this dichotomy. For example, the Program for Academic Survival Skills (PASS) and Procedures for Establishing Effective Relationship Skills (PEERS) programs are concerned, respectively, with building academic survival skills and adaptive social skills. In contrast, the Contingencies for Learning Academic and Social Skills (CLASS) and Reprogramming Environmental Contingencies for Effective Social Skills (RECESS) programs focus, respectively, upon the reduction of acting out and aggressive behavior.

Assessment methodologies geared toward children with mild behavior disorders would benefit from adoption of this simple bipolar classification system. Such methodologies would be tied directly to treatment prescription processes and the selection of appropriate services for remediation of specific disorders and behavior patterns. It would also be possible to establish normative levels of performance on behavioral profiles representative of this dichotomy for use in both screening and treatment evaluation tasks (Walker & Hops, 1976; Walker, Severson, & Haring, 1985; Walker, Severson, Haring, & Williams, 1986). Finally, summative measures of performance such as sociometric status and achievement level could be used as validation criteria for selecting intervention target skills and competencies that would have a maximum impact upon child development and school adjustment (Foster & Ritchey, 1979).

School Versus Nonschool Conceptualizations of Child Behavior

As noted earlier, school systems have traditionally relied upon conceptualizations of disordered child behavior supplied by the medical and clinical professions which are generic in nature and do not take performance within specific settings into account. The relevance of substantial portions of these conceptualization systems for school-related behavior disorders is obscure; until recently, however, educators rarely questioned their utility or content.

It can be argued, for example, that stimulus conditions, performance demands, behavioral expectations, and social relationships are radically different in the school and home setting. Disordered child behavior in these settings may be quite different in both form and content. In those cases in which a child's behavior pattern is disordered in both the school and home settings, there is no guarantee that specific behavior problems will be identical in the two settings or that they are a function of the same causal factors. Separate conceptualizations by setting are needed for disordered child behavior. The specific content of each conceptualization should be determined by direct measures of child behavior within the setting, by information on the characteristics and performance demands of the setting, and by the perceptions of key social agents (teachers versus parents) within the setting regarding child behavior therein.

In the authors' view, a school-based conceptualization of behavior disorders should focus equally upon academic and social development. Child behavior problems should be identified which compete or interfere with normal development in each of these major areas and measurement strategies should be developed which can assess their occurrence in natural settings.   Such strategies would include, at a minimum, teacher rankings/ratings of child behavior and direct observations recorded in the appropriate setting(s). The Influence of Setting and Behavioral Expectations Upon Child Behavior

Observers of child behavior are continually impressed with how different child behavior can be from setting to setting in terms of content, level, topography, and form. Mischel (1968, 1969) has provided an eloquent conceptualization of the situational specificity of human behavior. This specificity doubtless reflects strong differences between settings (e.g., home versus school, classroom to classroom, playground versus classroom) on such variables as: (a) existent stimulus conditions, setting events, and behavioral contingencies; (b) the behavioral/performance expectations of social agents in the setting; and (c) the tolerance levels of these agents for problematic, maladaptive, or disordered child behavior. At present, the extent to which each of these variables contributes to the definition and labeling of child behavior is unclear. It is well established, however, that children who are labeled as mildly behavior disordered by one teacher are not similarly perceived by all teachers to whom they are exposed (e.g., Fabre & Walker, 1986). The more extreme the behavior disorder, however, the more likely consistency in labeling will be observed. In the authors' opinion, teachers' behavioral expectations play a major role in this process and subsequently affect teacher-child interactions in a direct and substantial manner.

The work of Brophy and Good (1970, 1974), for example, provides compelling evidence that classroom teachers not only hold differential performance expectations for children in their classes, but behaviorally express them in their interactions with them. In their sample, teachers demanded better performance from those children for whom they had higher expectations, and were more likely to praise good performance when it was elicited. In contrast, they were more likely to accept poor performance from students for whom they held low expectations, and were less likely to praise good performance when it occurred. The achievement of high expectation students appeared to be maximized by the teachers in the Brophy and Good samples and minimized for the low expectation students. As a rule, pupils for whom teachers hold low expectations are low achievers, disadvantaged, and handicapped. It appears that teachers hold equally well-developed standards and expectations for adaptive and maladaptive types of child social behavior with clearly differentiated treatment of children whose behavior patterns fall within and outside them. Pupils with behavior disorders would likely be especially at risk for such treatment.

The senior author is currently engaged in research on the mainstreaming process (Hersh & Walker, 1983; Walker, 1984; Walker, 1986; Walker & Rankin, 1983; Walker, Reavis, Rhode, & Jenson, 1985) that systematically takes the receiving teacher's social behavior standards and expectations into account in the placement and integration process. He has developed, validated, and standardized an assessment system for use in measuring this variable (Walker, 1986; Walker & Rankin, in press). This assessment system contains one instrument that requires the teacher to make rating judgments in relation to 56 descriptions of adaptive skills and competencies that contribute to success in the regular classroom setting and 51 descriptions of maladaptive behavioral pinpoints that disrupt or interfere with satisfactory classroom adjustment. A second instrument contains descriptions of correlates of child handicapping conditions that may cause resistance to the placement/integration process. These instruments have generalized applicability to the task of assessing teacher expectancy effects in relation to mild behavior disorders in the school setting. They make it possible to assess the specific behavioral demands (i.e., required competencies and unacceptable social behaviors) that exist in less restrictive settings and provide an assessment of their social or behavioral ecology. This research has documented substantial agreement among samples of regular teachers in the ideal behavioral profiles required for success in mainstream settings. However, analysis of individual teacher responses to these instruments indicates extreme variability within samples of teachers regarding the intensity or relative narrowness of their behavioral demands and expectations. This variability has powerful implications for the screening, placement, and treatment of behavior disorders in the school setting. It suggests that, whenever possible, the level and nature of teachers' expectations should be assessed in the process of evaluating child behavior in any given setting for the purpose of determining whether it is disordered.

The Role of Social Agents' Tolerance Levels in Defining Disordered Child Behavior

Although behavioral expectations and standards obviously play an important role in the assessment of problematic child behavior on a case-by-case basis, the tolerance levels of classroom teachers may play an even more direct role in this process. Ross (1980) and Ullman and Krasner (1969) have emphasized the important role that the tolerance levels of social agents play in defining child behavior as abnormal or disordered. In fact, Ullman and Krasner (1969) note:

> Behavior which is called abnormal must be studied as the interaction of three variables: the behavior itself, its social context, and an observer who is in a position of power. No specific behavior is abnormal in itself. Rather, an individual may do something (e.g., verbalize hallucinations, hit a person, collect rolls of toilet paper, refuse to eat, stutter, stare into space, or dress sloppily) under a set of circumstances (e.g., during a school class, while working at his desk, during a church service) which upsets, annoys, angers, or strongly disturbs somebody (e.g., employer, teacher, parent, or the individual himself) sufficiently that some action results (e.g., a policeman is called, seeing a psychiatrist is recommended, commitment proceedings are started) so that the society's professional labelers (e.g., physicians, psychiatrists, psychologists, judges, social workers) come into contact with the individual and determine which of the current sets of labels (e.g., schizophrenic reaction, sociopathic personality, anxiety reaction) is most appropriate (p. 21). Notwithstanding the examples, settings, and agents in the above example, these authors could have been discussing behavior problems and disorders of children in the school setting.

Behavior disorders obviously cannot be judged in isolation. Judgments of problematic child behavior by important social agents (e.g., teachers, parents, peers) and the context within which child behavior occurs must both be taken into account systematically in the referral and evaluation process. Ross (1980) notes that, in certain instances, the tolerance levels of social agents in the natural settings (e.g., parents, teachers) may have to change, otherwise a child is asked to adjust to an intolerable situation. In those cases, where this is not possible, it may be necessary to consider alternative placement settings. Research on the mainstreaming and social integration of handicapped pupils indicates that handicapped children are often placed in normalized regular classroom environs where it is impossible for them to meet teacher and peer controlled behavioral demands (Gottlieb, 1979; Gresham, 1982).

Gersten, Walker, and Darch (in press) recently conducted a study in which they examined the relationship between teachers' (a) standards/expectations regarding adaptive and maladaptive pupil behavior, (b) tolerance for handicapped pupils' behavioral characteristics and attributes, and (c) a measure of their teaching effectiveness. Results of this study showed a powerful relationship between teachers' resistance to placement of handicapped pupils (i.e., their tolerance levels) and their teaching effectiveness. Ironically, the more effective teachers were less likely to accept handicapped pupils into their classes.

Similarly, Gerber and Semmel (1984), in a review and analysis of LEA referral/certification practices for mildly handicapped pupils, argue that teachers continually evaluate individual pupils against a teachability standard (Kornblau & Keogh, 1980; Kornblau, 1982) that defines a pupil's perceived ability to profit from placement in a regular classroom setting. They cite evidence to indicate that there is a broad consensus among teachers and school staffs regarding the appropriate academic-behavioral dimensions and the unacceptable social behavior(s) that comprise this teachability standard. Gerber and Semmel assert that teachers refer pupils to special services who (a) deviate too far from this teachability standard, (b) are difficult to teach and manage, and (c) consume too large a share of the teacher's time, energy, and expertise. This referral process has the effect of transferring responsibility for the child's instruction/management to someone else, reducing the complexity of the classroom ecology and generating a larger share of teacher-controlled resources for distribution among a smaller pool of more teachable pupils. This practice can contribute to a narrowing of the teacher's tolerance level(s) to a point where normal behavioral diversity is regarded as inappropriate or outside normal limits.

It is likely that classroom teachers' tolerance levels show the same degree of variability as do their standards/expectations for pupil academic performance and social behavior. Teachers likely also show differences among themselves in terms of their tolerance for specific types or patterns of child behavior and the age at which certain child behaviors are exhibited. However, research conducted to date indicates considerable agreement across teachers regarding the ideal behavioral profile(s) preferred by them in mainstream settings (Gresham & Reschly, in press; Hersh & Walker, 1983). As noted, studies of the referral process show that teachers are much more likely to refer hyperactive, aggressive, oppositional, and disruptive children than they are withdrawn, phobic, or depressed children. Doubtless, one reason for this is that teachers are generally much less tolerant of disruptive, acting out forms of child behavior—perhaps because disorders of this type place severe pressures upon the management and instructional skills of most teachers. What does this mean in a practical sense? It means that many children with nondisruptive behavior disorders, who are in need of existing services, are much less likely to be referred and placed in contact with needed services. It probably also means that many children with minimal repertoires of acting out or disruptive behavior are referred and labeled who should not be. Therefore, we should not rely exclusively upon idiosyncratic teacher tolerance levels and spontaneously initiated teacher referrals to define children who are in need of behavioral services. Mass screening procedures, which are highly cost effective, have been developed that require each child in a classroom to be evaluated by teachers regularly in relation to their risk status for a range of specific learning or behavioral problems that interfere with long term development and/or achievement (Greenwood, Walker, Todd, & Hops, 1979a; Kirschenbaum, Marsh, & Devage, 1977). Additional work needs to be done in this area to develop cost-effective, mass screening methods that take advantage of the power and sensitivity of teacher judgment while structuring these judgments in a manner which insures that the entire range of learning and behavior disorders for all children are systematically evaluated and considered for possible referral.

Criteria for Determining Disordered Behavior in the School Setting

Unfortunately, we have characteristically approached the problem of identifying disordered child behavior in the school setting as though it were a disease process capable of being isolated and reliably diagnosed. In fact, many of our assessment strategies attempt to apply this exact model to the analysis of problematic child behavior. Our traditional efforts in this area represent much of what is wrong with current assessment and remediation services.

For example, we act as though we have access to definitional criteria, classification systems, and measurement procedures that allow us to: (a) separate disturbed children from populations of nondisturbed children, (b) distinguish such children reliably from other categories of disability (e.g., learning disabled, mentally retarded), and (c) reliably diagnose different child behavior disorders. It appears that nothing could be further from the truth. For instance, using current definitions, criteria, and methods, prevalence estimates of emotional disturbance in school age populations range anywhere from 0.05% to 40% (Balow, 1979). A recent review of seven national prevalence studies in the ED/BD area conducted by separate organizations produced estimates that ranged from 2 to 30% of the school age population. Further, in a longitudinal study of 1,586 elementary school pupils in over 200 school districts in Minnesota, Rubin and Balow (1978) found that, in annual ratings of the sample children in grades K-6, 23-31% were judged by their teachers to be behavior problems in any one year. For children receiving three or more annual ratings, the figure was 59%. Among those receiving six annual ratings, 68% of the boys and 51% of the girls were considered a behavior problem by at least one teacher. Similar findings have been reported by Wherry and Quay (1971), who found that 49.7% of the boys in presumably normal K-2 classes were rated as having behavior problems. Surveys of this type frequently: (a) use checklists of problematic child behavior, (b) have teachers rate all children in their classes on them, and (c) compute the percentage of children who receive positive ratings on at least one item.

What are we to make of these prevalence estimates? Are we really to believe that half of our elementary-school-age population is behavior disordered in some sense? Perhaps there are occasional locales or settings where such is the case. However, this would be analogous to arguing that half of the adult population is neurotic and in need of intensive mental health services. Few professionals would dispute the absurdity of this assertion. Rather, it appears normal for children to receive some positive ratings, particularly on some of the more innocuous items included in these checklists (e.g., restless, distracted, daydreaming). Most children engage in these behaviors at one time or another.

To make a more refined judgment about the impact of these behaviors upon child adjustment or achievement, we need to know their frequency, rate, or the proportion of time each child engages in them. For example, if a child daydreams 80-90% of the time, obvious implications can be derived for his or her development or achievement. In contrast, if a child does so 1-2% of the time, there probably are no such implications. In making judgments of this nature, we need to know the kinds of behavioral items checked, as well as the number of items checked. A child who is characterized by 25 out of 50 problematic items on a checklist is likely to be very different from one for whom two, three, or four items apply. Similarly, two children can receive the same number of items checked but also be very different (e.g., descriptors of severe versus relatively innocuous behavioral problems with equally different implications for development).

In the authors' opinion, we need to stop trying to isolate child behavior disorders as unique forms of psychopathology which must be diagnosed in the traditional sense. Even across clinically trained professionals, existing classification systems do not generate acceptable levels of diagnostic reliability (Achenbach & Edelbrock, 1978). It is unlikely that we will ever be able to completely separate child behavior disorders in the school setting from other categories of disability.

We would be better off to develop school-based conceptualization systems and measurement procedures of those factors that interfere with, disrupt, or are incompatible with educational achievement and social development. We have available to us excellent criterion measures for both academic and social functioning (e.g., achievement tests for academic performance and sociometric measures for social competence). The predictive validity of both standardized achievement tests and sociometric measures have proven to be quite strong (Gottman, 1977; Van Hasselt, Hersen, Whitehill, & Bellack, 1979; Ysseldyke & Algozzine, 1982). We know which classes of academically related child behavior (e.g., attending, compliance, volunteering) facilitate academic achievement (Cobb, 1972). We have an excellent knowledge-base relating to disruptive or maladaptive behaviors that actively compete with academic performance. Similarly, Gottman and his colleagues (Gottman, Gonso, & Rasmussen, 1975) have empirically identified social skills that discriminate between popular and unpopular children. They found differences on referential communication skills, knowledge of how to make friends, and frequency of distributing and receiving positive peer social behavior. These measures and empirically based knowledge give us the means to develop cost-effective screening and identification methods and also make it possible to identify dimensions of child academic and social functioning which directly affect child achievement and social competence. We have the technology to increase children's achievement and social competence levels through direct instruction and intervention in the school setting. As long as we cling to our archaic and often irrelevant systems for defining, classifying, and identifying behavior disorders in the school setting, however, many children who desperately need these services will not get them.

We should establish a policy to systematically and regularly screen all children in two broad areas (i.e., academic and social functioning) and make services available to those children who need them, regardless of status or category of disability. Children will, and should, be identified in this process, whose general pattern of classroom behavior is either disruptive of or incompatible with expected rates of growth in academic achievement and social development.

Procedural Issues

Procedural, as used in this context, refers to assessment practices applied to behavior disordered children for purposes of supporting decision-making processes in the areas of screening, identification, certification, program planning and implementation, placement, and mainstreaming and social integration. This section begins with a discussion of variables that directly affect assessment practice. These are: (a) the model of psychological assessment used to guide practice, (b) the persons responsible for conducting assessments, and (c) the settings within which assessments are conducted. In the remainder of the section, issues and best practice standards are presented for a series of assessment tasks that are integral to serving the needs of behavior disordered children.

Models of Psychological Assessment

Coulter and Morrow (1977) argue that psychological assessment has two fundamentally distinct purposes. These are identification and intervention. Each requires different tests and interpretations of results. They note, as have other investigators (Hobbs, 1975; Kauffman, 1977), that diagnostic labels resulting from the identification process have almost no implications for the treatment process. They view assessment for intervention purposes as the primary concern of psychologists. However, it appears that in traditional assessment practice in this area, we have invested far more energy, time, and effort in identification and problem definition areas than in assessment for intervention.

There are a variety of assessment models available to guide assessment practice. Coulter and Morrow (1977) describe three models (i.e., medical, social system, and task analysis) for use in assessment for identification and intervention purposes. The authors recommend the application of a behavioral-ecological approach to the full range of assessment tasks relating to the delivery of services to behavior disordered children in the school setting. This approach incorporates many of the assumptions, principles, and recommended practices of the social system and task analysis models described by Coulter and Morrow (1977) which are based upon behavioral assessment principles.

A behavioral-ecological approach to assessment and intervention is based upon four primary assumptions: (a) individuals cannot be adequately assessed outside the context of their social environments; (b) environmental settings, as well as individuals, can be directly assessed; (c) persons and environments can be matched to provide optimal opportunities for growth, development and adjustment; and (d) the behavior of individuals and the structure of environments can be both modified to facilitate achievement of a satisfactory person-environment fit (Romer & Heller, 1983; Schalock, 1985). This model provides an excellent foundation for evaluating disordered pupil behavior in relation to environmental demands and expectations, for analyzing referral practices and for conducting assessments for social integration into less restrictive settings. As a rule, two assessment profiles are developed in this model (i.e., a person analysis and a setting analysis). The person analysis analyzes the target individual's skills, competencies, deficits, and resource requirements; the setting analysis analyzes the demands, performance requirements, and available resources of target environs. Semmel, Lieber, and Peck (in press) have argued for the adoption of this conceptual model to govern improvement of practices in relation to serving the full range of mildly handicapped pupils in schools. Anderson-Inman, Purcell, and Walker (1984) and Walker (1984) have described transition models for mainstreaming and social integration that operationalize these practices for use in school settings.

Rodgers-Warren (1984) has explicated an ecobehavioral model, within the field of applied behavior analysis, for analyzing person-environment interactions that incorporate principles of behavioral ecology, applied behavior analysis, and behavioral assessment. The nature of behavioral assessment, its assumptions, and practices are described in detail by Nelson and Hayes (1979). They describe this assessment model as "the identification of meaningful response units and their controlling variables (both current environmental and organismic) for the purposes of understanding and altering human behavior" (p. 491). Within this model, behavior is viewed as a sample of responding in a particular assessment situation. Unless empirical justification exists, inferences are not made beyond the present behavior and situation to underlying causes, other responses, or different settings. Behavioral assessment can include the measurement of overt motor, physiological-emotional, and cognitive-verbal behaviors. The model encourages recording of multiple measures to ensure a broad-band assessment. Characteristically, overt motor behavior is measured via direct observations by trained observers; physiological-emotional and cognitive-verbal behavior is measured by rating scales, checklists, questionnaires, and academic tests. Behavioral assessment measures both organismic variables and environmental factors within the setting or situation where functioning is considered disordered. Organismic variables include individual differences produced by past learning and physiology. Often, these variables are not alterable but may contribute to an adequate understanding of the disordered behavior. In some cases, however, they are alterable (e.g., some sensory or motor impairments may be corrected with prostheses and/or training).

Assessment of current environmental variables refers to the measurement and analysis of disordered behavior within natural settings and the variables that influence or control it. The situational specificity of behavior, along with its implications for assessment and programming, is a basic assumption of behavioral assessment. Situations differ in terms of expectations, stimulus conditions, and social contingencies, with corresponding differences produced in child behavior. Therefore, it is important to assess child behavior in multiple settings to determine its status and potential for change. Social agents' perceptions of the child's behavior, including generalized behavioral expectations, are an important element in this assessment.

In the remainder of this chapter, specific assessment practices that incorporate and expand many of the principles and practices of the behavioral-ecological and ecobehavioral models are reviewed and discussed. In the authors' opinion, these models have the potential to solve a substantial number of the measurement problems that have traditionally plagued attempts to deliver services to behavior disordered children in the school setting. Assessment Personnel

In the authors' opinion, assessments of children in the school setting should be coordinated by a "behavioral-ecological consultant". Qualifications for this position should be determined by training and experience rather than job title. In many cases, this person could be the school psychologist. In addition to conducting traditional behavioral assessments, the behavioral-ecological consultant would also conduct assessments of ecological variables such as those discussed in this chapter. If assessments of a specialized nature are required, (e.g., neurological, neuropsychological, or medical), referrals can be made as deemed appropriate. Whenever possible, behavioral observations should be conducted in those settings where child behavior is considered disordered and by individuals under the behavioral-ecological consultant's direct supervision (e.g., teachers, counselors, aides, student observers).

The classroom teacher's input should be weighed carefully in decisions relating to serving behavior disordered children in the school setting. Traditionally, teacher judgment has not been regarded as either valid or reliable. Wickman's (1928) monograph comparing the attitudes of teachers and clinicians toward the classroom behavior problems of children raised serious questions about the validity of teacher judgments. In this study, the judgments of psychologists were accepted as the validation criterion against which teacher judgments were compared. The general lack of agreement between the two groups was interpreted as a measure of the teacher's inaccuracy in identifying problematic child behavior. The Wickman study did not test the accuracy of teacher judgment of child behavior--only whether it corresponded with clinicians' judgments. Actual studies of teacher judgment show it to be very accurate (Bolstad, 1974; Greenwood, Walker, Todd, & Hops, 1979b; Gresham, 1986; Nelson, 1971; Schaefer, 1982; Walker, 1970). In particular, teacher judgment is most accurate at the extremes of the distribution, where child behavioral attributes are most salient.

Classroom teachers are in an ideal position to identify behavior disordered children. Teachers probably spend more time observing the behavioral characteristics of children in their classes than anyone except parents. It has been estimated that teachers spend 7,000 hours with their pupils in the elementary grades alone. Given this amount of time, teachers have the opportunity to amass considerable information for use in making judgments about the behavior of children in their classes. Gerber and Semmel (1984), in discussing the accuracy of teacher judgment of child behavior, suggest that the classroom teacher should be the criterion variable for validation of the assessments conducted by MDTs in school rather than vice versa.

Indeed, increasing empirical evidence supports the position that teachers are very accurate judges of student behavior. Greenwood, Walker, Todd, & Hops (1979b) assessed the accuracy of teacher rankings of child verbal frequency for identifying socially withdrawn children. Of the 26 teachers in the study sample, 23% had identified the lowest interacting child within their first rank. Given three ranks, 77% had identified the lowest interacting child. Presumably, teachers would be even more accurate in identifying acting out or disruptive child behavior because of its increased salience. Teacher nominations, rankings, and ratings can be extremely useful sources of information in the identification and assessment of behavior disorders. Teacher expectations also contribute a great deal of information about the behavioral ecology of the classroom and should be systematically measured in the process of defining and evaluating child behavior (Walker, 1984, 1986; Walker & Rankin, 1983; Walker, Reavis, Rhode & Jenson, 1985).

Assessment Settings

Behavioral assessment requires a demonstration that conclusions based on data from the assessment situation can be generalized to the criterion "real-life" situation; that is, the setting(s) in which the behavior is considered disordered. Too often, assessments of school behavior disorders fail this simple test of relevance and validity. If a child is exhibiting highly aggressive behavior on the playground, his or her behavior should be assessed in that setting, not in the clinician's office. As a rule, the child's behavior and social agents' perceptions of same, should be assessed in each setting where it is considered disordered and also in control, nonproblem settings. In vivo assessments of this type are often time consuming and sometimes difficult to obtain. The relevance and quality of the information produced by such assessments, however, will contribute significantly to the delivery of appropriate services to behavior disordered children.

Assessment of child behavior in the home setting, as a response to behavior disorders exhibited at school, may be a questionable and problematic procedure. As a rule, reliance must be placed upon anecdotal reports and ratings from parents in order to make such a determination. In some cases, parents may be willing to collect data on certain aspects of child behavior or on family interactions. Parent-collected data, however, should be interpreted cautiously in these situations, as it would be highly vulnerable to demand characteristics and response biases (Johnson & Boldstad, 1973).

Assessment Tasks

School professionals are charged with completing a sequence of assessment tasks if behavior disordered children's needs are to be served effectively in the school setting. These are: (a) screening, (b) defining the problem, (c) determining eligibility, (d) selecting target behaviors for interventions, (e) establishing baseline performance, (f) monitoring interventions, (g) evaluating outcomes, (h) conducting follow-up assessments, and (i) conducting assessments for mainstreaming and social integration purposes. In the remainder of this section, issues, procedures and best practice standards are presented in relation to each of these tasks.
Screening
Screening studies show that teachers usually refer from 2-6% of the school age population for special services (Hyde, 1975; Nicholson, 1967; Robbins, Mercer, & Meyers, 1967). The majority of these referrals are for children with academic rather than behavior problems (Kirschenbaum, Marsh, & Devage, 1977). Those behavior disordered children who are referred tend to exhibit maladaptive behavior patterns that are directed toward the external social environment (i.e., externalizing) and disturb classroom atmosphere (e.g. acting out, disruptive, hyperactive, aggressive forms of behavior). All children in regular classrooms should be screened regularly so that they have an equal chance to be identified for a variety of behavior problems that can interfere with their social and academic development. The teacher referral process, as it traditionally operates, does not accomplish this goal. Systematic screening procedures are needed which require the teacher to regularly evaluate all children in relation to criteria that affect their behavioral status and development.

Kirschenbaum, Marsh, and Devage (1977) have demonstrated the feasibility of a mass screening procedure that requires only 10 to 40 minutes per classroom. A brief teacher rating form, the AML (Cowen et al., 1973), was used as the primary screening instrument in this study. Previous research on the AML had established its ability to discriminate between groups of maladjusted and normal children. This study found that teachers directly referred 6.9% of the primary grade level children in three inner city schools (n=698). Mass screening procedures, using the AML, subsequently identified an additional 9.7% of this population as in need of services. Both groups exhibited significantly more maladaptive behavior than did a normative comparison group on the CARS (Child Activity Rating Scale) (Lorian, Cowen, & Caldwell, 1974), indicating that teachers did not naturally refer all children in need of behavioral services.

Economical, effective screening procedures of this type have significant applicability to the field of behavior disorders. They utilize teacher knowledge of child behavior, yet structure the teacher's judgment so that all behavior disorders have an equal chance to be identified. Other excellent systems of this type are available (Clarfield, 1974; Greenwood, Walker, Todd, & Hops, 1979a) for the screening of both school age and preschool populations in relation to common, school related behavior disorders.

The authors have found teacher rankings of child behavior to be extremely accurate and predictive of status on criterion measures at the extremes of the distribution. Teacher rankings of child academic achievement are also very accurate (Greenwood, Hops, Walker, Guild, Stokes, & Young, 1979). Rather than relying upon teacher nominations for referral purposes, teachers could be regularly asked to rank children in their classrooms on such variables as social competence, appropriate classroom behavior, and achievement. Children at the extremes of the distribution could then be studied and evaluated more thoroughly using such methods as: (a) anecdotal records, (b) checklists, (c) rating scales, and (d) observational data. This approach to screening improves cost-effectiveness because teachers would not have to complete rating instruments on all children in the classroom. An excellent resource for the screening and assessment of behavior disorders in school age pupils is by Wood, Smith and Grimes: *The Iowa Assessment Model in Behavior Disorders: A Training Manual* (1985) and is available through the Iowa Department of Public Instruction.

During the past two years, the present authors and their colleagues have been involved in the design and testing of a multiple gating screening system for behavior disordered pupils, K-6 grades, that standardizes the screening process and gives each child in a regular classroom setting an equal chance to be identified for externalizing and internalizing behavior disorders (Walker, Severson, & Haring, 1985; Walker, Severson, Haring & Williams, 1986). The model provides for the cost effective, mass screening of all children who are enrolled in regular classrooms and links (a) definitional criteria; (b) screening and assessment procedures; and (c) normative based, eligibility decision making into a single, self-contained system. Figure 1 provides an overview of this screening system which has, as a primary goal, improvement of the quality of teacher referrals to special

Figure 1

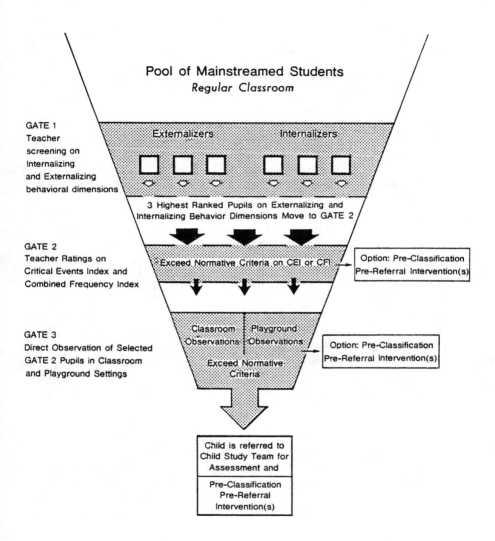

Multiple-Gating Assessment Procedure for Identification
of Behavior Disordered Students

services.

The *Standardized Screening and Identification of Behavior Disordered Pupils in the Elementary Age Range: Rationale, Procedures, and Guidelines* (SSBD) (Walker, Severson, & Haring, 1985) is patterned after models developed by Greenwood, Walker, Todd, & Hops (1979a) for the identification of socially withdrawn, preschool pupils and by Loeber, Dishion, and Patterson (1984) for the screening of children at risk for adoption of a delinquent lifestyle. The SSBD relies upon structured teacher judgment of pupil behavioral characteristics in stages one and two and uses normatively referenced, observation data to provide independent, in vivo assessments of the pupil's behavioral status in stage three within academic and free play settings. The results of screening decisions in each gate are cross validated by increasingly more intensive and complex assessments within subsequent stages.

Research conducted to data on the SSBD indicates that (a) the instruments comprising it have excellent psychometric properties, (b) it reliably identifies certified BD pupils in mainstream settings, (c) teachers show high levels of interrater agreement in their rankings and ratings of pupils using criteria and procedures contained in the system, and (d) pupils identified as externalizers and internalizers in stage one are clearly differentiated by both teacher ratings in stage two and by direct observations in stage three. In a year long test of the system's efficacy involving 18 classrooms and teachers in grades K-6, the SSBD correctly classified 89.47% of externalizing, internalizing, and normal pupils in these settings. The senior author and his colleagues recently received a three year, field initiated grant from the US Special Education Programs office to validate, standardize, and field test the SSBD. The system is currently available from the senior author for the cost of reproduction and mailing.

Defining the Problem

Once a child has been screened and identified as in need of behavioral services, it is important to define carefully the specific content of the behavior disorder and to measure the teacher's behavioral expectations and/or tolerance levels in relation to adaptive and maladaptive child behavior in general (Walker, 1984, 1986). There are a variety of checklists and rating instruments available for describing the content of child behavior disorders in school and home settings (e.g., Wood, Grimes & Smith, 1985). Some popular instruments for this purpose are: (a) the Devereux Child Behavior Rating Scales (Spivack & Levine, 1964), (b) the Behavior Problem Checklist (Quay, 1977), and (c) the Walker Problem Behavior Identification Checklist (Walker, 1983). Traditionally, the content of these instruments has been heavily weighted toward problematic child behavior. However, it is also important to obtain descriptive information on adaptive child behavior (Achenbach, 1978). Several recently developed instruments contain extensive descriptions of both adaptive and maladaptive child behavior (Achenbach, 1979; Gersten, 1976).

The authors propose a three-dimensional model for describing the content of child behavioral status after systematic screening efforts are concluded. In this model, classroom behavior is rated along a frequency dimension and a critical events dimension. The frequency index (i.e., ratings, counts, codings) is applied to both adaptive and maladaptive forms of classroom behavior. The purpose of this index is to identify the maladaptive behaviors that the child engages in too frequently (i.e., excesses) and adaptive behaviors that are engaged in too infrequently (i.e., deficits). A sample list of such pinpoints is included in Table 2.

Table 2
Frequency Index of Adaptive and Maladaptive Classroom Behaviors

-Follows classroom rules	-Talks out of turn
-Complies with teacher demands	-Gets out of seat
-Takes turns	-Whines
-Listens to teacher instructions	-Disturbs others
-Makes assistance needs known	-Defies the teacher
-Produces work of acceptable quality	-Disrupts the class
-Attends to assigned tasks	-Does not complete assignments
-Volunteers	

It is also important to obtain teacher assessments of critical behavioral events that are relatively independent of frequency, yet have serious implications for child behavioral or developmental status. A single occurrence of any of the events listed in Table 3 would be a cause for serious concern by service providers and should initiate a prompt referral to special school or psychological services.

The referred child's social competence should be rated by the teachers in specific social skills areas and, whenever possible, assessed with sociometric procedures. The authors recommend assessment in the following social skills areas: (a) affective skills, (b) interactive skills, (c) approaching others, (d) conversation skills, (e) cooperation, (f) coping skills, and (g) making friends. The child should be compared to peers in each area to determine whether the child is less skilled, as skilled, or more skilled than his/her peers.

Table 3
Critical Event Index

-Child masturbates in public
-Child assaults an adult
-Child attempts to seriously physically injure another
-Child engages in self-mutilation, e.g., head banging, biting, or cutting him/herself
-Child's verbal behavior is irrational and/or incomprehensible
-Child is not in contact with reality
-Child sexually molests another child
-Child threatens suicide
-Child shows evidence of physical abuse
-Child shows evidence of drug use

An excellent review and analysis of social skills assessment and intervention procedures is contained in Gresham and Reschly (in press). Walker and McConnell (in press) have also developed a 43 item teacher rating scale of pupil's social skills for use in grades K-6. It provides normative data on total score and three subscales that measure respectively (a) teacher preferred social behavior (b) peer preferred pupil behavior and (c) school adjustment behavior. Normative comparisons of the type referred to above are strongly recommended for both indirect (i.e., teacher ratings) and direct (i.e., behavioral observations) measures of child behavior. These comparisons are helpful in ensuring that the referral is based on actual disordered and/or deficient child behavior and is not a result of other idiosyncratic or extraneous factors. As a general rule, a peer of the same sex should be selected for comparative purposes (Walker & Hops, 1976) in referral setting evaluations. If clear differences are found, the referral is, in all likelihood, more appropriate than if no or only minimal differences exist between the referred and nonreferred pupil(s).

The authors also recommend that direct observational data be recorded on the child's behavior in those settings where it is considered problematic and, if one exists, in at least one setting where it is not considered problematic. Normative peer comparisons should be conducted, if possible, in each setting. This comparison could provide valuable information on levels of appropriate and inappropriate behavior in each setting. There are a number of observational codes and procedures available for use in classroom and playground settings which are easy to use and not too time consuming (Alessi, 1980; Keller, 1980; Walker, 1979). The data yield by these assessments is extremely valuable and the information generated usually has substantial relevance to the task of problem definition. As noted above, teacher expectations should be measured and the child's perceived behavior problems evaluated in relation to the teacher's behavioral standards or demands. Finally, if deemed appropriate, parent ratings may be obtained to compare perceptions of parents and teachers regarding child behavior across home and school settings.

Determining Eligibility

If a pupil is referred for problematic behavior in the classroom, the child and/or the teacher is probably in need of some form of service or assistance. As noted earlier, the factors that prompted the referral are unaffected by whether the child meets local, state, and/or federal eligibility criteria. We need to replace our current system of certifying a referred child as SED or BD` before any services or assistance become available which correspond to the type and severity of the referral problem. This would, of course, be determined only after a careful analysis of the child's behavior within the referral setting(s) and the social agents' perceptions of the child's behavior problem(s). Eligibility decisions should focus on which services or assistance the child's behavior problems require. These could range from consultant assistance in the classroom to an intensive behavior management program administered in a special setting. In some cases, referral to an outside agency may be warranted.

A number of states and LEAs have begun experimenting with prereferral interventions. That is, before a referral to special services is allowed, one or more interventions, designed to address the referral problem(s), are implemented. If the target pupil fails to respond to the intervention, it provides a further validation of the referral.

In developing the CORBEH behavior management packages referred to earlier (e.g., CLASS, PASS, PEERS, AND RECESS), the senior author used a combination of indirect and direct measures to establish eligibility criteria. These were teacher ratings on specific behavioral pinpoints and behavioral observations recorded on the child's performance in referral setting(s). The purpose of this dual criterion was to obtain a direct measure of the child's behavior, as well as, the teacher's perception of the child's behavior. The goal was to ensure that the child to whom the program was applied actually warranted the investment of time and energy required in the implementation process. Children who did not qualify were usually exposed to components of the program or to some other, less intensive intervention procedure. Children for whom the program was not successful were recommended for more intensive treatment services.

Waksman and Jones (1985) have developed an excellent procedure for determining the eligibility of behavior disordered pupils referred for evaluation and special services. The system relies upon empirically verifiable information regarding the referred pupil's behavioral status in a range of school settings. In order to be certified as eligible, target pupils must display problematic behavior across more than one school setting, at intense levels of severity, persisting over considerable periods of time. This model is considered by the present authors to be exemplary and is highly recommended for use in the certification process. A copy of the system can be obtained from the Oregon Department of Education, Division of Special Education (Attention: Howard Smith or Robert Siewert). Selecting Target Behaviors for Intervention

A great deal of research remains to be done in empirically identifying behavioral correlates of successful classroom adjustment, academic achievement, and social competence. Some important conceptual (Foster & Ritchey, 1979) and empirical (Gottman, Gonso, & Rasmussen, 1975) work has been directed toward identifying social skills that determine social competence. Similarly, Cobb (1972) empirically identified academic survival skills that were predictive of achievement. However, until relatively recently, little attention had been directed toward identifying those behavioral competencies and maladaptive social behaviors that distinguish successful and nonsuccessful classroom adjustment within mainstream school settings.

Careful descriptive studies in these areas will make future interventions far more precise and cost-effective than is presently possible. It is apparent that the same intervention procedure, applied to empirically determined target behavior versus nonempirically determined behaviors, will have vastly different effects on a child's overall adjustment. To date, we have developed a very powerful intervention technology that is applicable to the field of behavior disorders. When our technology of empirically based, target behavior selection approaches that for intervention, we will be in a more advantageous position to deliver cost-effective, intervention services in the school setting.

Until this technology is completely developed, the selection of behaviors will have to rely, to some extent, upon the advice of experts, logical analysis, and arbitrary judgment. Social validation techniques have been particularly effective in structuring our judgments for this purpose (Hersh & Walker, 1983; Kazdin, 1977; Van Houten, 1979; Walker, 1984, 1986; Walker & Hops, 1976). Social validation refers to the use of experts, consumers, or significant social agents in rating the importance of behaviors judged to be important as targets of intervention, and whether target responses selected for intervention have changed sufficiently for the treatment to be considered successful. Usually, a Likert-type of scale is used for this purpose.

As part of research focusing on the mainstreaming process, Walker (1984, 1986) assessed "receiving" teachers' expectations regarding classroom behavior. A broad range of regular and special education teachers responded to an inventory which required them to rate the importance of specific adaptive skills and competencies, as well as, the degree to which they were (or were not) accepting of the maladaptive child behaviors listed. The results indicated that teachers view classroom control and compliance behaviors as most important. In contrast, peer-to-peer social skills were viewed as least important. The least accepted child social behaviors of a maladaptive nature included stealing, self-abuse, teacher defiance, inappropriate sexual behavior, and tantrums. Interestingly, this list would be characterized as consisting of high intensity, low base rate pinpoints. Again, the most acceptable maladaptive behaviors were deficient peer-to-peer social skills. These outcomes provide valuable information about areas of child performance that teachers view as important. It also identifies areas of child performance, such as social skills, that are viewed as relatively unimportant by teachers, but which, nevertheless, are powerful determinants of social competence (Van Hasselt, Hersen, Whitehill, & Bellack, 1979).

When designing interventions for behavior disordered children, it is, of course, very important to respond to the specific problems that prompted the referral. It is equally important, however, to assess the child's status in behavioral domains that teachers in general see as predictive of good adjustment and also on those that teachers may not view as important, but that are empirically related to academic achievement, social competence, or general school success.

Establishing Baseline Performance

Baseline status on target behaviors selected or identified should be assessed, whenever possible, using direct observational procedures in natural settings so that treatment effects can be evaluated in both intervention and nonintervention settings. Nontarget but relevant corrollary behaviors should also be assessed to determine whether the intervention has only specific or more generalized effects (Kazdin, 1973) upon the target pupil's behavioral repertoire.

Indirect assessments of child behavior on these pinpoints using ratings or checklists contributed by teachers and/or parents also provide a basis for assessing the perceived impact of an intervention--although these are often less sensitive to the direct effects of intervention. The combination of direct and indirect assessment can provide a precise analysis of an intervention's overall effects. Normative peer comparisons on measures are also recommended during this assessment stage (Alessi, 1980; Walker & Hops, 1976).

Monitoring Interventions

"Fidelity of implementation" is a very important factor in the success of any intervention. We cannot assume that interventions are implemented by social agents (e.g., parents and teachers) in the intended manner. For the behavioral-ecological consultant, the social agent implementing an intervention can actually become the target of a behavioral intervention. Thus, the implementation process should be measured and documented whenever possible to increase the likelihood of high quality treatment. This would involve keeping careful records on such variables as praise rate, number of time outs, points awarded, points subtracted, privileges selected, frequency of reprimands, and alterations in stimulus conditions. These are essentially "process" measures that document the extent to which implementation goals are realized. They make it possible to identify and remediate implementation failures.

Evaluating Outcomes

Child outcomes should be evaluated according to (a) absolute gain from pre- to post-assessment time points, (b) relative gain in terms of movement toward a normative standard, and (c) assessments of the social significance of the achieved gains. To assess treatment outcomes adequately, baseline measures should be administered at pre-, during, and post-time points. The measurement data obtained during intervention provides an assessment of the maximum impact of the intervention on child behavior. The post-measure provides an indication of the intervention's short-term maintenance effects. Data recorded on nonreferred peers will make it possible to determine whether the intervention has moved the treated child into the normal range for the target behavior(s). Social validation measures from teachers and parents provide information on how the consumer views the changes (Kazdin, 1977). Treatments that move student performance into the normal range are generally considered successful (Walker & Hops, 1976). Conducting Follow-up Assessments

Until the beginning of the 1970s, it was largely assumed that treatment effects automatically generalized to nontreatment settings and were maintained indefinitely after intervention was terminated. Systematic assessments in natural settings showed that the opposite was true (Johnson, Boldstad, & Lobitz, 1976; Stokes & Baer, 1977; Walker & Buckley, 1972; Walker, Hops., and Johnson, 1975). Unprogrammed generalization and maintenance of treatment gains is an extremely rare occurrence (see Kohler & Greenwood, 1986, for a recent review). When it does occur, investigators are usually not able to identify the specific features, elements, or attributes of the intervention which accounted for the generalization and/or maintenance effects. Baer, Wolf, and Risley (1968) suggest that generalization should be programmed rather than expected, or later, lamented.

In conducting follow-up assessments of treatments administered to behavior disordered children in the school setting, it is strongly recommended that data be collected in each setting where treatment effects are expected to occur. Furthermore, long-term assessments should be made to determine the durability of achieved treatment effects. In those cases where effects are not maintained, low-cost variations of the original intervention can be implemented to bring child behavior back to criterion levels. Conducting Assessments for Mainstreaming and Social Integration

The special education and rehabilitation fields' collective experience with mainstreaming, deinstitutionalization, and the transition from school to adult life have dramatically highlighted the importance of planning careful transitions from more to less restrictive settings. The authors strongly recommend that ecological assessments be conducted to evaluate the appropriateness of less restrictive school settings as potential placements for mainstreamed behavior disordered pupils and that the transition process be planned carefully based upon such information. As a minimum, it is recommended that (a) the behavioral and academic demands of target mainstream settings be directly assessed prior to social integration, (b) target pupil behavioral/performance status be assessed in relation to the most critically important academic and behavioral demands, (c) this information be used to assist in selecting mainstream placements, and (d) that it constitute an integral component of the transition plan that prepares the pupil for entry into a more demanding, less restrictive setting. As noted, Anderson-Inman, Purcel, and Walker (1984) and Walker (1984, 1986) have designed and partially validated assessment systems for conducting these assessments in both academic and behavioral areas.

Conclusion

In the authors' view, there needs to be a radical reconceptualization of behavior disorders in the school setting. The assumptions we make about child behavior have a dramatic impact upon assessment practices and the way in which we interpret assessment information. In turn, conclusions based on this information determine the remediation services eventually made available to behavior disordered children. Accompanying this reconceptualization, new definitions of disordered child behavior in the school setting need to be developed, operationalized, and translated into assessment practice. In the authors' view, this process can ultimately result in the delivery of relevant, individualized treatment services to children with behavior disorders in the school setting.

The authors are aware of the complex philosophical, economic, legal, and logistical barriers that impinge upon these tasks. In many respects, the practices suggested in this chapter represent idealized versions of assessment practice. Professional time and actual school district programming options are always critical elements in considerations relating to progress that depends upon such radical changes in traditional practices. Obviously, these exemplary practices will require years to achieve. It is apparent, however, that behavior disordered children are not being adequately assessed or served under our current system. Given diminishing school resources, it will be interesting to observe how the current intense pressures for change in this area are translated into progress during the next few years.

References

Achenbach, T. (1974). *Developmental psychopathology*. New York: Ronald Press.

Achenbach, T. (1978). Psychopathology of childhood: Research problems and issues. *Journal of Consulting and Clinical Psychology, 46*(4), 759-776.

Achenbach, T. (1979). The child behavior profile: An empirically based system for assessing children's behavioral problems and competencies. *International Journal of Mental Health, 7*(3), 24-40.

Achenbach, T., & Edelbrock, C. (1978). The classification of child psychopathology: A review and analysis of empirical efforts. *Psychological Bulletin, 85*(6), 1275-1301.

Alessi, G. (1980). Behavioral observation for the school psychologist: Responsive-discrepancy model. *School Psychological Review, 9*(1), 31-44.

Allport, G. (1966). Traits revisited. *American Psychologist, 21*, 1-9.

Allport, G. (1974). Personalistic psychology: A trait approach to personality. In W. S. Sahakian (Ed.), *Psychology of personality: Readings in theory*. Chicago: Rand McNally & Company.

American Psychiatric Association. (1980). *Diagnostic and statistical manual of mental disorders* (3rd ed.). Washington, DC: Author.

Anderson-Inman, L., Walker, H. M., & Purcell, J. (1984). Programming for handicapped students in the mainstream. In W. Heward, T. Heron, D. Hill, & J. Trap-Porter, *Focus on behavior analysis in education*. Columbus OH: Charles Merrill.

Baer, D., Wolf, M., & Risley, T. (1968). Some current dimensions of applied behavior analysis. *Journal of Applied Behavior Analysis, 1*, 91-97.

Balow, B. (1979). Definitional and prevalence problems in behavior disorders of children. *School Psychology Digest, 8*, 348-353.

Becker, W. C., & Krug, R. (1964). A circumplex model for social behavior in children. *Child Development, 35*, 371-396.

Bolstad, O. (1974). *The relationship between teachers' assessment of students and students' actual behavior in the classroom*. Unpublished doctoral dissertation, University of Oregon.

Brophy, J. E., & Good, T. (1970). Teachers' communication of differential expectations for children's classroom performance: Some behavioral data. *Journal of Educational Psychology, 61*, 365-374.

Brophy, J. E., & Good, T. (1974). *Teacher-student relationships: Causes and consequences*. New York: Holt, Rinehart & Winston.

Bruner, J. (1968). *Toward a theory of instruction. New York: W. W. Norton.*

Carlson, C., & Lahey, B. (1983). Factor structure of teacher rating scales for children. School Psychology Review, 12(3), 285-293.

Clarfield, S. (1974). The development of a teacher referral form for identifying early school maladaption. *American Journal of Community Psychology, 2*, 199-210.

Clarizio, H., & McCoy, G. (1976). *Behavior disorders in children* (2nd ed.). New York: Thomas Y. Crowell.

Cobb, J. (1972). The relationship of discrete classroom behavior to fourth grade academic achievement. *Journal of Educational Psychology, 63*, 74-80.

Coulter, A., & Morrow, H. (1977). *The concept of emotional disturbance within special education*. Austin TX: Austin Regional Resource Center, University of Texas.

Cowen, E., Dorr, D., Clarfield, S., Kreling, B., McWiliams, S., Pokracki, F., Pratt, D., Terrel, D., & Wilson, A. (1973). The AML: A quick screening device for early detection of school maladaption. *American Journal of Community Psychology, 1*, 12-35.

Cullinan, D., Epstein, M., & Lloyd, J. (1983). *Behavior disorders of children and adolescents*. Englewood Cliffs NJ: Prentice Hall.

Edelbrock, C. (1979). Empirical classification of children's behavior disorders: Progress based on parent and teacher ratings. *School*

Psychology Digest, 8(4), 355-369.

Fabre, T. R., & Walker, H. M. (1986). Teacher perceptions of the behavioral adjustment of primary grade level handicapped pupils within regular and special education settings. Manuscript submitted for publication.

Forness, S. (1985). *Psychologizing special education. Who needs it?* Keynote address at the Annual Behavior Disorders Conference. Phoenix AZ: Arizona State University.

Foster, S., & Ritchey, W. (1979). Issues in the assessment of social competence in children. *Journal of Applied Behavior Analysis, 12,* 625-638.

Freemont, T., & Wallbrown, F. (1979, Spring). Types of behavior problems that may be encountered in the classroom. *Journal of Education,* 5-23.

Galagan, J. (1985). Psychoeducational testing: Turn out the lights, the party's over. *Exceptional Children, 52*(3), 288-299.

Gerber, M., & Semmel, M. (1984). Teacher as imperfect test: Reconceptualizing the referral process. *Educational Psychologist, 19*(3), 137-148.

Gersten, E. (1976). Health Resources Inventory: The development of a measure of the personal and social competency of primary grade children. Journal of Consulting and Clinical Psychology, 44, 775-786.

Gersten, R., Walker, H. M., & Darch, C. (in press). Relationships between teachers' social behavioral standards/expectations and their teaching effectiveness. *Exceptional Children.*

Gottlieb, J. (1979). Placement in the least restrictive environment. In L. Morra (Ed.), *LRE: Developing criteria for evaluation of the least restrictive environment provision.* Philadelphia: Research for Better Schools.

Gottman, J. (1977). Toward a definition of social isolation in children. *Child Development, 48,* 513-517.

Gottman, J., Gonso, J., & Rasmussen, B. (1975). Social interaction, social competence and friendship in children. *Child Development, 46,* 709-718.

Greenwood, C., Hops, H., Walker, H. M., Guild, J., Stokes, J., & Young, R. (1979). Standardized classroom management program: Social validation and replication studies in Utah and Oregon. *Journal of Applied Behavior Analysis, 12*(2), 235-254.

Greenwood, C., Walker, H. M., Todd, N., & Hops, H. (1979a). *SAMPLE (Social assessment manual for preschool level).* Eugene, OR: Center at Oregon for Research in the Behavioral Education of the Handicapped (CORBEH), Clinical Services Building, University of Oregon.

Greenwood, C., Walker, H. M., Todd, N., & Hops, H. (1979b). Selecting a cost-effective device for the assessment of social withdrawal. *Journal of Applied Behavior Analysis, 12*, 639-652.

Gresham, F. (1982). Misguided mainstreaming: The case for social skills training with handicapped children. *Exceptional Children, 48*, 422-433.

Gresham, F. (in press). Conceptual issues in the assessment of social competence in children. In P. Strain, M. Guralnick, & H. M. Walker (Eds.), *Children's Social Behavior: Development, assessment, and modification.* New York: Academic Press.

Gresham, F., & Reschly, D. (in press). Issues in the conceptualization, classification and assessment of social skills in the mildly handicapped. In T. R. Kratochwill (Ed.), *Advances in School Psychology.* Hillsdale, NJ: Lawrence Erlbaum.

Grosenick, J., & Huntze, S. (1980a). *National needs analysis in behavior disorders: Adolescent behavior disorders.* Columbia, MO: University of Missouri, Department of Special Education.

Grosenick, J., & Huntze, S. (1980b). *National needs analysis in behavioral disorders: Severe behavior disorders.* Columbia MO: Department of Special Education, University of Missouri.

Hersh, R., & Walker, H. M. (1983). *Great expectations: Making schools effective for all children* (Special issue), 2(1), 147-188.

Hobbs, N. (1975). *The futures of children.* San Francisco: Jossey-Bass.

Huntze, S. (1985). *Statement to support replacing the term seriously emotionally disturbed with the term behaviorally disordered as a descriptor for children and youth who are handicapped by their behavior*(Position paper). Columbia MO: Council for Children with Behavior Disorders.

Hyde, E. (1975). School psychological referral in an inner city school. *Psychology in the Schools, 12*, 412-420.

Hyman, I., Bilus, F., Dennehy, N., Feldman, G., Flanagan, D., Lovoratano, J., Maital, S., & McDowell, E. (1979, Spring). Discipline in American education: An overview and analysis. *Journal of Education*, 51-68.

Jenson, W. (1984). *Severely emotionally disturbed versus behavior disorders: Consideration of a label change.* Salt Lake City, UT: University of Utah, Department of Educational Psychology.

Johnson, S. M., & Boldstad, O. (1973). Methodological issues in naturalistic observation: Some problems and solutions for field research. In L. A. Hamerlynck, L. C. Handy, & E. J. Mash (Eds.), *Behavior change: Methodology, concepts, and practice.* Champaign IL: Research Press.

Johnson, S., Boldstad, O., & Lobitz, G. (1976). Generalization and contrast phenomena in behavior modification with children. In E. J. Mash, L. A.

Hamerlynck, & L. C. Handy (Eds.), *Behavior modification and families*. New York: Brunner/Mazel.

Jones, V., & Jones, L. (1986). *Comprehensive classroom management: Creating positive learning environments* (2nd Ed). Boston: Allyn & Bacon.

Kauffman, J. M. (1977). *Characteristics of children's behavior disorders. Columbus OH: Charles E. Merrill*.

Kauffman, J. M. (1980). Where special education for disturbed children is going: A personal view. Exceptional Children, 46, 522-527.

Kauffman, J. M. (1982). Social policy issues in special education and related services for emotionally disturbed children and youth. In M. Noel & N. Haring (Eds.), *Progress or change: Issues in educating the emotionally disturbed*. Seattle: University of Washington.

Kazdin, A. (1973). Methodological and assessment considerations in evaluating reinforcement programs in applied settings. *Journal of Applied Behavior Analysis, 6,* 517-531.

Kazdin, A. (1977). Assessing the clinical or applied importance of behavior change through social validation. *Behavior Modification, 1,* 427-452.

Keller, H. (1980). Issues in the use of observational assessment. *School Psychological Review, 9*(1), 21-29.

Kirschenbaum, D., Marsh, M., & Devage, J. (1977). The effectiveness of a mass screening procedure in an early intervention program. *Psychology in the Schools, 14(4),* 400-406.

Kohler, F., & Greenwood, C. R. (1986). Toward a technology of generalization: The identification of natural contingencies of reinforcement. The Behavior Analyst, 9, 19-26.

Kornblau, B. (1982). The teachable pupil survey: A technique for assessing teachers' perceptions of pupil attributes. *Psychology in the Schools, 19,* 170-174.

Kornblau, B., & Keogh, B. (1980). Teachers' perceptions and educational decisions. *Journal for Teaching and Learning, 1, 87-101.*

Kulik, J., Stein, K., & Sarbin, T. (1968). Dimensions and patterns of adolescent antisocial behavior. Journal of Consulting Psychology, 32, 375-383.

Lentz, F. (1985). Evaluating outcomes in programs for behavior disordered children and youth. *Education and Treatment of Children, 8*(4), 321-356.

Levitt, E. (1971). Research in psychotherapy with children. In A. E. Bergin, & S. L. Garfield (Eds.), *Handbook of psychotherapy and behavior change: An empirical analysis*. New York: John Wiley & Sons.

Loeber, R., Dishion, T., & Patterson, G. (1984). Multiple gating: A multistage assessment procedure for identifying youths at risk for delinquency. *Journal of Research in Crime and Delinquency, 21*(1), 7-32.

Lorian, R., Cowen, E., & Caldwell, R. (1974). Problem types of children referred to a school based mental health program. *Journal of Consulting and Clinical Psychology, 42*, 491-496.

Mischel, W. (1968). *Personality and assessment.* New York: John Wiley & Sons.

Mischel, W. (1969). Continuity and change in personality. *American Psychologist, 24*(11), 1012-1018.

Neel, R., & Rutherford, R. (1981). Exclusion of the socially maladjusted from services under P.L. 94-142. Why? What should be done about it? In F. Wood (Ed.), *Perspectives for a new decade: Educators' responsibilities for seriously disturbed and behaviorally disordered children and youth.* Reston VA: Council for Exceptional Children Publications.

Nelson, M. (1971). Techniques for screening conduct disturbed children. *Exceptional Children, 37*, 501-507.

Nelson, R., & Hayes, S. (1979). The nature of behavioral assessment: A commentary. *Journal of Applied Behavior Analysis, 12*, 491-500.

Nicholson, C. (1967). A survey of referral problems in 59 Ohio school districts. *Journal of School Psychology, 5*, 280-286.

Noel, M. (1982). Public school programs for the emotionally disturbed: An overview. In M. Noel & N. Haring (Eds.), *Progress or change: Issues in educating the emotionally disturbed* (Vol 2). Seattle: University of Washington.

Patterson, G. (1964). An empirical approach to the classification of disturbed children. *Journal of Clinical Psychology, 20*, 326-337.

Patterson, G. (1982). *Coercive family process.* Eugene, OR: Castalia Press.

Peterson, D. (1965). Scope and generality of verbally defined personality factors. *Psychological Review, 72*, 48-59.

Phillips, B. (1968). Problem behavior in the elementary school. *Child Development, 39*, 895-903.

Quay, H. (1964). Dimensions of personality in delinquent boys as inferred from the factor analysis of case history data. *Child Development, 35*, 479-484.

Quay, H. (1972). Patterns of aggression, withdrawal, and immaturity. In H. Quay & J. Wherry (Eds.), *Psychopathological disorders of childhood.* New York: John Wiley & Sons.

Quay, H. (1977). Measuring dimensions of deviant behavior: The behavior problem checklist. *Journal of Abnormal Child Psychology, 5, 277-288.*

Reichler, R., & Schopler, E. (1976). Developmental therapy: A program model for providing individual services in the community. In E. Schopler

& R. Reichler (Eds.), *Psychopathology and child development*. New York: Plenum Publishing.

Reitz, A. (1985). Comprehensive evaluation of programs for exceptional children: Summary and future directions. *Education and Treatment of Children, 8*(4), 357-365.

Robbins, R., Mercer, J., & Meyers, C. (1967). The school as a selecting-labeling system. *Journal of School Psychology, 5*, 270-279.

Rodgers-Warren, A. (1984). Ecobehavioral analysis. *Education and Treatment of Children, 7*(4), 283-305.

Romer, D., & Heller, T. (1983). Social adaptation of mentally retarded adults in community settings: A social-ecological approach. *Applied Research in Mental Retardation, 4*, 303-314.

Ross, A. (1971). *Behavior disorders of children*. New York: General Learning Corporation.

Ross, A. (1980). *Psychological disorders of children: A behavioral approach to theory, research and therapy* (2nd ed.). New York: McGraw-Hill.

Ross, A., Lacey, H., & Parton, D. (1965). The development of a behavior checklist for boys. *Child Development, 36*, 1013-1027.

Rubin, R., & Balow, B. (1978). Prevalence of teacher identified behavior problems: A longitudinal study. *Exceptional Children, 45*, 102-113.

Schaefer, E. (1982). Development of adaptive behavior: Conceptual models and family correlates. In M. Begab, H. Barber, & H. C. Haywood (Eds.), *Prevention of retarded development in psycho-socially disadvantaged children*. Baltimore: University Park Press.

Schalock, R. (1984). Comprehensive community services: A plea for interagency collaboration. In R. H. Bruininks & C. Lakin (Eds.), *Living and learning in the least restrictive environment*. Baltimore: Paul H. Brookes.

Semmel, M., Lieber, J., & Peck, C. (in press). Special education environments and their effects: Beyond mainstreaming. In J. Meisels (Ed.), *Mainstreaming*. Hillsdale, NJ: Lawrence Erlbaum.

Shepherd, M., Oppenheim, B., & Mitchell, S. (1971). *Childhood behavior and mental health. New York: Grune & Stratton*.

Smith, C. (1985). *Identification of handicapped children and youth: A state agency perspective on behavioral disorders. Remedial and Special Education, 6*(4), 34-41.

Spivack, G., & Levine, M. (1964). The Devereux child behavior rating scales: A study of symptom behaviors in latency age atypical children. *American Journal of Mental Deficiency, 68*, 700-717.

Spivack, G., & Swift, M. (1966). The Devereux elementary school behavior rating scales: A study of the nature and organization of achievement related disturbed classroom behavior. *Journal of Special Education, 1*, 71-90.

Stokes, T., & Baer, D. (1977). An implicit technology of generalization. *Journal of Applied Behavior Analysis, 10(2)*, 349-358.

Ullmann, L., & Krasner, L. (1965). *Case studies in behavior modification.* New York: Holt, Rinehart & Winston.

Ullmann, L., & Krasner, L. (1969). *A psychological approach to abnormal behavior.* Englewood Cliffs, NJ: Prentice-Hall.

US Department of Education. (1985). *Seventh annual report to congress on the implementation of public law 94-142: The education for all handicapped children act.* Washington, DC: Author.

US Department of Education. (1986). *Eighth annual report to congress on the implementation of public law 94-142: The education for all handicapped children act.* Washington, DC: Author.

Van Hasselt, V., Hersen, M., Whitehill, M., & Bellack, A. (1979). Social skills assessment and training for children: An evaluative review. *Behavior Research and Therapy, 17*, 413-437.

Van Houten, R. (1979). Social validation: The evolution of standards of competency for target behaviors. *Journal of Applied Behavior Analysis, 12*, 581-592.

Wahler, R. (1969). Setting generality: Some specific and general effects of child behavior therapy. *Journal of Applied Behavior Analysis, 2*, 239-246.

Waksman, S., & Jones, V. (1985). *A suggested procedure for the identification and provision of services to seriously emotionally disturbed students* (Technical Assistance Paper #5). Salem, OR: Oregon Department of Education.

Walker, H. M. (1970, revised 1976). *The Walker problem behavior identification checklist (WPBIC)* (Test and manual). Los Angeles: Western Psychological Services.

Walker, H. M. (1977, May). Administrative, logistical, and fiscal considerations in the implementation of CORBEH's behavior management package for the remediation of specific classroom behavior disorders. *Proceedings of the CORRC/Mideast Regional Resource Center Conference on Programming for the Emotionally Handicapped*, 18-30. Washington, DC: Mideast Regional Resource Center.

Walker, H. M. (1979). *The acting out child: Coping with classroom disruption.* Boston: Allyn & Bacon.

Walker, H. M. (1980). *The SBS (social behavior survival) inventory of teacher expectations and social behavior survival* (Initial validation results). Eugene, OR: Center on Human Development, Clinical Services Building, University of Oregon.

Walker, H. M. (1983). *The Walker Problem Behavior Identification Checklist (WPBIC)* (rev. ed.). Los Angeles: Western Psychological Services.

Walker, H. M. (1984). The social behavior survival program (SBS): A systematic approach to the integration of handicapped children into less restrictive settings. *Education and Treatment of Children, 6*(4), 421-441.

Walker, H. M. (1986). The AIMS (Assessments for Integration into Mainstream Settings) assessment system: Rationale, instruments, procedures and outcomes. *Journal of Clinical Child Psychology, 15(1)*, 55-63.

Walker, H. M., & Buckley, N. (1972). Programming generalization and maintenance of treatment effects across time and across settings. *Journal of Applied Behavior Analysis, 5*, 209-224.

Walker, H. M., & Hops, H. (1976). Use of normative peer data as a standard for evaluating classroom treatment effects. *Journal of Applied Behavior Analysis, 9*, 159-168.

Walker, H. M., & Hops, H. (1979). The CLASS program for acting out children: R & D procedures, program outcomes and implementation issues. *School Psychology Digest, 8*, 370-381.

Walker, H. M., Hops, H., & Greenwood, C. R. (1976). Competency-based training issues in the development of behavior management packages for specific classroom behavior disorders. *Behavior Disorders, 1*, 112-122.

Walker, H. M., Hops, H., & Greenwood, C. R. (1984). The CORBEH research and development model: Programmatic issues and strategies. In S. Paine, G. T. Bellamy, & B. Wilcox (Eds.), *Human Services that work*. Baltimore: Paul H. Brookes.

Walker, H. M., Hops, H., & Johnson, S. M. (1975). Generalizations and maintenance of classroom treatment effects. *Behavior Therapy, 6*, 188-200.

Walker, H. M., & McConnell, S. R. (in press). *The Walker-McConnell test of children's social skills*. Austin, TX: PRO-ED.

Walker, H. M., & Rankin, R. (1983). Assessing the behavioral expectations and demands of less restrictive settings. *School Psychology Digest, 12*, 274-284.

Walker, H. M., & Rankin, R. (in press). *Manual for the SBS inventory and child behavior rating scale*. Los Angeles: Western Psychological Services.

Walker, H. M., Reavis, H., Rhode, G., & Jenson, W. (1985). A conceptual model for delivery of behavioral services to behavior disordered children in educational settings. In P. Bornstein & A. Kazdin (Eds.), *Handbook of clinical behavior therapy with children*. Homewood IL: Dorsey Press.

Walker, H. M., Severson, H., & Haring, N. (1985). *Standardized screening and identification of behavior disordered (SSBD) pupils in the elementary age range: Rationale, procedures and guidelines*. Eugene, OR: Center on Human Development, Clinical Services Building, University of Oregon.

Walker, H. M., Severson, H., Haring, N., & Williams, G. (1986). Standardized screening of behavior disordered (SSBD) pupils in the elementary age range. *ADI News, 5*(3), 15-18.

Wherry, J., & Quay, H. (1971). The prevalence of behavior symptoms in younger elementary school children. *American Journal of Orthopsychiatry, 41*, 136-143.

Wickman, E. (1928). *Children's behavior and teachers' attitudes*. New York: The Commonwealth Fund.

Wood, F. (1985). Decision making: Eligibility and programming options. In F. Wood, C. Smith, & J. Grimes (Eds.), *The Iowa assessment model in behavioral disorders: A training manual*. Des Moines: Department of Public Instruction, State of Iowa.

Wood, F., & Lakin, K. (1979). *Disturbing, disordered, or disturbed? Perspectives on the definition of problem behavior in educational settings*. Minneapolis: Advanced Training Institute, University of Minnesota.

Wood, F., Smith, C., & Grimes, J. (Eds.). (1985). *The Iowa assessment model in behavioral disorders: A training manual*. Des Moines: Department of Public Instruction, State of Iowa.

Ysseldyke, J., & Algozzine, B. (1982). *Critical issues in special and remedial education*. Boston: Houghton Mifflin.

Ysseldyke, J., Algozzine, B., & Epps, S. (1982). A logical and empirical analysis of current practices in classifying students as handicapped. *Exceptional Children, 49*.

Ysseldyke, J., Algozzine, B., Shinn, M., & McGue, M. (1982). Similarities and differences between underachievers and students classified learning disabled. *Journal of Special Education, 16*, 73-85.

Ysseldyke, J., Christenson, S., Pianta, B., & Algozzine, B. (1983). An analysis of teachers' reasons and desired outcomes for students referred for psychoeducational assessment. *Journal of Psychoeducational Assessment, 1*, 73-83.

Ysseldyke, J., Thurlow, M., Graden, J., Wesson, C., Algozzine, R., & Deno, S. (1983). Generalizations from five years of research on assessment and decision making. *Exceptional Education Quarterly, 4*, 75-93.

THEORY INTO PRACTICE: AN OVERVIEW OF PUBLIC SCHOOL PROGRAMS FOR THE BEHAVIORALLY DISORDERED[1]

Margaret J. McLaughlin

Educational intervention and management of behaviorally disordered (BD) students have a relatively short history. Although public school programs began to be developed only about 25 years ago, there has always been a certain schizophrenia surrounding the responsibility for and nature of programs for behaviorally disordered. These students have been, and to a significant degree continue to be, "treated" or "managed" in psychiatric or mental health facilities and "educated" in school programs. This chapter will focus on the nature of public school education. As such, it is limited to a review and discussion of some of the program models that can operate within the public schools.

Clearly evident from the review is that present public school programs for the behaviorally disordered lack a comprehensive conceptual model. Programs that have been developed for this population reflect several different theoretical approaches. These differences influence the programs in terms of focus of intervention as well as administrative arrangements. The diversity in programming appears to be, in large part, the result of at least one pervasive issue confronting the field of emotional disturbance. The issue of inadequate definition consistently emerged in the literature as a major impediment to the provision of special education services and reflects the complexity of the problems presented to educators who work with behaviorally disordered students.

This chapter has been organized to present a brief historical review of general programming efforts and an overview of the major conceptual models that have developed within special education for the behaviorally disordered. Finally, examples of current programming strategies will be presented and recommendations or observations regarding future directions will be suggested.

History

Special education for the behaviorally disordered has a relatively short history. Paul and Warnock (1980), in an overview of the changes that have occurred within the field, note that educational responsibility for these students did not become a major emphasis until the early 1960s. Prior to that time, BD students were generally considered to be the responsibility of the mental health system. Paul and Warnock attribute the shift in responsibility to several factors, including a lack of mental health professionals, a growing realization that psychiatric and institutional treatment were inadequate as well as inhumane, and a questioning of the legitimacy of use of the medical paradigm of emotional "sickness" or "illness."

The failure of the mental health movement of the 1930s and 1940s to deal effectively with behaviorally disordered youth provided the major impetus for the development of special programs within the public schools (Haring & Phillips, 1962; Morse, Cutler, & Fink, 1964). Whether due to lack of resources, such as personnel, or of a basic knowledge base, child guidance clinics, mental health centers, and other similar psychiatrically oriented facilities were failing to meet the needs of the behaviorally disordered. Not only were the programs in these facilities ineffective, they were, in fact, considered to have negative effects on children because they necessitated the separation of the child from the home and community.

The more mildly to moderately BD students, not considered serious enough for institutional placement, had no options. They frequently dropped out of school or, more likely, were given disciplinary expulsion, considered unteachable, and removed from the school system (Paul & Warnock, 1980). In general, the public schools had few programs and few intervention models, and furthermore, had no useful way of classifying these students. In 1948 only 90 school districts in the entire United States were operating programs for what was termed the emotionally disturbed (Mackie, 1969). In 1958, as the dissatisfaction with the mental health movement reached crisis proportion, Knoblock (1963) sampled 5000 public school districts in the U.S. and found that only 500–a tenth–were providing some sort of service to emotionally disturbed students.

As educational programs and services began to be developed in the late 1950s and early 1960s, the lack of a common set of characteristics of classifications for the behaviorally disordered student began to be noted. Knoblock (1963), citing the reasons for the slow development of these programs, noted the problem of the wide array of symptoms and characteristics presented by the students; this diversity coupled with the related problem of role conflict between educators and mental health professionals had resulted in confusion and a lack of cohesive program models for public schools. Earlier, Quay (1963) cautioned that, while public schools may have been in a rush to create programs for the emotionally disturbed in response to community demands, the field had inadequate knowledge about these students to guide program development. In particular, he expressed concern that classifications, placements, and programs were being based on clinical impressions and quasi-personality theory and were failing to recognize the variety of behaviors exhibited by these students.

In fact, many early programs for the emotionally disturbed were marked by a confusion over the role of mental health and traditional psychodynamic treatment models and that of education. Lacking both a body of empirical knowledge regarding treatment or management and a concept of emotional disturbance, public schools developed programs that ran the gamut from psychiatric to traditional education. The results of two surveys of public school programs conducted during the 1960s, the well-known Morse, Cutler, and Fink (1964) study, and a national survey conducted by Adamson (1968), both demonstrated this lack of a common conceptualization for emotional disturbance an program orientation.

One of the major observations noted by Morse and his colleagues was the variability in classifications and definitions used by states. While some states maintained a very clinical psychological classification system, others varied between the more behavioral and descriptive to defining the population as simply "socially maladjusted." The programs provided by the schools reflected the same lack of cohesiveness and were characterized by general goals and a variety of administrative arrangements and philosophical orientations.

Morse identified seven categories of programs that were in operation across the states. These included: (a) psychiatric dynamic–programs in which education played a secondary role to "therapy"; (b) psychoeducational– programs representing a blend between psychodynamic concepts an education; (c) psychological-behavioral–programs based on learning theory and representing a more structured approach; (d) educational–programs characterized by formal, accepted, regular education procedures and curricula, with little or not theoretical design; (e) naturistic–programs with no specific design or organized approach in which teachers responded to behavior as it came; (f) primitive–programs with aloof teachers who maintained control through domination and fear; and (g) chaotic–classes in which there was not order or no organized program. The type found most often was the formal educational variety, followed by the psychoeducational approach. Regardless of philosophical orientation, however, all of the school programs tended to exist in isolation from other treatments or interventions. There was little or no communication or cooperation with other agencies or individuals serving the behaviorally disordered student, thus no continuity of treatment existed across settings. In addition, while these programs were in public schools, they were frequently run in special segregated classrooms, and only a third provided some degree of integration of the behaviorally disordered students with nonhandicapped peers.

Adamson's (1968) survey provided some substantiation that programs for the behaviorally disordered were growing. He identified a total of 2,800 classrooms in the United States which were serving 35,000 children. Seventy-five percent of these classes, however, were in states that had no requirements for specially trained teachers or provided any program guidelines. This lack of program direction was also noted by Knoblock and Johnson (1967). However, while they recognized the conceptual and organizational problems within the field, they were optimistic that the public schools were beginning to define better their role as service providers. They expressed optimism that there was impetus from within the field for change and that, coupled with increases in federal funding, a wide range of programs with proven effectiveness would be developed.

This optimism was not realized, however as the situation did not improve during the early part of the next decade. Schultz, Hirshoren, Manton, and Henderson (1971), reporting data from a survey conducted in 1970 of all 50 states and the District of Columbia, found that six different terms were being used to define emotional disturbance, and while a range of 12 different service delivery options was defined, there was no consistent methodology for program organization. They too attributed the scattered and slow growth of programs and services to the problems in defining and identifying the population. In terms of service delivery arrangements, they found that the most frequent service option being provided was the special class (47 states). Forty states reported having resource room programs for behaviorally disordered students. Thirty-eight states, however, also indicated that homebound instruction was a frequently used option. Of particular note is that no measures of program effectiveness were provided by any state. This lack of program evaluation data was also noted by Vacc (1972), who questioned the fact that the professional literature was concentrating on describing projects or suggesting methodologies, but was providing little data on overall program effectiveness.

Even with the lack of data, some positive trends were becoming apparent at the beginning of the 1970s. Most notably there appeared to be a shift toward more integration of the emotionally-disturbed into the regular education mainstream through use of resource rooms or a form of consultant-teacher models. There was also a recognition of the importance of developing comprehensive community-based treatment programs that involved the public schools as the major "treatment" option, in cooperation with other child-centered agencies (Joint Commission on Mental Health of Children, 1970). The notion that special education was pivotal in the overall programming for BD children seemed firmly established. Some individuals, notably Morse (1970), remained concerned that public school

programs for the behaviorally disordered continued to be "muddled," and that existing programs were characterized by "futility." He felt that the public schools had lost confidence in all the traditional treatments, but were still without a unified treatment approach.

The decade of the 1970s saw some of the most massive changes in special education. The national right-to-education movement resulted in the Education for All Handicapped Children Act that became Public Law 94-142 in 1975. With this new legislative mandate, public schools began to spur development of educational programs for their handicapped students. The impact of PL 94-142 on the education of handicapped children has been monumental. The effect on service delivery to the behaviorally disordered, however, may be questionable. First, there was the lack of a unifying theory that could serve as the basis for program development (Apter, 1977; Paul, 1977; Rhodes & Paul, 1978). In addition, there was concern that programs were not "flexible" or eclectic enough to match the wide range of characteristics of the behaviorally disordered. A second area of concern surrounded the concept of education in the least restrictive environment (LRE), which required public schools to provide a continuum of service options, such as special classes and resource rooms, which would allow for placement based on educational need and not on disability label.

From the inception of the field, the trend had been to segregate the behaviorally disordered from the nonhandicapped to "relieve tensions" and to protect the nonhandicapped. In 1979, Hirshoren and Heller published the results of a national survey of services being provided to behavior disordered adolescents. While they were specifically interested in secondary programs, they felt that their data reflected program development for all behavior disordered students. Once again, the most frequently utilized service model was the special segregated classroom. In addition, while 42 states had their programs administered by LEAs, some states turned their program administration and operation over to state hospitals or private mental health facilities.

Perhaps the most current statement regarding educational service delivery was compiled by the National Needs Analysis Project (Grosenick & Huntze, 1983). This project collected and analyzed data from a number of sources, the most extensive being the Annual Program Plans submitted by states to Special Education Programs (formerly the Office of Special Education). Information was collected on a number of major issues, including definition, teacher training and certification, personnel, and service delivery options.

The results of this survey do not speak well for the growth of the field. The most striking statistic is that, even based on conservative estimates, it appears that three-fourths of the children and youth with serious behavior disorders, some 741,000 students, were not being provided special education services. In addition, the report indicated that there was a prevalent feeling within the field that many of the programs that did exist were inappropriate or of poor quality, primarily because of the lack of trained and certified teachers.

In terms of service delivery, the survey did find that between 85 and 95% of all students who were labeled "Seriously Behaviorally Disordered" were being served in public school facilities. In addition, most states indicated that they provided several types of program options; however the most commonly used option was still the within-district special class. Some variety of resource room was the next most frequent option, although the report stated that districts fluctuated greatly in use of this type of program.

With respect to use of more restrictive placements, such as special day schools, residential placement, or homebound instruction, states varied considerably. In several states where such options were used, emotionally-disturbed students were placed more often than those with other types of handicaps. The data on use of homebound instruction were particularly notable, as nearly 40% of all handicapped students who were receiving this service were identified as "Seriously Behaviorally Disordered." The report concluded that these dismal statistics may be indicative of the overall "frustration and difficulty" public schools face in dealing with these students.

After nearly two decades of public school involvement with the behaviorally disordered, one must question the progress that has been made in providing educational services. Despite the influx of federal monies and the creation of legal mandates for service, the optimism expressed by Knoblock in 1963 has not been confirmed. However, neither the dismal statistics nor the professional lamentation reflect total lack of progress in the development of interventions or programs. In fact, there has been, from the field's inception, a body of literature that represents several schools of thought or conceptual models related to identification of and intervention with the emotionally disturbed. The major models have been identified and organized through the work of William Rhodes and Michael Tracy and their colleagues at the University of Michigan (Rhodes & Tracy, 1972a, 1972b). They identified six basic conceptual models for intervention with behaviorally disordered students. While all six models have contributed to the general knowledge base in the area of emotional disturbance, four of the models (i.e., the psychodynamic, the psychoeducational, the behavioral, and the ecological) have had more wide-reaching applications within the public schools. These four models for intervention will be reviewed briefly in the following sections. In addition, a fifth approach, the psychoneurological, will also be discussed. While this approach was initially more closely identified with education of the "minimal brain damaged" student, it was not uncommon for children who exhibited behavior disorders such as impulsivity and hyperactivity, or who were generally acting out, to be diagnosed and treated as minimally brain damaged (Clements, 1966).

Conceptual Models

The six conceptual models, identified by Rhodes and Tracy, were drawn from the literature in the field of emotional disturbance and include: biophysical theory, psychodynamic theory, learning theory, ecological theory, sociological theory, and counter-theory. Each model is defined by its basic principles or theories regarding the origin of behavior deviance as well as the nature of its interventions. The influence of each of these models on special education progress has varied over the past 20 years. However, as noted earlier, four of the models have had a more pronounced impact on educational programming.

Psychodynamic and Psychoeducational Models

Perhaps the most prevalent intervention models in the late 1950s and early 1960s were the psychodynamic and the psychoeducational. The former was derived from traditional psychoanalytic theory, with its emphasis on internal states and its focus on the subconscious as the cause of disturbance. Intervention strategies were focused on individual therapy. Two approaches that epitomized the psychodynamic model were developed by Berkowitz and Rothman (1960) and Redl (1959). In general these approaches viewed education as an extension of the therapy process. The basic goals for programs within those models reflect classical psychodynamic therapy, with its concern for id, ego, and superego. Education was oriented toward achieving self-awareness and knowledge of the environment, building relationships with others, and in general defining the building the ego.

Thus, the educational programs organized within these models were characterized by a more permissive approach, stressing communication, "active" learning, sensory involvement, and child-defined goals. The curriculum and learning activities focused on the student's feelings and encouraged exploration of inner thoughts and expression of feelings.

The traditional psychodynamic therapeutic models constituted a major approach to treatment of behaviorally disordered children at all levels of severity. As public schools began to assume a primary responsibility for the education of the behaviorally disordered, however, it became apparent that the psychodynamic model was neither cost effective nor time efficient. Specifically, it was not appropriate for classroom adaptation because treatment methodology relied exclusively on the direction of psychiatrists, child psychologists, and other clinical professionals. The recognition of the importance of education in its own right became the major impetus for development of the following models.

The psychoeducational model emerged in the late 1950s (Long, Morse, & Newman, 1971; Morse, 1975) and represents a compromise between educational and psychotherapy. While psychoeducational programs recognized the importance of the individual child's psychosocial developmental level as well as the internal dynamics of behavior, they also stressed the importance of education and achievement in the total treatment plan. Special education teachers were not viewed as mere technicians operating at the direction of psychiatrists, but rather as program managers who used clinicians as adjuncts.

Psychoeducational programs were focused on "therapeutic education" (Morse, 1976) and were guided by educational goals and objectives and characterized by comprehensive assessment, including psychological and educational measurement. Individualized instruction plans were based on both academic achievement and the student's emotional and social developmental levels. While the need for classroom "limits" and structure was noted, there was also concern for developing a warm and accepting learning environment, fostering positive relationships between teacher and child, and strengthening the child's sense of self-control.

The content of individual school programs was compatible with both the student's educational and emotional needs. As such, educational experiences, including behavior management, were utilized to help the child cope with the daily environment. The "crisis teacher," a concept developed by William Morse (1976), is perhaps one of the clearest examples of the blend of education and psychological therapy in the psychoeducational approach to managing the behaviorally disordered student. This individual, a combination of a special educator and clinical worker, serves as a resource to the classroom teacher, and can work as tutor as well as quasi-therapist in assisting children in dealing with their behaviors.

The psychoeducational model became one of the first educational approaches to programming for the behaviorally disordered. At the same time that Morse and his colleagues were defining this concept of "clinical" education, however, a new educational technology, based on the concepts of learning theory, began to surface in special education.

Behavioral Model

The behavioral approach to management of the behaviorally disordered in public schools first began to reach prominence with the publication of the Haring and Phillips (1962) work, Educating Emotionally Disturbed Children. The authors presented a model for programming for the BD student which was founded on the basic premises of learning theory. The strategies of the program incorporated principles such as reinforcement and extinction within a structured, orderly environment that included reduced stimuli, direct instruction, and immediate feedback. Another major example of a program based on behavioral principles was the Engineered Classroom developed by Hewett (1968).

The behavioral programs were guided by the principle that the behaviors exhibited by BD students should be the focus for "treatment." While the behaviorists were not unconcerned about the student's feelings or the need for an accepting environment, the programs focused on the precise identification of maladaptive or "disturbed" behaviors, identification of the events in the immediate environment which maintained that behavior, and changes in the environment which facilitated the learning of appropriate behaviors.

The behavioral model places responsibility for the education of the behaviorally disordered squarely on the special educator, whose role is that of learning specialist. The role of the clinician is moved outside the classroom, and the development of specific academic skills and appropriate behaviors becomes the goal of the intervention strategies.

Like the psychoeducational model, the behavioral model espoused individual assessment and individualized instruction. In the latter model, however, assessment consists of direct observation, and results in the precise definition of observable behaviors, as opposed to the clinical interpretation of those behaviors. Instructional programming in both cases recognizes that learning occurs in stages or sequences. The behaviorist, however, does not define a child's level of instruction in terms of normalized theories of emotional or affective development. Rather, learning sequences or hierarchies are derived from the principle of behavior shaping.

While the behavioral model and the psychoeducational model dominated the field during the 1960s, the end of the decade saw the rise of a fourth major conceptual model, vased on the ecological perspective.

Ecological Model

The ecological theorists assume what they call an "interactionist perspective" (Paul & Warnock, 1980). That is, behavior disorders are viewed as an interaction between the individual's behavior and the norms and expectations of the environment. As such, this perspective incorporates thinking from sociology as well as developmental theory and focuses on the discrepancy between what an individual is doing and what his or her "normal" peers are doing. Accordingly, these theorists acknowledge that specific behaviors are contingent upon events and expectations from the environment. Educational interventions are thus designed to include the total environment in which the child is expected to function.

Two of the major proponents of ecological interventions include William Rhodes (1967, 1970) and Nicholas Hobbs (1966). Hobbs's Re-Education (Re-Ed) Program, initially developed as a residential program, provides comprehensive intervention or treatment, including active participation of families, schools, various child service agencies, and neighborhoods. The major goals of Re-Ed encompass both positive academic and behavioral changes in the child, as well as change in the child's ecology or environment. Education is a major component of the ecological approach–a recognition of the learned nature of behavior. As such, education becomes the major strategy for changing the child's behavior as well as the behavior of those with whom he or she interacts.

Biophysical or Psychoneurological

Among the early public school programs for handicapped students were those based on biophysical or psychoneurological theories. These programs focused on specific behavior disorders that were seen as a result of a dysfunction within the central nervous system. Major researchers and theoreticians representing this school of thought have included Strauss and Lehtinen (1947), Cruickshank, Bentzen, Ratzeburg, and Tannhauser (1961), and Rapaport (1951), and the major educational intervention or treatment strategy that grew out of this perspective has been called the structured approach.

Specific treatment plans included an in-depth analysis of an individual's strengths and deficits; the development of an individual educational prescription, focusing heavily on motor, perceptual, and attentional disorders; and the management of behavior through use of a structured or stimulus-controlled environment. As hyperactivity and poor impulse control are characteristics shared by the minimally brain damaged and many "behaviorally disordered" students, some programs for the latter incorporated the structured environment into their design.

Only five of the more dominant conceptual models for intervention in education for the behaviorally disordered have been reviewed; it should be acknowledged, however, that other models, specifically the humanistic and counter-culture, have contributed to development of programs. For a more thorough review, the reader is referred to Rhodes and Tracy (1972a, 1972b).

Recent Approaches

This section reviews the more current literature and what is currently being done to educate behaviorally disabled students within the public schools. Particular attention has been devoted to identifying trends in the conceptual orientations of programs as well as to examining the nature of services that are being provided to these students. The review was limited to the programs either known to be currently in operation or those that have been reported in the literature over the past ten years. The specific intent was to determine if an organizing framework or a general conceptual model for educating behaviorally disordered students is evident within the field.

The lack of a consistent approach to programming for the behaviorally disordered student has long been discussed. Harshman (1969) cited the wide variety of approaches in use during the 1960s, and eight years later, Paul (1977) and Feiner and Tarnow (1977) were all decrying the lack of a single organizing framework or model. While there appeared to be less reliance on psychodynamic approaches and more eclecticism, a need for coordinating and integrating services across agencies was cited. While these authors believed that services should be delivered by the public schools, they also felt that the services should be developed in coordination with other disciplines, such as medicine, psychiatry, and social work. This need for combining services "to provide flexible adaptations of intervention" also was noted by Wood (1979), who felt that pure educational interventions were limited. In addition, Wood specifically noted the need for eclectic and flexible interventions, ranging from highly-structured environments to the more unstructured and "therapeutic" classrooms.

More recently, Grosenick and Huntze (1983) and Lakin (1982) reviewed the literature on public school programs and practices for behaviorally disordered students and concluded that there was sparse information about the characteristics of programs, leading Grosenick and Huntze to conclude that the literature "was not reflective of well-conceptualized programs" (p. 20). Nonetheless, Stainback and Stainback (1980) did identify several trends in programming for the behaviorally disordered. These include increased application of "direct and functional methods for identification and programming" as well as intensive, individualized instruction. In addition, these authors note a trend in educational programs to focus on a student's total environment and to move away from isolated treatments. These statements would suggest that the field is, at last, responding in an organized fashion to the educational needs of the behaviorally disordered student. However positive this may appear, the authors did not provide specific examples of programs.

Thus, a review of public school administered programs is justified, if only to affirm the aforementioned trends. This review was limited to programs reported in the professional literature and included journal articles, reports, conference papers, and dissertations, as well as a review of 30 current federally funded model demonstration programs that are serving behaviorally disordered students (Mirkes, 1981). Only programs that specifically served behaviorally disordered or emotionally disturbed students were included. Thus, programs serving the "mildly handicapped" or similar generic programs were not reviewed. Also not reviewed were programs that were administered solely by agencies other than the public schools. Finally, this review excluded "practices," that is, isolated interventions or strategies that have been used with the behaviorally disordered. For purposes of organization the programs have been divided into the following categories: (a) basic instructional, (b) interagency programs, (c) special schools, (d) vocational programs, and (e) preschool programs. Each program was examined in terms of its major focus according to category as well as its conceptual or theoretical approach.

Instructional Programs

These programs, defined by their basic emphasis on academic instruction, represent by far the largest category. This should come as no surprise, as basic academic instruction has long been advocated for programs for the behaviorally disordered (Haring & Phillips, 1962; Hewett, 1968; Morse, 1976). Among the recent programs reviewed, some clearly adhered to a specific identifiable model or theoretical orientation, while others appeared more eclectic or were undefinable.

Among the 30 federal projects that reported serving "seriously behaviorally disordered" students, eight have a basic educational focus, including in-depth assessment of academic achievement, assessment of behavior problems, and the subsequent development of prescriptive educational plans. While differences exist among these programs in terms of specific curricula, they are alike in terms of their orientation to academic instruction. Four of these programs are noncategorical and include variations on the basic instructional approach, such a use of peer tutors or a computer system for generating instructional objectives and daily programs (Mirkes, 1981).

The general literature was perhaps less definitive, perhaps due to the move toward noncategorical programs for the mildly to moderately handicapped. Since the mid-1970s there has been a focus on children with learning and behavior disorders (see Blankenship & Lilly, 1981; Hallahan & Kauffman, 1977; Hammill & Bartel, 1978; Stephens, 1977; Wallace & Kauffman, 1978). Despite the inclusion of behavior disorders, the bulk of these programs is more commonly referred to as learning disabled programs. In general, they include precise academic assessment, individualized programming, and direct instruction.

Full Service Programs. Included in this category were programs in both special classes and resource rooms that provided academic instruction, behavioral interventions and all other services to the BD student, utilizing public school staff. Several special class programs (Buck & Markson, 1982; District of Columbia Public Schools, 1981; Hannafin, 1978; Vetter-Zemitzsch, Bernstein, Johnston, Larson, Simon, & Smith, 1984) were described in the literature as focused on developing basic academic and personal skills with "behavioral interventions" and group counseling. The primary focus of these programs appeared to be basic skill training with all services provided within the public school classroom by teachers or counselors. Among the full service instructional programs were several resource room or partial day arrangements which again had, as their primary focus, academic instruction and behavior management. Examples of these resource room programs include one reported by Gottlieb (1976) in New York which provided basic academic skill instruction and employed a token reinforcement program. Two other resource room programs were reported by Klein (1980) and Toker and Hoeltke (1978). The former, which operates in a junior high school in Minnesota, provides one to three hours a day of specialized academic instruction along with a systematic behavior management program. The program utilizes behavioral contracts and a token system that includes awarding points for demonstrating appropriate behaviors within the regular classrooms.

The second program is described as a basic resource room approach for behaviorally disturbed students in which the intervention plans focus first on the student's behaviors and "attitudes" and then on the individual academic needs. Specific techniques employed include providing structure, developing communication abilities, developing "awareness" and interests, and encouraging self-expression.

Consultant or Support Models. Among the variations of the instructional program, the consultant model (Blankenship & Lilly, 1981; Nelson & Stevens, 1981; Tharp & Wetzel, 1970) was one of the more widely used. This model involves the provision of support services and training to classroom teachers who are in turn responsible for delivering service directly to the student who is experiencing learning problems or exhibiting inappropriate behavior.

One variation of this model was described by McGlothlin (1978), who developed a School Referral Committee (SRC) comprised of regular classroom teachers, special education teacher, a school psychologist, and the building principal for the purpose of receiving referrals, defining specific student problems, and developing classroom-based interventions. The major purpose of the SRC is to maintain the student in the regular classroom. Thus, in this model, classroom teachers are heavily involved in developing specific realistic interventions and are provided with direct assistance and training in implementing the interventions.

Wixson (1980) also reported a successful implementation of a variation of the consultant model in an educational service district in Pennsylvania. In this program the special education teacher provided direct service to learning and emotionally disordered students in a special resource room, and indirect services, such as assessment, evaluation, and teacher consultation, in the regular classroom.

Nagrodsky (1977) utilized a team approach, including special education teachers and a Title I reading specialist, to provide consultation on program modifications and support to regular classroom teacher who had behaviorally disordered and learning disabled students in their classes. A somewhat less academic approach reported by Carroll et al. (1978) was essentially a modification of the crisis teacher approach in that the special teacher provided support and consultation to regular classroom teachers in the management of behavior and academic problems of mainstreamed behaviorally disordered students. The special teacher also served as a back-up teacher responsible for counseling students in crisis. A further example includes a secondary school program reported by Anderson (1980) for behaviorally disordered adolescents that provided outreach counselors in the public schools to assist mainstreamed students.

A major variation of a consultant model is the Adaptive Learning Environments (ALE) model, which has been developed by Wang and her colleagues at the University of Pittsburgh. The ALE is a noncategorical model that calls for the provision of special education services within the context of the regular classroom. Thus, any child who is experiencing learning or behavior problems can receive services within the regular classroom either directly from a specialist or from the classroom teacher in cooperation with the special teacher. In the latter case, the specialist assists the classroom teacher in modifying or adapting the child's academic program and learning experience (Mirkes, 1981).

Alternative approaches focusing on educating the behaviorally disordered student within the regular classroom have included both direct instruction to teachers and provision of special programs or materials. Two recent examples of such an approach are those developed by Edwards (1980) and Kaeck (1978). Both utilize an external behavior manager who develops individual student management programs, modifies curricula and provides training to teachers in implementing the programs. Walker and his colleagues (Walker & Hops, 1979; Walker, Hops, & Greenwood, 1976) developed four comprehensive behavior management packages, CLASS, PEERS, PASS, and RECESS, designed specifically for use by classroom teachers. These packages, which contain identification and assessment criteria, include specific interventions for use with children who have low academic skills, are acting out, withdrawn, or aggressive. The packages provide a systematic approach for pinpointing problem behaviors and selecting an appropriate target behavior for training. They focus on maintaining the behavior disordered student in the regular classroom.

A final example of a consultant or support approach is one based on ecological and developmental theory, which has been developed by the Intervention by Prescription Project at the University of Michigan–Dearborn. This program utilizes a full-team approach; the team consists of special teacher, diagnostician, psychologist, and social worker. The team conducts an ecological assessment of children who have been referred from the regular classroom for behavior problems and then develops individualized interventions that match both the developmental level and the specific environment of the child (Mirkes, 1981). Again the major intent is to maintain the child in the regular classroom.

Within the general category of "instructional programs," it appears that the behavioral model has had a major influence, particularly as evidenced by the emphasis on direct assessment and instruction. The efficacy of the basic academic orientation with behaviorally disabled student has been demonstrated in the past (Glavin, Quay, & Werry, 1971), and if the numbers of instructional programs are indicative of the future, it will undoubtedly remain a major program type for the behaviorally disordered student in the public school.

Interagency Programs

A secondary major category of programs includes those that provide general instruction in basic skills with additional services, such as psychological counseling or psychiatric treatment, social skill training, and vocational training provided in cooperation with another agency. By far the most common of these types of programs involve cooperative arrangements between the public school and a community mental health agency. The defining characteristics of the programs include a structured academic remediation program and the provision of some type of individual or group therapy, provided by mental health professionals. While the notion of providing therapy within a school-based program is closely aligned with both the psychoeducational and Re-Ed models, many of the current programs within this category have strong behavioral orientations, particularly those operating in the classroom setting.

The concept of providing mental health services in conjunction with the public schools is not new. Knoblock and Garcea (1965) proposed a model that utilized mental health professionals in public school classes to provide both direct therapeutic counseling to students as well as training to teachers. In 1970, Clarizio and McCoy, noting the fragmentation of services which exists when both the mental health agency and public school are intervening with behaviorally disordered students, proposed a centralization of services. They recommended that the public school become the treatment site for the behaviorally disordered student and that mental health professionals provide consultant services, such as diagnostic evaluation, teacher support, and emergency or crisis treatment.

Among the current programs, there are essentially two types of school/mental health agency arrangements. The first involves a special class or resource room placement within a public school setting, staffed with special education teachers who work in direct cooperation with mental health counselors or psychologists. An early example of this model was reported by Marrone (1970). This program consisted of special classes that operated within a regular public school. The intervention plan included intensive academic remediation, chemotherapy, group and individual therapy, and some behavioral interventions. Mental health professionals provided direct services to students, including group and individual therapy as needed within the mental health setting.

Some of programs for the behaviorally disordered involve cooperation between the public schools and mental health agencies. Most of these programs follow the same model, which includes provision of a traditional educational program within public school classrooms with group and/or individual therapy provided by mental health professionals. A more typical example was described by Marshall and Lowenstein (Mirkes, 1981) operating in Dade County, Florida. Students in this program are provided academic instruction within a special self-contained class, modeled after Hewett's Engineered Classroom. As part of their total educational plan, therapeutic services are provided directly by mental health counselors working within the public school building. Similar programs were described by Bostrom and Thunder (1976), Cobberly (1978), Garrett et al. (1979), LeVine, Rittenhouse, Smith, and Thompson (1981), Patton (1979), Thompson (1978), and Wasserman and Adamany (1976). While these programs differed somewhat in terms of age group addressed, all described structured academic classrooms with some behavioral "treatment" or "modification" and individual and group therapy provided by mental health professionals. The programs did vary in the degree to which this therapy was an integral part of the students' program versus an optional support service that could be available to selected students and in some cases their families.

A variation of the cooperative model was reported by Lillesand (1977) and combined a behavioral and psychotherapeutic approach. This special class program, designed for severely behavior disordered elementary age students, is sponsored by the Department of Youth Services and operates in cooperation with the public schools. The special classes, located in classrooms outside of the public school building, provide instruction focused on developing appropriate classroom behaviors, such as attention to task and independent learning, while providing remediation of academic deficits. The students progress through a series of steps, beginning with a highly structured token economy that is faded until students are receiving naturally occurring reinforcers and are phased back into the public school. Therapy and counseling are provided to students and families on an as-needed basis.

Another version of the school/mental health model, reported by Purdon (1979), is based on Redl's "therapeutic milieu" concept, and incorporates basic therapy into the total educational program. This program employs the combined resources of the public school and the community mental health agency. The student's "educational" plan stresses group process goals, individual therapy and counseling, and related psychotherapeutic interventions. A further example of the dual approach to intervention with the behaviorally disordered is a program operated at Children's Hospital in San Francisco (Linnibran, 1977), which provides a partial day program for behavior disordered adolescents. The program consists of individual and group psychotherapy and provides structured social interaction through art and recreation. Students participate for three hours a day and for the remainder of the time are involved in normal community programs, such as public school or vocational training. The center program is designed to support and subsidize, rather than supplant, existing educational services.

Special Programs

Included within this category are all programs that are separate from the basic academic instructional program operating in a regular comprehensive public school. Such programs include alternative schools or programs within schools, or supplementary programs like social skill training and career/vocational education. Of the alternative programs, or those providing a nontraditional approach to curricula, none were evident in the literature. A number of special schools or centers were described that provided specialized services to the behaviorally disordered adolescent, but all offered a basic academic and/or vocational training program. For example, Johnson (1977) and Ramsey and Sickles (1978) reported on an alternative school in Florida serving severely emotionally disturbed adolescents. The school offers a highly structured program of academic and vocational training organized around a token economy and employing precision teaching. A second alternative school, located in Illinois, was described by Lane, Bonic, and Wallgren-Bonic (1983). This school, also for high school students with "significant behavioral and/or emotional problems", was also a full-time educational program that included adaptive physical education, socialization training, and a reality therapy approach. Webster (1981) also described an alternative school that provided academic training and also offered vocational training through job training. Other examples of such special schools include the Madison School in Minneapolis (Braaten, 1979); the Woodward School in Massachusetts (Kennedy, Mitchell, Klerman, & Murray, 1976), the Mark Twain School in Montgomery County, Maryland (Laneve, 1979), and Cheltenham School in Prince Georges County, Maryland (Leone, 1984; Stetson & Rhead, 1984). While the programs offered within these schools differ somewhat in philosophical approach, they all provide, as part of the total educational program, specialized related services such as counseling or therapy and/or vocational and prevocational training. The schools function as total units, separate from the normal public school environment, and the degree of daily integration with nonhandicapped peers is limited or nonexistent.

The lack of alternative, nontraditional school programs for the behaviorally disordered is apparently reflective of what exists in the field, for as Grosenick and Huntze (1983) note in their review, behaviorally disordered students are, in fact, usually not served in these programs, as evidenced by the lack of such programs in this present review.

Vocational/Career Awareness Programs

Of all of the programs, among the more common were those that provided some form of vocational or career training either as the sole intervention or as a major part of an academic program. These programs are generally designed for junior high and high school students and employ specialized curricula designed to increase career awareness. In general they also provide structured and systematic training of critical employability skills, such as communication and social interactions. In addition, the programs offer functional skill training in reading and computation as an alternative to the standard school curricula for those students with significant achievement deficits.

One example of a comprehensive vocational program is the Experience Based Career Education (EBCE) model. Initially developed in the late 1960s by Appalachia Regional Education Laboratory, this model has been successfully replicated with mildly handicapped adolescents (Mirkes, 1981) and constitutes a total vocational program. While there are a number of variations, the basic program provides structured career awareness, through both classroom activities and on-site job sampling, and then moves students into employment sites for training. Intensive support and supervision are provided to students and employers. In the latter case EBCE staff provide specific techniques for training or managing the student on the job site. Academic instruction is individualized and functional in that it relates to the world of work.

Another example is Project ADVANCE (Adams & Bielicki, 1981; Waller, 1978) which is jointly administered by a public school and vocational/technical school. The highly structured behavioral program provides a dual focus on academic performance and vocational training. Simek et al. (1980) described a program for emotionally disturbed secondary students that provided career experience studies and monitored and supported job placements. At least two of the vocational programs (Tomalesky & Jackson, 1984; Stein et al., 1976) provided individual and/or group counseling along with academic and job training.

A final example of a program with a career awareness emphasis is an adapted Foxfire model, Project Sense of Pride (Mirkes, 1981). The program is offered for behaviorally disordered students within the public schools and is considered a supplement to the prescribed educational program. Students involved in the classes produce and market their own magazine, which contains interviews with handicapped adults who have made successful life adjustments as well as with employers in a variety of job and career settings.

A less intensive type of vocational program is the part-time program that supplements the regular education program. Richmond (1978) described a highly-structured, part-time prevocational program for behaviorally disordered adolescents conducted in an off-campus leased building. Students attended the program for several hours each day and received job skill training in several vocational areas. They also participated in a structured recreation program. A major focus of this program was the development of appropriate social skills, and living skills such a sewing, cooking, and reading the newspaper. All students were enrolled in a regular high school for some portion of the day, but could also receive instruction in functional reading and computation as well as tutoring within the part-time program.

A similar program operated by the Minneapolis Public Schools is the Out of School Youth Program (Mirkes, 1981). Designed for mildly handicapped adolescents who have voluntarily left school, the program provides vocational training as well as assistance in job seeking and job "survival." The program also provides training in adult living skills, such as parenting, and provides basic academic tutoring as will as individual mental health counseling.

Social Skill Training

A second major type of supplemental program that was noted includes the social skill training programs. These programs reflect the increased attention in recent years to the concept of social skills; specifically the direct teaching of behaviors that are considered essential for survival in a regular classroom or job site. The recognition that social behaviors could be effectively taught, much as academic skills are taught, is not new. In fact a number of procedures for teaching social skills have been demonstrated to be effective (Minkin et al., 1976; Werner et al., 1975; Willner, Braukman, Kirigin, Fixsen, & Wolf, 1977).

While the importance of such training was frequently noted by early program developers, only recently have packaged social skill training curricula or programs begun to be developed. Two examples of such programs include Social Effectiveness Training (SET) (Mirkes, 1981) and the Social Behavior Survival (SBS) curriculum (Walker et al., 1983). The SET program teaches 13 specific social behaviors through use of role playing and behavioral rehearsal. The structured program is designed to supplement existing instructional curricula and can be used within the classroom or other settings. The SBS curriculum, also designed for small groups, provides direct instruction of five essential classroom behaviors and 28 peer-to-peer social skills. The teaching procedures involve verbal instruction, modeling through use of video-taped vignettes, and role playing. The curriculum focuses on facilitating the integration of handicapped students into the mainstream.

A somewhat different approach to training socialization and survival skills is being implemented at the Judge Baker Guidance Center in Boston, Massachusetts (Mirkes, 1981). This curriculum addresses a wide range of areas, including problem solving and decision making, social awareness, sexual development, peer relations, drug abuse, "law-related" issues, and career awareness. The instructional approach involves role playing and problem solving in small group settings. A similar program is conducted at the Yellowstone Boys and Girls Ranch School (Bryngleson, 1980). This program teaches school survival skills and basic academics along with "life survival" skills.

Absent from this review of recent programs were references to supplemental programs in art, music, dance, and recreation. Of all education programs reviewed, none reported utilizing any of these types of therapeutic interventions. Several cross-categorical programs in adaptive physical education and recreation indicated that they served behaviorally disordered students; however, it was difficult to determine what special adaptations or additional activities were being provided to the mildly handicapped students. Several recreational programs involving Outward Bound or wilderness training and camping and hiking were also noted in the literature. All of these programs, however, were conducted by agencies other than the public schools and were offered as voluntary, extra-curricular activities.

The final category of programs reviewed included those for the behavior disordered preschooler. All of the programs discussed so far have been reported as designed for school age children. While several have been implemented with primary age children, the majority have been targeted for upper elementary age children, preadolescents, and adolescents.

Preschool/Early Childhood Programs

Early childhood programs began to be developed prior to the passage of PL 94-142, which mandated education for children as young as three years old. Stimulated by federal grant programs such as Head Start and the Handicapped Children's Early Education Program, hundreds of programs were developed, a number of which have been widely replicated. Among these are relatively few that have been developed for behavior disordered children as well as for the mildly to moderately handicapped.

Meisels and Friedland (1978) commented on the lack of services available to the preschool behavior disordered child. They cite several reasons for this, among which is the notion that the child's disordered behavior represents a developmental stage that will be "outgrown." With respect to the identification of these students, specifically the more mildy behavior disordered preschoolers, there are both proponents and opponents. While proponents cite the need for early intervention in order to avoid the cumulative effects of failure, opponents are primarily concerned with the effects of misdiagnosis and subsequent labeling of young children as handicapped. It is not within the scope of this chapter to provide a detailed discussion of these issues or to provide a complete review of early childhood programs. However, there appear to be several general characteristics of early childhood programs that have been developed for the more mildly to moderately handicapped children, including those for the behavior disordered.

First, almost all programs are characterized by strong parent and family involvement, which frequently includes training parents in how to manage their child's behavior as well as in how to stimulate learning. A second feature is the major emphasis placed on language and communication. The programs, some of which have a developmental perspective and some of which take a behavioral or task analytic approach, focus much time and specialized instruction in developing communication competency. A third feature is the way in which social and emotional problems are handled. The programs typically include basic behavior management techniques in parent training as well as in the context of the instructional program. However, serious emotional problems tend to be dealt with by social workers, child psychologists, or child development specialists through family therapy and/or counseling.

These early childhood programs that have been developed specifically for disturbed children have been designed for children with more severe maladaptive behaviors. One example of such a program is the Rutland Center in Athens, Georgia (Hoyt, 1978; Wood, 1972). The program employs what is called Developmental Therapy and has a basic psychoeducational orientation. Children in the program attend regular public school programs on a part-time basis, and spend about two hours a day in the special program at the center. The center staff include mental health and special education personnel and other child development specialists. The program has a strong educational focus and provides training in communication and preacademicas as well as in developing socialization and age-appropriate behaviors. Developmental Therapy was also the basic model employed in a joint public school and mental health program conducted in a child study center in Tacoma, Washington (Barr & DelFava, 1980). This program provided individual educational and therapeutic activities to the preschoolers and also involved parents through bi-weekly home visits. For a more complete review of models of eary childhood programs, the reader is referred to Evans (1975) and Glasscote and Fishman (1974).

Summary

To make any definitive statements about program development for the behaviorally disordered within the public schools may, in fact, be fool-hardy. Certainly when considering a summary, one conclusion did appear unarguable, and that is the fact that these students are underserved. Substantive evidence exists to suggest that public schools are not providing a full range of programs options for the behaviorally disordered. Looking only at the Grosenick and Huntze (1983) and Hirshoren and Heller (1979) data, there is little indication that the concept of least restrictive environment is guiding the development of programs.

Paul (1985) recently addressed the gains made in the field of educating the emotionally disturbed. A major gain noted by Paul is the increase in the numbers and availability of special education programs for the behaviorally disordered youngster as well as the concomitant gain in number of trained teachers who work with these students. Among the other gains cited was a move toward acceptance of the "utility of different perspectives" in programming for the behaviorally disordered and away from behavior modification as a sole intervention. However, other gains noted include assumptions that the behaviorally disordered are being educated in the least restrictive environment and that programs are developed with a focus on the full "social history" of the child.

The present review of programs would certainly support the increase in numbers of programs and variety of programs. There has been program development. In fact there is a sense of almost frenetic, not to be confused with flexible, program development. Indeed, several perspectives are represented in the more recent programs. A variety of programs are described and together appear to respond to the call for eclectic programming, but it is difficult to determine if the programs represent isolated approaches or if they are only part of a full continuum of services for the behaviorally disordered. Only one program mentioned the reintegration of its students into the mainstream.

The fact that the programs reviewed were presented as isolated and autonomous units may not be unusual; however, the absence of reported effectiveness data is noteworthy. The vast majority of the programs were simply described as "successful," yet in only four instances were any supporting data presented. Even in these instances, data were limited to measures of short-term effects, and only one program (Leone, 1984) indicated any follow-up evaluation.

A further impediment to any summarization is the lack of clearly defined target populations. While the programs purport to serve emotionally disturbed, behavior disordered, or seriously behavior disordered, there generally was no specification of the characteristics or behaviors of the students who are involved in the programs. The general lack of population description makes it difficult to ascertain who is being served by the public schools and in what setting.

In terms of conceptual models or theoretical approaches, it seems that there are two predominant influences. Clearly, the principles and technology developed out of the behaviorist model are evident in the vast majority of programs. While there were few programs that were characterized by strict applications of the behavioral approach, most descriptions noted use of such techniques as "token economies," "point systems," or "time out." The behavioral influence is also evidenced by the number of programs that include direct academic instruction as their major focus.

Also predominant among the programs is a continuing commitment to "therapeutic" interventions, involving group and individual counseling and psychotherapy, although these interventions are designed to support or complement a strong educational program and did not comprise the total intervention.

In general, all of the programs appear to reflect a narrow perspective of behavior disorders. That is, the interventions are heavily child directed and seem to cling to the notion that treatment should address specific deficits, be they social, academic, or intrapsychic. There is little evidence that the ecological perspective is being widely applied.

Recommendations

There appear to be three major or priority needs with respect to program development for the behaviorally disordered. First is the critical need to define the population. There are no specific references to levels of severity. There are no distinctions made between the mild, moderate, and severe forms of behavior disorders and the characteristics of the students. This inability to distinguish between mild, moderate, and severe emotional disturbance is also markedly apparent throughout the field's literature, which appears to further reinforce the notion that educational policy and procedures have evolved from an inadequate and incomplete concept of the basic population to be served.

A second need is for thorough evaluations of existing programs. There is a need for empirical data that clearly demonstrate the effectiveness of various programs, including curricula, service setting, and support services. Such evaluations must begin to consider the long-term results of programs. Specifically, are effects maintained over time and generalized across environments? Program evaluations must also include precise descriptions of the child populations served by the program. It is imperative that a program's effectiveness be presented in relation to specific student characteristics or behaviors.

The final need is for comprehensive full-service educational planning for the behaviorally disordered. Consideration should be given to providing program options within a system which allows for structure and restriction as well as for fully integrated service delivery. The options should be defined in terms of specific student behaviors or needs. In addition, given a variety of placement options, an educational policy must be developed that recognizes the variability among these students and allows for changes in placement based on educational needs that may change frequently.

With respect to comprehensive educational planning and measurement of overall program effect, the evaluation of the effectiveness of various related services, such as counseling and therapy, should take place in terms of their contribution to educational goals. Such services appear to be frequently provided because of a particular conceptual or theoretical bias with no knowledge if they ultimately enhance program effects. Once it is determined what services are supportive of educational programs, then policy makers or administrators can begin to explore more creative and more cost-efficient cooperative arrangements for providing such services.

Finally, the need to reconceptualize behavior disorders in terms of the environment and the social context in which they occur is not only apparent, but has perhaps the greatest potential for the development of future intervention models. Keogh (1980) has suggested that the traditional global approaches to children's atypical behavior are no longer tenable, given new theories and constructs which are emerging from the child development research. She argues that all atypical behaviors, including emotional problems or behavior disorders, must be viewed in terms of the environment in which they occur. Paul (1977) also has asserted that many children who are considered behaviorally disordered are in reality victims of the interaction between the educational system and their own characteristics. Further, he suggests that this variance should be viewed in terms of cultural and value differences and the ineffective or outdated educational philosophies which govern the public school system. This notion has been seconded by Apter (1977), who recommends that future programs shift away from the focus on the child's disordered behavior and instead attend to the disordered ecosystem in which that child must function, and by Kauffman (1979), who, while addressing the need for a reconceptualization of behavioral deviance, also argues that the individual cannot be viewed in isolation from his or her environment. Referring to the basic tenants of social learning theory, Kauffman's position is that the behavior of the student is a function of a continuous reciprocal interaction between the environment and the student's perceptions of that environment. The implications of all of these perspectives to the provision of special education services for the behaviorally disordered is clear. Intervention cannot occur in isolation from the total environment, neither can programs continue to focus solely on the child and his or her specific behavioral deficits.

There has been progress in the area education for the behaviorally disordered. The fact that programs have continued to emerge during the past 20 years is indicative that schools are making some response to the behaviorally disordered student. Whether that response is self-serving, representing an attempt to maintain harmony in the system, or is, in fact, a legitimate response to the needs of these students may be arguable. The fact is that programs do exist, but their quality or effectiveness is, to a large degree, unknown. These statements are broad and certainly not new; however, if one overall recommendation can be made, it is to stop scattered, episodic program implementation and to begin to develop system-wide service plans based both on empirical evidence of what works and the precise student needs that are being addressed.

References

Adams, W. H., & Bielicki, R. J. (1981, April). *Alternative design for vocational and necessary cognitive education for secondary emotionally disturbed students*. Paper presented at the annual international convention of the Council for Exceptional Children (59th), New York, NY. (ERIC Document Reproduction Service No. ED 204 947)

Adamson, G. (1968). Study on programs on the emotionally disturbed. *Exceptional Children, 34*, 756-757.

Anderson, C. C. (1980). *Manstreaming emotionally disturbed/behavior disordered adolescents: An outreach model*. Ann Arbor, MI: University of Michigan.

Apter, S. J. (1977). Applications of ecological theory: Toward a community special education model. *Exceptional Children, 43*, 366-373.

Barr, W., & DelFava, C. (1980). *Public school and community mental health interagency cooperation for treatment of the child with special educational needs*. Tacoma, WA: Pierce County Health Department Child Study and Guidance Clinic.

Berkowitz, P. H., & Rothman, E. P. (1960). *The disturbed child*. New York: New York University Press.

Blankenship, C., & Lilly, M. S. (1981). *Mainstreaming students with learning and behavior problems*. New York: Holt, Rinehart and Winston.

Bostrom, B., & Thunder, S. (1976). Dealing with the angry ones. *Today's Education, 65*(4), 60-61.

Braaten, S. (1979). The Madison school program: Programming for secondary level severely emotionally disturbed youth. *Behavioral Disorders, 4*, 153-162.

Bryngleson, J. (1980). The Yellowstone plan: Individualized Education Program for emotionally handicapped boys and girls. (ERIC Document Reproduction Service No. ED 195 122)

Buck, M. H., & Markson, H. J. (1982). *Desiderata programs: A unit of Phoenix Union High School District #210*. AZ: Phoenix Union High School District. (ERIC Document Reproduction Service No. ED 217 667)

Carroll, J., Katz, S. G., Waters, C., & Zaremba, S. (1978, May). *An effective model for mainstreaming emotionally impaired students*. Paper presented at the Annual International Convention of the Council for Exceptional Children. (ERIC Document Reproduction Service No. ED 153 406)

Clarizio, H. R., & McCoy, G. F. (1970). *Behavior disorders in school-aged children*. Scranton, PA: Chandler Publishing Co.

Clements, S. D. (1966). *Minimal brain dysfunction in children: Terminology and identification* NINDB Monograph, No. 3. Washington, D.C.: U.S. Department of Health, Education, and Welfare.

Cobberly, L. (1978). *Providing therapeutic support services for emotionally handicapped secondary students through cooperation with a community agency*. Jacksonville, FL: Nova University. (ERIC Document Reproduction Service No. ED 184 285)

Cruickshank, W. M., Bentzen, F. Z., Ratzeburg, F. H., & Tannhauser, M. T. (1961). *A teaching method for brain-injured and hyperactive children*. Syracuse: Syracuse University Press.

District of Columbia Public Schools. Division of Research, Planning and Evaluation. (1975). *Morse Crisis Intervention Center-Project Advance. Title III project final evaluation report*. Alexandria, VA: Commonwealth Learning.

District of Columbia Public Schools. Division of Research, Planning and Evaluation. (1981). *Youth in psycho-educational services program (special education). E.S.E.A. Title IV-C final evaluation report,*

1979-1980. Washington, DC: Author.

Edwards, L. L. (1980). Curriculum modification as a strategy for helping regular classroom behavior-disordered students. *Focus on Exceptional Children, 12*, 1-11.

Evans, E. D. (1975). *Contemporary influences in early childhood education*. New York: Holt, Rinehart, & Winston.

Feiner, J. S., & Tarnow, J. D. (1977). Expanding the base for child mental health service and training. *Journal of Special Education, 11*, 99-158.

Garrett, G. H., Chem, T. M., Montague, E., McDaniel, W. C., Paavala, J., Rich, H. L., Randalls, C. M., & Dean, G. H. (1979, April). *Project TREAT: An inter-agency approach to serving severely emotionally disturbed children in a public school setting and Sequoyah Mental Health Center*. Paper presented at the annual international convention of the Council for Exceptional Children (57th), Dallas, TX. (ERIC Document Reproduction Service No. ED 171 037)

Glasscote, R., & Fishman, M. E. (1974). *Mental health programs for preschool children*. Washington, D.C.: American Psychiatric Association and National Association for Mental Health.

Glavin, J. P., Quay, H. C., & Werry, J. S. (1971). Behavioral and academic gains of conduct problem children in different classroom settings. *Exceptional Children, 37*, 441-446.

Gottlieb, J. (1976). *Transitional classes program: School year 1975-76 evaluation report*. Brooklyn, NY: New York City Board of Education, Office of Educational Evaluation. (ERIC Document Reproduction Service No. ED 135 465)

Grosenick, J. K., & Huntze, S. (1983). *More questions than answers: Review and analysis of programs for behaviorally disordered children and youth*. Columbia, MO: National Needs Analysis/Leadership Training Project, University of Missouri.

Hallahan, D. P., & Kauffman, J. M. (1977). Categories, labels, behavioral characteristics: Ed, LD, and EMR reconsidered. *Journal of Special Education, 11*, 139-149.

Hammill, D. D., & Bartel, N. R. (1978). *Teaching children with learning and behavior problems* (2nd ed.). Boston: Allyn and Bacon, Inc.

Hannafin, M. H. (1978). *Adapt: Alternative direction for adjustment and personal training, part 1 and 2*. Gilbert, AZ: Gilbert Public Schools. (ERIC Document Reproduction Service No. ED 167 932)

Haring, N. G., & Phillips, E. L. (1962). *Educating emotionally disturbed children*. New York: McGraw-Hill Inc.

Harshman, H. W. (Ed.). (1969). *Educating emotionally disturbed: A book of readings*. Thomas Y. Crowell Company, Publishers.

Hewett, F. M. (1968). *The emotionally disturbed child in the classroom.* Boston: Allyn and Bacon, Inc.

Hirshoren, A., & Heller, G. G. (1979). Programs for adolescents with behavior disorders: The state of the art. *Journal of Special Education, 13*, 275-281.

Hobbs, N. (1966). Helping disturbed children: Psychological and ecological strategies. *American Psychologist, 21*, 1105-1115.

Hoyt, J. H. (1978). Georgia's Rutland Center. *American Education, 14*, 27-32.

Johnson, S. B. (1977). *An initial evaluation of students in attendance prior to June, 1977; final report.* Gainesville, FL: Alachua County Schools. (ERIC Document Reproduction Service No. ED 149 559)

Joint Commission on Mental Health of Children. (1970). *Crisis in child mental health: Challenge for the 1970s.* New York: Harper & Row.

Kaeck, D. J. (1978). *The modification of emotionally disturbed behavior through teacher and peer training.* Unpublished dissertation. Utah State University. ERIC Document EC 122 279.

Kauffman, J. M. (1979). An historical perspective on disordered behavioral and alternative conceptualization of exceptionality. In F.H. Wood & K.C. Lakin (Eds.), *Disturbing, disordered, or disturbed? Perspectives on the definition of problem behavior in educational settings.* Minneapolis: Advanced Institute for Trainers of Teachers for Seriously Emotionally Disturbed Children and Youth, Department of Psychoeducational Studies.

Kennedy, J., Mitchell, J. B., Klerman, L. V., & Murray, A. (1976). A day school approach to aggressive adolescents. *Child Welfare, 55*, 712-724.

Keogh, B. K. (Ed.). (1980). *Overview in advances in special education* (Vol. 1). Greenwich, CT: Jai Press Inc.

Klein, J. S. (1980, August). *Responsibility resource room.* Paper presented at Topical Conference of the Council for Exceptional Children, Minneapolis, MN.

Knoblock, P. (1963). Critical factors influencing educational programming for disturbed children. *Exceptional Children, 30*, 124-129.

Knoblock, P. (Ed.). (1964). *Educational programming for emotionally disturbed children: The decade ahead.* New York: Syracuse University Press.

Knoblock, P. (1973). Open education for emotionally disturbed children. *Exceptional Children, 39*, 358-365.

Knoblock, P., & Garcea, R. A. (1965). Toward a broader concept of the role of the special class for emotionally disturbed children. *Exceptional Children, 31*, 329-35.

Knoblock, P., & Johnson, J. L. (1967). *The teaching-learning process in educating emotionally disturbed children.* Syracuse: Division of Special Education and Rehabilitation, Syracuse University.

Lakin, K. C. (1982). Research-based knowledge and professional practices in special education for emotionally disturbed students. In C. R. Smith & B. J. Wilcots (Eds.), Iowa monograph: *Current issues in behavior disorders - 1982.* Des Moines, IA: Iowa Department of Public Instruction.

Lane, B., Bonic, J., & Wallgren-Bonic, N. (1983). The group walk-talk: A therapeutic challenge for secondary students with social/emotional problems. *Teaching Exceptional Children, 16,* 12-17.

Laneve, R. (1979). Mark Twain School: A therapeutic educational environment for emotionally disturbed students. *Behavioral Disorders, 4,* 183-192.

Leone, P. (1984). A descriptive follow-up of behaviorally disordered adolescents. *Behavioral Disorders, 9,* 207-214.

LeVine, E., Rittenhouse, J., Smith, G., & Thompson, T. (1981). A cojoint operant model for assisting profoundly behaviorally disordered adolescents. *Adolescence, 16,* 299-307.

Lillesand, D. B. (1977). A behavioral-psychodynamic approach to day treatment for emotionally disturbed children. *Child Welfare, 56,* 613-619.

Linnibran, P. C. (1977). Adolescent day treatment: A community alternative to institutionalization of the emotionally disturbed adolescent. *American Journal of Orthopsychiatry, 47,* 679-688.

Long, N. J., Morse, W. C., & Newman, R. G. (Eds.) (1971). *Conflict in the classroom.* (2nd ed.) Belmont, CA: Wadsworth.

Mackie, R. P. (1969). *Special education in the United States: Statistics 1948-1966.* New York: Columbia University Teachers College Press.

Marrone, R. T. (1970). Innovative public school programming for emotionally disturbed children. *American Journal of Orthopsychiatry, 40,* 694-701.

McGlothlin, J. E. (1978, Summer). The resource room: A model for increasing its effectiveness. In R. R. Rutherford, Jr., & A. G. Prieto (Eds.), *Monograph in severe behavior disorders in children and youth.* Arizona State University, Teacher Educators for Children with Behavioral Disorders and Council for Children with Behavioral Disorders.

Meisels, S. J., & Friedland, S. J. (1978). Mainstreaming young emotionally disturbed children: Rationale and restraint. *Behavioral Disorders, 3,* 178-185.

Minkin, N., Braukman, B. J., Minkin, B. L., Timbers, G. D., Timbers, B. J., Fixsen, D. L., Phillips, E. L., & Wolf, M. M. (1976). The social validation and training of conversation skills. *Journal of Applied Behavior Analysis, 9*, 127-140.

Mirkes, D. Z. (Ed.). (1981). *Overview, Directory & Product Guide 1980-81*. Seattle: Program Development Assistance System, College of Education, University of Washington. (ERIC Document Reproduction Service No. ED 213 157)

Morse, W. C. (1970). If schools are to meet their responsibilities to all children. *Childhood Education. 46*, 299-303.

Morse, W. C. (1975). The education of socially maladjusted and emotionally disturbed children. In W. M. Cruickshank & G. O. Johnson (Eds.), *Education of exceptional children and youth* (3rd ed.). Englewood Cliffs, NJ: Prentice Hall, Inc.

Morse, W. C. (1976). The crisis or helping teacher. In N. J. Long, W. C. Morse, & R. G. Newman (Eds.), *Conflict in the classroom* (3rd ed.). Belmont, CA: Wadsworth.

Morse, W. C., Cutler, R. L., & Fink, A. H. (1964). *Public school classes for the emotionally handicapped: A research analysis*. Washington, D. C.: Council for Exceptional Children.

Nagrodsky, J. R. (1977). The LD/ED child. The practitioner's point of view from a Title I program perspective. *Behavioral Disorders, 2*(3), 152-156.

Nelson, C. M., & Stevens, K. B. (1981). An accountable consultation model for mainstreaming emotionally disturbed children. *Behavioral Disorders, 6*(2), 82-92.

Patton, P. L. (1979). *A model for teaching rational behavior therapy in a public school setting*. San Diego, CA: San Diego State University. (ERIC Document Reproduction Service No. ED 169 415).

Paul, J. L. (1977). Mainstreaming emotionally disturbed children. In A. J. Pappanikou & J. L. Paul (Eds.), *Mainstreaming emotionally disturbed children*. New York: Syracuse University Press.

Paul, J. L. (1985). Where are we in the education of emotionally disturbed children? *Behavior Disorders, 10*(2), 145-151.

Paul, J. L., & Warnock, N. J. (1980). Special education: A changing field. *The Exceptional Child, 27*, 3-28.

Pearl, S. (1979). The responsibility resource rooms and resource center: A program administrator looks at training needs of teachers of emotionally disturbed students in secondary school programs. *Behavior Disorders, 14*, 163-167.

Purdon, D. (1979, April). A public school comprehensive interdisciplinary day treatment program for pre-adolescents and adolescents with severe hearing and behavioral disturbances. Paper presented at Annual International Convention, The Council for Exceptional Children. Dallas, TX. (ERIC Document Reproduction Service No. ED 171 081)

Quay, H. C. (1963). Some basic considerations in the education of emotionally disturbed children. *Exceptional Children, 30*, 27-31.

Ramsey, R. W., & Sickles, W. L. (1978). *The alternative school: Alachua County Florida public schools. Descriptive materials covering the secondary center for emotionally disturbed adolescents in Alachua County, Florida.* Gainesville, FL: Alachua County Schools. (ERIC Document Reproduction Service No. ED 149 526)

Rapaport, D. (1951). *Organization and pathology of thought.* New York: Columbia University Press.

Redl, F. (1959). The concept of the life space interview. *American Journal of Orthopsychiatry, 29*, 1-18.

Rhodes, W. C. (1967). The disturbing child: A problem of ecological management. *Exceptional Children, 33*, 637-642.

Rhodes, W. C. (1970). A community participation analysis of emotional disturbance. *Exceptional Children, 36*, 309-314.

Rhodes, W. C., & Paul, J. L. (1978). *Emotionally disturbed and deviant children.* Englewood Cliffs, NJ: Prentice-Hall, Inc.

Rhodes, W. C., & Tracy, M. L. (Eds.). (1972a). *A study of child variance, Vol. 1: Theories.* Ann Arbor: University of Michigan Press.

Rhodes, W. C., & Tracy, M. L. (Eds.). (1972b). *A study of child variance, Vol 2: Interventions.* Ann Arbor: University of Michigan Press.

Richmond, C. A. (1978, May). *Practical applications of a behavior modification management system project.* Paper presented at the Annual International Convention. The Council for Exceptional Children, Kansas City, MO. (ERIC Document Reproduction Service No. ED 153 423)

Schultz, E. W., Hirshoren, A., Manton, A. B., & Henderson, R. A. (1971). Special education for the emotionally disturbed. *Exceptional Children, 38*, 313-319.

Simek, T. S., Poyourow, R., & Marchek, M. (1980, April). *Project PISCES: Career education curriculum and work experience for secondary emotionally disturbed/learning disabled students.* Paper presented at the annual international convention of the Council for Exceptional Children (58th), Philadelphia, PA. Washington, DC: Bureau of Elementary and Secondary Education (DHEW/OE). (ERIC Document Reproduction Service No. ED 196 202)

Stainback, S., & Stainback, W. (1980). *Educating children with severe maladaptive behaviors.* New York: Grune & Stratton.

Stein, E. M., Ball, H. E., Jr., Conn, G. J., George, T., Haran, J., & Strizver, G. L. (1976). A contingency management day program for adolescents excluded from public school. *Psychology in the Schools, 13*, 185-191.

Stephens, T. M. (1977). Teaching learning and behavioral disabled students in least restrictive environments. *Behavioral Disorders, 2*, 146-151.

Stetson, F. H., & Rhead, J. C. (1984). A conceptual framework for providing services to seriously emotionally disturbed children and adolescents. In S. Braaten, R. B. Rutherford, Sr., & C. A. Kandash (Eds.), *Programming for Adolescents with Behavioral Disorders*. Reston, VA: Council for Children with Behavioral Disorders of the Council for Exceptional Children.

Strauss, A. A., & Lehtinen, L. E. (1947). Psychopathology and education of the brain-injured child. New York: Grune & Stratton.

Tharp, R. G., & Wetzel, R. J. (1970). *Behavior modification in the natural environment*. New York: Academic Press.

Thompson, J. L., Harris, J. H., Balfour, M. J., & Braham, B. J. (1978). *School-based adolescent groups: The Sail Model*. Hopkins, MN: Hopkins Public Schools. (ERIC Document Reproduction Service No. ED 165 386)

Toker, M. L., & Hoeltke, G. M. (1978). Pilot models for mainstreaming secondary students who are mild to moderate behaviorally disordered. Lincoln: Nebraska State Department of Education. (ERIC Document Reproduction Service, No. ED 155 853)

Tomalesky, M., & Jackson, R. (1984). The Safety Harbor exceptional student center: Multiphasic academic/therapeutic program model. In S. Braaten, R. B. Rutherford, Jr., & C. A. Kardash (Eds.), *Programming for adolescents with behavioral disorders* (pp. 52-58). Reston, VA: The Council for Children with Behavior Disorders.

Vacc, N. A. (1972). Long term effects of special class intervention for emotionally disturbed children. *Exceptional Children, 39*, 15-22.

Vetter-Zemitzsch, A., Bernstein, R., Johnston, J., Larson, C., Simon, D., & Smith, A. (1984). The on campus program: A systemic/behavioral approach to behavior disorders in high school. *Focus on Exceptional Children, 16*(6), 1-8.

Walker, H. M., & Hops, H. (1979). The CLASS program for acting out children: R & D procedures, program outcomes and implementation issues. *School Psychology Digest, 8*, 370-381.

Walker, H. M., Hops, H., & Greenwood, C. R. (1976). Competency-based training issues in the development of behavior management packages for specific classroom behavior disorders. *Behavioral Disorders, 1*, 112-122.

Walker, H. M., McConnell, S., Walker, J. L., Clarke, J. Y., Todis, B., Cohen, G., & Rankin, R. (1983). Initial analyses of the ACCEPTS curriculum: Efficacy of instructional and behavior management procedures for improving the social adjustment of handicapped children. *Analysis and Intervention in Developmental Disabilities, 3*, 105-127.

Wallace, G., & Kauffman, J. M. (1978). *Teaching children with learning problems* (2nd ed.). Columbus, OH: Charles E. Merrill Publishing Company.

Waller, J., Jr. (1978). *Emotional disturbance: A behavior modification management model.* Paper presented at Kansas City, MO. (ERIC Document Reproduction Service No. ED 153 422)

Wasserman, T., & Adamany, N. (1976). Day treatment and public schools: An approach to mainstreaming. *Child Welfare, 55*, 117-124.

Webster, R. E. (1981). Vocational-technical training for emotionally disturbed adolescents. *Teaching Exceptional Children, 14*, 75-79.

Werner, J. S., Minkin, N., Minkin, B. L., Fixsen, D. L., Phillips, E. L., & Wolf, M. M. (1975). Intervention package: An analysis to prepare juvenile delinquents for encounters with police officers. *Criminal Justice and Behavior, 2*, 55-83.

Willner, A. G., Braukman, C. J., Kirigin, K A., Fixsen, D., L., Phillips, E. L., & Wolf, M. M. (1977). The training and validation of youth-preferred social behaviors with child-care personnel. *Journal of Applied Behavior Analysis, 10*, 219-230.

Wixson, S. (1980). Two resource room models for serving learning and behavior disordered pupils. *Behavioral Disorders, 5*(2), 116-125.

Wood, F. H. (1979). Issues in training teachers for the seriously emotionally disturbed. In R. B. Rutherford & A. G. Prieto (Eds.), *Severe behavior disorders of children and youth.* Reston, VA: Council for Children With Behavioral Disorders, The Council for Exceptional Children.

Wood, M. M. (Ed.). (1972). *The Rutland Center model for treating emotionally disturbed children* (3rd Ed.). Athens, Georgia, Rutland Center: Prototype for the Georgia Psychoeducational Center Network Limited Distribution Copy.

Note

[1] This review originally appeared in Margaret M. Noel and Norris G. Haring (Eds.), (1982), *Progress or Change: Issues in Educating the Emotionally Disturbed, Volume 2: Service Delivery*; Seattle: University of Washington, Program Development Assistance System; produced under US Department of Education contract no. 300-79-0062; ERIC Document Reproduction Service ED 229 949. The author wishes to acknowledge the assistance of Peter Leone in updating the review of current programs.

METHODS OF INSTRUCTION

Gregory J. Williams

For too many years, special education personnel assumed total responsibility for remediating the problems (both academic and behavioral) of SBD students. However, Public Law 94-142, the Education of the Handicapped Act, has authorized the education of these students in the least restrictive environment, which (in most cases) is the regular education classroom. Thus these students have become the responsibility of the regular education program. Yet the assumption that special education professionals alone are best suited to meet the needs of SBD students cannot be erased by the passage of a law. Therefore, special education must provide regular educators with the support and training that are necessary in order for SBD students to succeed in the mainstream. This involves training in skills as well as accomplishing an attitudinal change. One aim of any program that seeks to facilitate the mainstreaming of these students must be to expand regular educators' tolerance for the variety of behaviors that students will display. Subsequently, educators must receive training in a methodology to modify extreme, unacceptable behaviors. Skill training and attitudinal change can be facilitated by a special education program that actively supports regular educators. The consultant teacher model (Reisberg & Wolf, 1986) is now the method of choice to accomplish this goal.

Given these concerns, what competencies are required by regular educators for the successful placement of SBD students into regular classes? Certainly, if we are to expect SBD children and youth to succeed in a regular class environment, the teachers who work with them on a day-to-day basis must possess certain skills that ensure successful student placement in which social and academic growth is encouraged, and deficits are remediated. These teacher competencies fall in three areas: (1) an instructional methodology that is appropriate for use with a handicapped population; (2) the use of environmental adaptations that enhance social and behavioral growth; and (3) the use of behavioral management strategies that control and decelerate deviant, inappropriate behaviors, encourage and foster appropriate interpersonal behaviors, and attempt to generalize positive behaviors outside of the educational setting.

Special education has developed such a teaching technology. This technology emphasizes the use of behavioral interventions with students that have learning and behavior problems. Behavioral interventions in order to increase or decrease target behaviors are based on the systematic application of learning principles. Knowledge of principles such as extinction and reinforcement can provide teachers with a broad repertoire of strategies to help those students who exhibit problematic behaviors in their classes.

For the regular classroom teacher, an initial focus on environmental planning is recommended. Grounded in ecological theory, environmental planning dictates that manipulation of the physical and psychological environment helps to insure optimal student performance. Regarding the physical environment, the teacher can insure organization and structure in the classroom. An open, unstructured, often chaotic classroom will only serve to exacerbate a behavior disordered student's problems. Rather, the teacher can focus on structuring curriculum materials, teacher directives, placement of desks and activity areas (Gallagher, 1979). The guidelines for organization and structure in a special education classroom are well documented (Haring, 1963; Hewett & Taylor, 1980). The key for the regular educator is to adapt these findings to a classroom with 25-30 students, 1 or 2 of whom may have significant behavioral problems. Use of preferential seating strategies can often obviate behavioral problems. Almost all strategies use common sense, such as seating a student away from windows and high level traffic areas. Seating students at the front of the room, near the teacher can work wonders, as can the use of rather isolated study areas for independent work. One strategy many teachers employ is seating a behavior problem student next to a "good model"—one who works hard, can sometimes provide needed directions, and can ignore inappropriate behavior when necessary!

Just as important as the physical variables noted above is the process of systematically establishing a connection between student behavior and its consequences and establishing clear expectations, rules, and guidelines for behavior. The teacher can achieve an optimal psychological environment by being consistent across the variables of scheduling, setting and enforcing rules, and providing feedback to students.

Scheduling. Hewett and Taylor (1980), Gallagher (1979), and Haring (1963) offer scheduling guidelines for special education classes and teachers. The regular educator can approximate these recommendations by maintaining consistency across days and weeks. Simply said, don't dive into activities haphazardly. A pre-planned day and week help to organize the teacher, and give the students concrete expectations for performance. In short, both teacher and student know what's coming next, can anticipate the variations and adapt to the changes.

Providing feedback as well as consistent and contingent presentation of consequences for behavior helps all students attain higher levels of appropriate behavior. For example, the teacher who throughout the day gives approval to students who get their assignments done or raise their hands to ask questions, is using an extremely powerful tool. Some researchers (Shores, 1981) believe that the ability to praise appropriate student responses may be *the* most important teacher competency.

Setting and enforcing rules. Rules are an integral component of establishing and maintaining a positive and consistent behavior patterns in the classroom. In order for rules to be effective, they must be fair, enforceable, and clear-cut. An important guideline is to state only those rules that you can follow through. The behavior disordered student is legendary for testing limits. By consistently following through, the teacher is predictable–and students' behavior will follow the teacher's model.

Attending to these concerns will obviate many of a teacher's management problems. Some individual cases, however, require a more planned and systematic approach. In these cases, a behavior change plan can be implemented.

The first step in intervening to modify behaviors is to target specific behaviors and assess their current operant levels. The next step is to select an intervention in a planned and systematic manner. The remainder of this chapter will discuss and illustrate the planned use of behavioral interventions. The illustrations take place in regular classroom settings, where regular educators receive help, support, and encouragement from a special education consultant teacher.

The use of *extinction* is a primary consideration when a teacher is faced with problematic student behavior. Extinction, or planned ignoring, reduces a target inappropriate behavior by terminating all reinforcement of that behavior (Alberto & Troutman, 1986). A teacher should be aware of several things regarding the use of extinction. First, the target inappropriate behavior must be under the control of the teacher's attention for extinction to be successful. Second, when a target behavior is put on an extinction schedule, it is going to increase before it will begin to decrease. Given these considerations, the use of extinction can be a basic strategy for the teacher to control inappropriate behaviors. Mr. Solar's 10th grade history class provides us with an example of the use of extinction.

JOE - AN ILLUSTRATIVE VIGNETTE

Joe, a good-looking 16-year-old, has been mainstreamed into Mr. Solar's history class after an entire school career in self-contained classes for the behavior disordered. Needless to say, Mr. Solar is apprehensive about this placement. So far, three weeks into the semester, things are OK. Joe has been provided with a lot of structure, high expectations for appropriate behavior, and clear communication about what is and is not appropriate for the class. Mr. Nottingham, the school district special education consultant teacher, has been very

helpful. He has supported Mr. Solar in his continuing efforts at providing an environment for Joe that is conducive to behavioral and academic growth. One problem, however, is that Joe will speak out in class, or interrupt other students who are trying to work. Every time this happens, Mr. Solar has said something to Joe, such as "Joe, please do your work", or "Joe, you'll have to wait and raise your hand if you want to contribute to the class discussion." This seems to work for awhile, but invariably Joe will begin talking again. It seems that the behavior has gotten worse over the last few days, and Mr. Solar definitely wants it to stop.

Mr. Solar went to Mr. Nottingham for some help. Mr. Nottingham told him that he had fallen into the "criticism trap:" even though in the short run it seemed that by responding to Joe with critical comments he was stopping him from talking so much, in the long run Joe was talking out more and more. In effect, Mr. Solar's criticism was increasing Joe's talking. The solution, Mr. Nottingham said, was to not say anything at all to Joe when he talked out inappropriately; perhaps that would do the trick.

REMEDIATING JOE'S PROBLEMS

The next day, Mr. Solar was ready. Three or four times during his lecture, Joe spoke without raising his hand. Mr. Solar steadfastly refused to say anything to him. Once, he raised his hand, and Mr. Solar called upon him immediately. However, Mr. Nottingham was right, he was talking out more. He was also interrupting other students more often, but they were trying to ignore him also; that is what they usually did anyway. Over the next four days, Joe gradually talked out and interrupted less and less. Mr. Solar was pleased, to say the least. It seems that it really was working! When Joe did interrupt, Mr. Solar did ignore him (at times it was extremely difficult) and, if he could, called on a student who had her hand raised by saying "Yes, June, your hand is up, did you want to say something?" It seems that something was right in this procedure, because by the end of nine days, Joe was no longer interrupting or talking out in class. Mr. Solar thought that this "extinction stuff" was just about the slickest idea he'd run across yet. Mr. Nottingham tried to convince him that it was nothing more than a planned, systematic approach to classroom management. Whatever the case, Joe, Mr. Solar, and Mr. Nottingham were very pleased with the mainstream placement to date.

There are, of course, times when extinction will not be the strategy of choice. In these cases, teachers can use strategies of *differential reinforcement* to accomplish behavior change. Differential reinforcement is a positive approach to behavior change; positive approaches to the management of behavior should always be the first choice in deciding upon a course of action. Differential attention strategies that can be used effectively in a regular classroom involve differential reinforcement of other behavior (DRO) and differential reinforcement of incompatible behaviors (DRI). DRO procedures involve delivering a reinforcing stimulus when the target behavior does not occur for a specified period of time (Reynolds, 1961) DRO reinforces zero occurrence of the target behavior. Consequently, DRO procedures require reinforcement of all behaviors except one (Ferster & Perrot, 1968). DRI strategies involve reinforcing a response that is incompatible with the target behavior. The two responses are mutually exclusive, one cannot occur in the presence of another; it literally is impossible for the student to exhibit both at the same time.

The key is to put these together in a package that can be used by the regular teacher! Perhaps a vignette will serve to illuminate these methods and procedures that have proven effective for use with behavior-disordered students in regular classrooms.

BOBBY - AN ILLUSTRATIVE VIGNETTE

Wednesday was like most any day for Mr. Johnson. He arrived at school at about 7:40, but had started to think about what to do with Bobby much earlier than that. It seems that this process was never ending. Each day, a new challenge presented itself. Bobby had caused more problems than any other child in the class. Mr. Johnson's description of 10-year-old Bobby's behavior sounds like the usual description of the behavior disordered population; in fact, Bobby has been labeled as such by the school multi-disciplinary team. He is disruptive, frequently turning around in his seat to bother other students. He will frequently get out of his seat to walk around the room and spend inordinate amounts of time at the pencil sharpener, fish tank, or looking out the window. It seems he is constantly in motion. Even when he is at his desk with something to do, Bobby does not complete his work. It seems he is distracted by even the slightest disturbance or activity occurring in other parts of the room. Bobby is falling further and further behind in his work because of these inappropriate behaviors. He just doesn't seem to have any self-control or direction. It's not that Bobby is malicious, or that he purposefully engages in these disruptive, off-task behaviors. He just seems to be "bouncing around the room."

The problems that Bobby presents to his teacher are not uncommon; indeed, many children that are not identified as "handicapped" behave in a similar way, albeit to a somewhat lesser degree in most cases. Fortunately, special education can help by offering the consultant teacher model to facilitate behavioral interventions (Reisberg & Wolf, 1986). As a consultant to the school district, what teaching methods would Mr. Nottingham recommend to Mr. Johnson to help him deal effectively with Bobby?

Mr. Nottingham believes that the differential reinforcement of other behavior (DRO), and the differential reinforcement of incompatible behaviors (DRI), would be a first step in remediating Bobby's problems. DRO and DRI strategies combine extinction with attention directed towards those behaviors identified by Mr. Johnson as appropriate for his classroom. Let's visit Mr. Johnson's classroom and see just how the consultant teacher can work with him to facilitate the implementation of these strategies.

REMEDIATING BOBBY'S PROBLEMS
It is Tuesday morning in Mr. Johnson's class. He had spent several hours Monday afternoon with Mr. Nottingham learning about ways to manage Bobby (indeed his entire class) by incorporating the principles of differential attention into his own behavioral repertoire. One of the first things that they had done was to identify target behaviors to increase (such as actively engaging with academic work on desk, complying with teacher requests) and target behaviors for reduction (e.g., noncompliance with teacher requests, looking around the room or out the window instead of working). So today he was going to try out these new strategies. The students entered the classroom, noisy and full of energy as usual. Mr. Johnson, remembering the strategy of clear directions followed by immediate positive consequences (*if* the directions were followed!), started giving the students directions for beginning the day's activities. The first thing, of course, was to get them all seated. He approached individual students and asked them to hurry and get to their desks. When he approached Jennifer, who was chatting with Julie at the back of the room, and asked her to get to her seat, he was pleasantly surprised when she said "O.K." and went to her desk. He immediately went to her and said "Jennifer, it's just great that you went to your seat like that!" Faced with this success, he tried the same thing with Tim. He was pleased to find the same response. Mr. Johnson then approached Bobby. "Bobby," he said, "please go to your seat now so we can begin class." Bobby started toward his seat. Mr. Johnson took this opportunity to put his hand on Bobby's shoulder and say, "It's great when you follow my directions like that, Bobby, you really are a great kid" (DRI). Mr. Johnson could have

sworn that he detected a smile on Bobby's face after that comment. Mr. Johnson repeated this procedure with a number of children, and before too many minutes had passed, the entire class was seated, ready to begin the school day.

Mr. Johnson then told the entire class how great they were to all be in their seats ready to work. "I look around this class and see so many students doing things that tell me they are going to work hard today. Just look at Suzie, she has her hands on her desk, feet on the floor, and she is looking at me; that's what I call good class behavior! And how about Bobby, he certainly looks ready to work also, he has his attention directed towards me, his hands are on his desk, why, he must be ready to work also!" (DRO).

Once the class had begun to work on their math assignments, Mr. Johnson remembered talking to Mr. Nottingham about DRI strategies. They had identified a behavior that was incompatible with Bobby getting out of his seat (i.e., simply being in his seat). Looking over at Bobby, Mr. Johnson noticed that he was seated at his desk actively engaged in his daily assignment. Mr. Johnson went to Bobby's desk, and immediately praised his behavior. He made it a point to tell Bobby exactly what it was he was doing right. "Bobby, just look at you, you are sitting nicely, you're working on your math workbook, you're just being a great kid today. I sure like it when you behave this way" (DRO, DRI). Mr. Johnson then circulated around the class and made it a point to notice and reinforce other students who were doing what they should. He did this for the remainder of the class period. He thought he detected a difference in the class; for one thing, he found himself paying attention to positive behaviors, and the students seemed to like being noticed for being good, rather than always being singled out for inappropriate behavior. "Hmmm, this isn't such a bad way to deal with my class," Mr. Johnson thought to himself.

The strategies that Mr. Johnson has employed are basic to good classroom management. Differential attention strategies can be incorporated into a teacher's behavioral repertoire and used on a daily basis. These strategies accomplish several things. First, they establish the teacher as a discriminative stimulus for appropriate behavior. When students see the teacher, they associate him or her with positive, appropriate school behaviors. Second, they set up a classroom environment that is positive. Appropriate behaviors are being noticed and reinforced, students are being "paid off" for those behaviors the teacher wants to increase. These strategies can help to make school a positive place to be, a place where students want to behave appropriately.

There are, of course, those instances when differential reinforcement strategies are not appropriate or sufficient to accomplish behavioral change. For example, if the target behavior is so intrusive that it simply cannot be tolerated for the length of time it might take for a DRO or DRI strategy to reduce and eliminate the behavior (e.g., hitting other children, yelling and screaming in class), you are obligated to try a more powerful procedure. Following the method of systematic application of learning principles, the teachers next choice would be a response cost strategy.

Response cost strategies involve removing desirable stimuli contingent upon exhibition of a target behavior (Haring & Schiefelbusch, 1967). Literally, "what you do will cost you." Response cost procedures are frequently used in conjunction with token economies. For the regular teacher, however, token economies take too much time and work to administer. In most cases they are simply not worth the trouble. How can teachers implement response cost procedures effectively in their classrooms? Let's return to Mr. Johnson's class and see if we can't find an illustration of this particular procedure.

SUSIE - AN ILLUSTRATIVE VIGNETTE

As usual for a Tuesday morning, Mr. Johnson has finished his math lecture, and it is time for independent seat work, when the students are expected to complete their workbook assignments. It is an opportunity for Mr. Johnson to move around the class and practice his DRI and DRO strategies. He has been using them for about three weeks now, with positive results, for the most part. Of course, there are always exceptions to the rule, and Susie is the exception. She was fine during the lecture, but not, when she should be working quietly at her desk--well, there is just no way that she accomplishes anything. She is always looking around the class, turning in her seat, talking to her neighbor, and so on. Sometimes she will leave her seat to go to the pencil sharpener, and never return! Mr. Johnson has attempted all of his tried and true interventions. He has seated Susie next to a high-achieving student, he has praised her according to the guidelines Nr. Nottingham had given him ("Be consistent, be contingent"), he has tried DRI and DRO to no avail. Susie is still not getting her work done. This math period is without a doubt the worst time of the day for Susie. He is at his wits' end; she will fail to learn math skills if she never practices them. He decides that he will call Mr. Nottingham – surely he will have some ideas.

When the two of them sat down to talk, Mr. Nottingham explained that some behaviors just aren't amenable to modification with DRI and DRO strategies. In Susie's case, it was much more reinforcing to look around the room and interact with other students than it was to be praised by Mr. Johnson every now and then. Mr. Johnson could continue to use these strategies indefinately and Susie would still be exhibiting her off-task behavior. Mr. Nottingham suggested that they take a close look at this behavior. Susie would complete more problems if she was off task less, and so perhaps a more powerful procedure would decrease Susie's inappropriate behavior. "What happens after math period?" Mr. Nottingham asked. "Why, it's recess," Mr. Johnson replied. Mr. Nottingham continued, "What if we fine Susie a certain number of minutes when she is not doing her work, and she has to wait that long before she can go out to recess? It really gets to kids when they see their classmates going out to have fun, and they can't go."

REMEDIATING SUSIE'S PROBLEMS

It was the following Friday morning, and Mr. Johnson was ready. He had written out a plan of action to deal with Susie's off-task behavior. After the math lecture he was prepared to explain the plan to her and then to implement it. When the lecture was over, he first made sure that all the students were beginning their independent seat work; then he went over to Susie's desk (sure enough, she had not even begun a problem, and was staring out the window). "Susie, I'd like to propose a plan to you so that we can work on your completing more math problems during this part of the class." Mr. Johnson went on to explain that it was important for her to finish her work, and that if all she ever did was look out the window or talk to other students, it would never get done. Mr. Johnson wasn't entirely sure if Susie was going to buy this or not–so he went directly to the heart of the matter. "Susie, I've decided that if you continue to look out the window, or turn around in your seat and talk to other students, or go fool around at the pencil sharpener, then I am going to have to do something. This is what I have decided to do–during independent work time, which is usually about 25 minutes long–I will look at you ten times. That means about every three minutes I will glance in your direction. I will be looking at you to determine if you are working on your assignment or not. If you are not–that is, if you are looking around, not working, then you will be fined three minutes. For each of the ten times that I look at you and you are off-task, those minutes will add up. They will be taken from your recess time. You will not be able to go out to recess with the other students until you spend that amount of time staying in." From the look on Susie's face Mr. Johnson could see she was not pleased with this state of affairs. He made sure, however, to speak as if he really meant business. He wanted to get this problem taken care of ...

Toward the end of his math lecture, Mr. Johnson couldn't help but think about the upcoming independent work period. He really wondered what would happen. But as Mr. Nottingham had said, it is an empirical question whether something will work or not–you just have to try it and see. You can make an informed prediction, but the proof is in the pudding, so to speak. Well, Mr. Johnson thought, we are just about ready to make the pudding! At the beginning of independent work time, Mr. Johnson went over to Susie and reminded her of the contingency in effect. She said she remembered. The first time Mr. Johnson glanced at Susie, she was looking right at him–as soon as they made eye contact, she went right to work. "Aha," Mr. Johnson thought, "she knows I mean business." Still, however, he fined her three minutes–after all, she was not working on her assignment when he looked at her. Over the next nine observations, Susie was working hard. She didn't get out of her seat once during that class period. And when he went to her desk to check her work at the end of the period, she had completed all but one of her math problems. Mr. Johnson explained to Susie why she had to stay in from recess for three minutes; she understood and agreed. It did not escape Mr. Johnson's attention that systematically applying this "response cost" was not too difficult, and that it certainly had occasioned an immediate change in Susie's behavior. "All right!", Mr. Johnson said, "I'm on the right track now!"

Mr. Johnson has applied a basic learning principle to decelerate an inappropriate classroom behavior, and found it to be extremely effective. At this point, Mr. Johnson has progressed from the teacher's "first line of offense," the use of extinction and differential attention strategies, to a second level, the use of decelerating, punishment procedures. Specifically, Mr. Johnson used a response cost strategy. Another type of punishment procedure that is at the same level is *time-out*. Time-out procedures deny the student access to reinforcement for a specified period of time, contingent upon the exhibition of a target inappropriate behavior (Alberto & Troutman, 1986). There are several ways that time-out can be used in a regular school classroom. Let's take a look at Ms. Sullivan's class for a good example of the use of time-out.

VANCE - AN ILLUSTRATIVE VIGNETTE
Vance was placed in Ms. Sullivan's class in mid-February. His progress in a self-contained classroom for the behavior disordered

called for a placement in the least restrictive environment, specifically the regular classroom. Ms. Sullivan is the type of teacher who provides a lot of structure for her students. She gives very clear directions, has rules for her classroom that she reviews with all the children and, most important, she provides consequences when students either follow or disobey those rules. She has a schedule that sets a brisk pace for instruction and activities throughout the school day. She is the type of teacher that multi-disciplinary teams love to have as a resource for SBD student placement. Vance was placed in her class for this reason. Vance is a very impulsive student who acts without thinking. He blurts out answers in class, speaks out of turn, and frequently jumps at answers before considering what might be the best response. Of course, he has many other problems, but Ms. Sullivan can tolerate his impulsiveness the least, and thus it is the first target for intervention. Ms. Sullivan has also determined when this problem is worst–during reading group instruction, when she simply can't tolerate interruptions. During this 20 minute period, she has counted Vance's interruptions and found that they occur about every two minutes (median number of interruptions: 12).

Mr. Nottingham has also been in to talk to Ms. Sullivan. He has also observed Vance to see how mainstream placement is going. The two of them have decided to implement a time-out procedure to decelerate his interruptive behavior. They have decided upon non-seclusionary time-out as the intervention. Non-seclusionary time-out involves removing a student to the periphery of an activity, thus denying that student access to reinforcement. In Vance's case, he will simply have to move to a chair that is next to the reading group area. He will still be able to see and hear what is going on but won't be able to take part in the activity. As Ms. Sullivan always reinforces her students, and generally makes her class and activities positive ones, Vance will be missing out on a considerable amount of reinforcement when he is removed from the group.

REMEDIATING VANCE'S PROBLEMS

Having decided upon this plan of action, on Tuesday morning Ms. Sullivan called Vance aside. She very carefully told him what the target behavior was. "Vance, every time you interrupt our reading group by talking out when you haven't been called on, you are going to have to sit in this chair [she points to a chair next to the reading group area] for three minutes. At the end of the three-minute period, I will tell you to come back and join the group. In order to come back though, you must be sitting quietly. If you are talking, or bugging other students, you will have to stay in time-out until you are quiet. Every time you talk out, you will have to sit there for three minutes."

And so reading group instruction began. Ms. Sullivan was pleased when after about seven or eight minutes, she noted that Vance was obviously attempting to control his talk-outs. After about 12 minutes, however, Vance did blurt out, "Johnny, quit looking at me that way!" Ms. Sullivan immediately told Vance, "Vance, you can't talk out like that in class, go to that chair until I tell you to return to the group." Well, Vance didn't want to go–that was obvious from the look on his face–but slowly, he got up and went to sit in the chair. Ms. Sullivan went on with the group activity, not even looking in Vance's direction. She remembered what Mr. Nottingham had said about not paying any attention to the student in time-out. To Ms. Sullivan's surprise, Vance sat quietly the entire three minutes. She made sure to actively engage all the other students' attention during that time so they wouldn't be tempted to look in Vance's direction. At the end of the three minutes, she said, "Vance, you're sitting quietly, you may return to the group." Vance walked to his seat, sat down, and participated in the group activity. Ms. Sullivan, remembering what Mr. Nottingham had said, praised him soon thereafter for sitting quietly and (most important), for waiting to be called on before talking. That day, Vance spoke out inappropriately only twice. The number of his inappropriate interruptions remained between one and three for the rest of the week. Ms. Sullivan was very pleased. "This is wonderful", she thought. "Spending effort on this procedure for a short period of time will give me so much more quality instruction time in the long run."

Ms. Sullivan has discovered that the systematic application of a learning principle (in this case, time-out) will effectively reduce the amount of time and energy she has to spend in dealing with some of the problematic behaviors that children exhibit in class. Such an application makes school time more satisfying for both students and teachers alike.

Teachers in the classrooms described above have demonstrated the use of behavior change strategies derived from the principles of learning. There are also certain special strategies that have been used, successfully, with many different individuals: contingency contracting, and social skill instruction. These procedures incorporate several of the behavior change strategies described above in a package, which is then applied in individual cases to achieve change.

Counselors, behavior therapists, and teachers have all used *contingency contracting* to remediate performance deficits. Cooper, Heron, & Heward (1987) define a contingency contract (behavioral contract) as a document that specifies a reward that is contingent upon the exhibition of a specified behavior. It is typically drawn up between at least two people, and assigns responsibilities to both. One person is usually in the position of delivering the reward, while the other is in the position of earning it. Contingency contracts are signed documents as well, and have an air of formality absent from informal contracting with students, in which conditions are usually only verbally specified.

In Ms. Wilson's class, we can look at a problem that could very well be addressed through the implementation of a contingency contract.

JEFF - AN ILLUSTRATIVE VIGNETTE

Well, Jeff was at it once again! Ms. Wilson was fed up with his argumentative, obnoxious behavior. At this point, she didn't care that he was a "handicapped" student; the fact was that his arguing with the other students and calling them names had to stop. She had tried telling him to stop, threatening to tell his parents, and sending him to the Vice Principal, but nothing seemed to work. She looked over in Jeff's direction, and saw that he was turned around in his seat having a heated discussion with Robert (it seemed like they were always at it!). Ms. Wilson walked over and said "Jeff, please stop that! You have to answer the questions at the end of the chapter, and you won't get that done unless you stop arguing and get with it." Jeff responded with, "How can I get anything done with him always bugging me? You always say that it's my fault–well it's not. He says bad things to me all the time. Most of the kids in this class do too. This class is !#?&$!, I hate it. It's dumb, I just don't care whether I pass or not."

Ms. Wilson listened quietly, and then just turned and walked away. She simply didn't know what else to say or do. The whole situation was out of control. This sort of altercation happened at least once a day–no matter what the activity. Thank goodness she was meeting with Mr. Nottingham, the district special education consultant teacher. Maybe he would have a few suggestions.

REMEDIATING JEFF'S PROBLEMS

Two days later, Ms. Wilson was sitting with Mr. Nottingham in her classroom after school. Mr. Nottingham suggested that perhaps a behavioral contract would help with Jeff's behavior. He felt that a contract with Jeff might be just the thing because of the negotiation involved in developing the contract. Mr. Nottingham went on to explain. "Contracts place an emphasis on student involvement and the use of behavior change strategies. In Jeff's case, perhaps having a say in what is happening to him will help to improve his behavior. In order for contracts to work effectively, they must meet certain criteria: first, there must be a goal for the student, and it must be one that they want and will be willing to work for. Second, a contract must specify in measurable and observable terms the target behavior. Third, a contract must specify consequences not only for meeting the requirements contained therein, but also the consequences for not meeting those requirements. There are also some other considerations." Mr. Nottingham at this point gave Ms. Wilson a list of guidelines for behavioral contracting (see Figure 1).

Figure 1

A behavior contract includes the following:

a. What is the goal of the contract?

b. What specific behaviors is the student required to exhibit?

c. What specific behaviors is the teacher required to exhibit?

d. What reinforcers will be used?

e. What punishers (if any) will be used?

f. How will the behaviors be monitored?

g. When will the contract be reviewed?

Mr. Nottingham continued, "You can write behavioral contracts in a number of forms. Here is one that I have found works well [see Figure 2]. As you can see, it's set up on an "if ... then ... " format. Basically, if Jeff does something you want him to, then you will be responsible for rewarding him. What is important to remember is that you and Jeff arrive at this contract together, you negotiate it with him. If he participates in its development, then he is more likely to abide by its constraints.

Figure 2

CONTRACT

Behavioral Goal

_____

_____

If _____   Then _____

_____   _____

If _____   Then _____

_____   _____

Bonus _____

Penalty _____

Signed _____   _____

_____   _____

This contract will be reviewed by _____.

                                        Date

"The procedure is like this," Mr. Nottingham went on to explain. "You sit down with Jeff and discuss both his and your expectations, perceptions, and feelings about this class. Through this discussion, you come to an agreement about what is acceptable and unacceptable behavior in this class. You, as the teacher, will outline for Jeff what your limits are, and he will do the same. A compromise can hopefully be reached. You identify a priority for change, which is noted at the top of the contract. Specific behaviors that lead to this goal are recorded, in observable and measurable terms on the contract. These are written in the "if ..." section. You and Jeff must be very clear about these. In a general sense, the "if ..." sections are Jeff's behaviors, and the "then ..." sections note the consequences when these behaviors occur. These sections are your responsibility. What are you willing to do when Jeff observes his part of the contract? Will you give him free time, buy him a new car, or what? Also, you must try and state contracts in positive terms, always focus on the positive with your students. Probably the most difficult part of writing a contract is identifying a reinforcer for the student. For Jeff, it might be best to just ask him what he would like to earn, and if he can't think of anything, then perhaps you can think of what he does most often in his free time, and use that."

The next morning Ms. Wilson made an appointment to see Jeff during her planning period. When they sat down to talk, Ms. Wilson made it a point to approach the problem from a positive perspective. She certainly didn't want to start out by getting Jeff mad and upset. "Jeff," she said, "I wanted to talk to you today because I'm upset about the way our class is going. In particular, you and I seem to have some difficulty. I'm sure you have felt it too, haven't you?" Jeff nodded his head. "Well, maybe it would help if I identified just what it is about your behavior in class that I find troublesome, and then you could tell me what you think about it as well. How does that sound?" "Well, I guess that's OK," Jeff replied.

Ms. Wilson went on to tell Jeff that her main concern was his turning around in class and talking to other students. It simply could not continue, and was hurting him most of all. If he could change that behavior, then she would be much happier, and he would get along better in class. She then asked him what he thought about making this change. Jeff replied that he would like to do better, that he didn't like arguing with other kids, but that they were always setting him up, they would bait him when she wasn't looking or listening. Ms. Wilson agreed that she just couldn't be aware of all the sutdents' behavior all the time. She said "That's a good reason why a contract between the two of us might help. It could assist you in managing to 'keep it together' when those kids say things to you. You know, Jeff, if you could just not turn around and say something back to them they would eventually stop–I'm sure of it. Do you want to try?" "Well, yeah, if it would stop them from bugging me." "This conference is going very well so far," she thought. Together, they filled out that portion of the contract that specified how Jeff was to behave: "If Jeff sits in his seat and faces the front of the class 90% of the time," and "If Jeff talks only appropriately (no name calling, no arguing) during the class period." "What can I do for you, if you abide by this contract, Jeff?", Ms. Wilson asked. Jeff replied, "How about letting me come in and use the computer during part of my study hall period?" That seemed reasonable to Ms. Wilson, and so she recorded this on the "Then ..." portion of the contract. They both agreed that the contract would begin the next day. Jeff then left, and Ms. Wilson was relieved. It had gone very well, and tomorrow would be a new day!

Ms. Wilson and Jeff have illustrated the use of a behavioral contract to facilitate improved classroom behavior. As Jones (1985) notes, these contracts can be especially effective with adolescents; the key is to have the student "buy into" the strategy for behavioral change. Once the adolescent is committed to making a change, then a strategy that assigns responsibility to the student as well as the teacher is the optimal course of action.

Ms. Wilson and Jeff have taken a big step towards solving their problems. Behavioral contracts can be extremely effective tools when working with adolescents. Not only do behavioral contracts target specific behaviors for change, they also address the developmental concerns of adolescents by giving students some responsibility for bringing about change. In many cases, it is the change strategy of choice when working with the adolescent with behavior problems, whether that student is identified as "behavior disordered" or not.

Instructional programs that explicitly teach *social skills* are essential for schools today. There has been an increasing emphasis on social skills for behavior disordered students and a number of curricula are now available (Coleman, 1986). As Goldstein, Sprafkin, Gershaw, and Klein (1980) state, "... educators ... have begun to realize that the solutions to many [of the B.D. students' interpersonal] problems may lie in concentrated efforts to build up the strengths and potentials of troublesome and troubled young people rather than interdisciplinary or remedial action" (p. vii). This positive perspective on the inappropriate behaviors that characterize the behavior disordered population certainly is prerequisite to working with these students. In Ms. Martini's class, we can see social skill instruction in action.

TONY - AN ILLUSTRATIVE VIGNETTE

Ms. Martini was concerned about Tony. He was having a difficult time. This fourth grade class of hers certainly had its share of problems this year, but Tony stood out above them all. He had severe academic deficits in math and reading, as well as in language arts. His off-task behavior in class certainly did not guarantee that he would catch up, and the other kids in the class were picking on him as well. Tony's world was one of failure and rejection; the future seemed to hold the same. What could she do? With a class of 28, she was overwhelmed with things to do, and it seemed that Tony was slipping between the cracks. She decided to call Mr. Nottingham, the district special education consultant, and get his ideas on strategies.

Several days later, sitting with Mr. Nottingham, Ms. Martini thought, "I sure hope something can be accomplished here, I'm just afraid that unless we do something Tony will continue to fall further behind." Mr. Nottingham first asked her to decide what was Tony's most serious deficit. "What do you think is the paramount concern with Tony now, Ms. Martini?" That was a tough one. Ms. Martini thought about it; she decided that, at this point, the emphasis should be on social behavior. If she could just help him to get along better with his peers, perhaps his life would be a little less miserable. Mr. Nottingham continued, "What we need to do now is identify, in specific, measurable, observable terms, just what his most serious behavioral deficit is. After that, we can identify a prosocial behavior to remediate this deficit, and teach it to Tony." "Well," Ms. Martini replied, "he should ignore the teasing of others; he just doesn't have a thick skin. Come to think of it, a few others in my class could use that skill." Mr. Nottingham indicated that perhaps a small instructional group could be set up to teach that skill. Mr. Nottingham said he could come into her class twice a week to teach "ignoring others" as a specific social skill for the students. "This type of instruction, given twice a week," said Mr. Nottingham, "will benefit all the students in the group, as well as Tony. Good, we'll start next Tuesday."

Mr. Nottingham is going to approach teaching social skills from a direct instruction perspective. This teaching methodology, first identified by Haring & Schiefelbusch (1967), is made up of four steps: 1. advance organizers, 2. modeling, 3. guided performance, and 4. independent performance.

In Step 1, the goal is to establish rapport with the students, to explain to all involved the steps in learning the skill, how the skill will be taught, and the rules of group participation. In Step 2, the skill is modeled for the participants. The model can be the group leader, a competent peer, or even video tapes. The model performs both correct and incorrect demonstrations of the skill. This enables students to see the skill performed both ways, gives them a chance to see the consequences (both positive and negative) of both, and provides an opportunity for discussion. Step 3 gives the students a chance to actually perform the skill themselves under the guidance of the leader, or a competent peer. This practice is needed for eventual successful performance of the skill. Establishment of a "safe environment" so the students can feel comfortable making mistakes is essential at this point. Students practice the skill until they have mastered it. A commitment to time is important in social skill instruction, as skill mastery will not occur in one or even two or three sessions. Once the skill is mastered, then students undertake Step 4. They perform the skill independently, first within and then outside the group. This skill should enter into natural systems of reinforcement present in the environment and subsequently maintain and generalize so that students can eventually demonstrate the skill outside of school. Let's go back to Ms. Martini's class and see how "social skill instruction" is going.

REMEDIATING TONY'S PROBLEMS

The following Tuesday, Mr. Nottingham conducted his first instructional session. There were five students in the group, including Tony. He started off by talking with the kids, introducing himself, having them introduce themselves, and finding out a little bit about each one. Then he asked the students if they were ever teased by others. "You bet!" said Paul. "Yeah, it happens a lot to me," said Tony. "They make fun of me because I don't wear fancy clothes." Tom said. "They make fun of me because I don't do so well in school." "What do you do when that happens?" Mr. Nottingham asked. "I tell them to shut up and leave me alone," said Paul. "Yeah!" said Tony. "But wait," said Mr. Nottingham, "does that make them stop? What happens when you respond that way?" "Well," Tony said, "I guess they just laugh and keep saying more things." "Exactly," Mr. Nottingham replied, "they will just make fun of you more. What I want to do with you kids is to teach you a skill–ignoring others–which will make it easier for you to put up with those kinds of situations. It might even decrease the number of times that other kids tease you. Wouldn't you like that?" There were affirmative replies all around. "Well, good, then let's get started!" Mr. Nottingham said.

Mr. Nottingham told the students that they could learn how to ignore others the same way you learn to drive a car or ride a bike. Just like those activities, ignoring others was made up of a bunch of smaller skills. He said that they would start by learning the small skills, and eventually they would know how to perform the larger skill of "ignoring others."

Next, Mr. Nottingham said, "How do you know if you are being teased?" Julie answered, "When others make jokes about you." Tim chimed in, "When others are whispering, looking at you, and laughing." "That's right," Mr. Nottingham said. "The next step is to decide how to respond to it. Watch me. Let's say that someone is calling me names during class, and Ms. Martini is working with another group of students, so she isn't nearby." Mr. Nottingham modeled looking at a book, getting out a piece of paper, and making no response to the imaginary name calling. "O.K. Tony, now I'll pretend that I am at my desk, and you tease me, and I'll show you again." This went on until the students clearly saw what the desired behavior was. Mr. Nottingham then exhibited responding *incorrectly* to teasing. "See the difference?" he said. "You sure have an easier time of it if you can ignore this, that's for sure!" The students agreed.

In subsequent class sessions, students were given the opportunity to practice the skill with Mr. Nottingham guiding them, and receiving feedback from others in the group. Once they mastered the skill, Mr. Nottingham told them to come back to the group with examples of how they used the skill in class, or even outside of class. At the same time, he told Ms. Martini to watch for successful examples of "ignoring others" and to praise the students for it.

After several weeks, Ms. Martini noticed a difference in Tony. He definitely was better at ignoring other students when they made fun of him. She reinforced him for it whenever she could. She was very pleased with his progress; to be sure, he still had his problems, but he was one step down the road in the right direction.

Up until recently, social skills were part of the "hidden curriculum" in our schools. In the last ten years or so, however, they have emerged as a distinct content area. Social skill instruction is especially needed for behavior disordered students such as Tony. Mr. Nottingham is providing social skill instruction in the regular classroom, not only to a behavior disordered student, but to all other students as well. This type of instruction, using a consultant in addition to the regular teacher in the classroom, is the merging of special education and regular education at their best.

SUMMARY

The teachers whose classrooms you have visited in the pages above have learned to use behavioral principles, and consequently managed student behavior to create more positive learning environments for not only the identified behavior disordered students in their classes, but for *all* the students in their classes. They have accomplished this with the help of special education support services in their district. In part because of this support, a mainstream placement has been able to succeed. The student has profited, an attitudinal change on the part of the teacher has been accomplished, and the regular teacher has developed new skills and competencies as well. All have profited.

This scenario need not be an isolated, unusual occurrence. It can be happening in many school districts. What teachers need to know is: first, what principles of learning can be used effectively to manage student learning and behavior, and second, what behaviors and circumstances dictate which type of intervention is indicated?

As Figure 3 indicates, our technology of behavioral change has progressed to the point that we can make predictions about which type of interventions will be most effective in managing which types of behavior. As mentioned above, this systematic use of behavioral interventions is optimal.

Being faced with a classroom full of thirty or so students can be an intimidating experience. This situation is exacerbated when one or more of those students are behavior disordered, and mainstreamed into your class. The disruptions that can occur create extremely difficult classroom management problems—sometimes serious enough for the regular teacher to resent the practice of integrating these students. Rather than being frustrated for a semester or an entire year, the solution is a planned, systematic application of behavioral principles. As Figure 3 illustrates, there are interventions which have been proved effective over a number of research studies with certain types of behaviors. Before going into those, however, it is worth reviewing some of the 'low profile' interventions which can obviate many behavior problems.

Comprehensive management strategies such as physical arrangement of the room can have a measureable impact on student behavior. For instance, if you want to encourage student interaction (both appropriate and inappropriate), seating students together at tables, or close to each other in individual desks, or randomly placing desks around the room, will serve to accomplish that end. On the other hand, systematic placement of students

Figure 3

Type of Intervention	Target Behaviors
Extinction	talk-outs (directed at teacher) disruptive classroom behaviors verbally aggressive behaviors non-study behavior
Differential Reinforcement of Incompatible Behavior	studying attendance at task hyperactivity inappropriate verbalizations aggressive behavior (hitting) talking-out
Differential Reinforcement of Other Behaviors	aggressive behavior talk-outs out of seat assignment completion
Response Cost/ Time-Out	hitting swearing spitting rule violation off-task
Contracts	attendance on-task inappropriate verbalizations aggressive behavior
Social Skill Instruction	on-task aggressive behavior numerous pro-social behaviors (see Goldstein et al., 1980)

can cut down on interaction. Seating problematic students near to the teacher will cut down on inappropriate, off-task behavior. Seating low functioning students at the front-center of the room will also facilitate improved behavior. Another strategy which can be effective is increasing the structure of your daily activities. Providing students with clear and explicit directions at the beginning of the period, telling them exactly what is to be done, and then providing the materials and activities for this to be carried out will communicate to the students that when they arrive in your class, it is time to work! Likewise, if you are unsure of what to do next and don't have your class activities planned and materials organized for each day, students will become aware of this and more off-task behavior will ensue. Finally, instructing students in the expectations and requirements for behavior in your class from the beginning will have a positive effect. You are, once again, making sure that each student knows what the rules are. Of course, following through with positive attention when they are good must naturally follow an emphasis on knowledge of the rules for behavior. Simply telling students what is expected, and not following through with consequences, will not necessarily result in more appropriate student behavior.

In the case of students with serious behavior disabilities, what happens when you have done all that, and you still have one or two students in your class who have chronic and more severe behavior problems? At this point, planning an intervention based on a careful perusal of the alternatives is called for–and the information in Figure 3 can provide this to you.

For instance, in the case of behaviors which are maintained by teacher attention, extinction can be used. If the teacher has been reacting to behaviors, such as talk outs and disruptive, attention-getting behaviors, then these are prime candidates for deceleration through planned ignoring. The key to extinction, or planned ignoring, is that you, as the teacher, must be maintaining the behavior through your attention. If that is not the case, the behavior may go on indefinitely without results. Behavior problems can be maintained by other sources of stimuli.

A second strategy which has shown positive results in increasing appropriate behaviors and decreasing target behaviors is differential attention. Differential attention strategies combine extinction with attention directed towards other, non-problematic behaviors. As Figure 3 indicates, DRO and DRI strategies have been effective with a number of classroom behaviors. On task behavior, inappropriate verbalizations, some type of aggressive behavior, out of seat behavior have all been modified through the use of differential attention. The key to these strategies lies in the power of your attention as a reinforcer. Your attention must be something that the student desires (not always the case); however, if your attention is known to be reinforcing, then systematically implement your attention as a consequence.

There are, of course, those circumstances and behaviors that dictate the use of more powerful decelerative techniques. When the behavior is potentially harmful for either the student or the others in the class (including yourself) then you are obligated to intervene with a powerful change procedure. Very firm, directive procedures such as time-out, overcorrection, and restitution have proven very effective for use with seriously maladaptive behaviors. It is important to remember, however, that these procedures do not teach students how you want them to behave–they only teach them how *not* to behave. So if you want to increase "good" behavior then you also have to target it and reinforce it whenever it is observed. This should always be a part of any program which uses response-cost or time-out.

In the final analysis, successful mainstream placements will depend upon the systematic use of behavior principles. As Mr. Johnson and Ms. Sullivan and others have illustrated, it *can* be accomplished. Mr. Nottingham, the special education consultant teacher for the district, certainly has helped. It serves to illustrate the power of not only systematic, planned interventions to help the behavior disordered youngster, but also the team approach to remediating problems. Special education and regular education have combined in these vignettes to form "effective education." What has been shown to be good for special children can be good for all children. Perhaps that is what the future will hold for education of the behavior disordered, as well as all children in our schools.

References

Alberto, P., & Troutman, A. (1986). *Applied behavior analysis for teachers* (2nd ed.). Columbus, OH: Merrill.

Coleman, M. C. (1986). *Behavior disorders, theory, & practice.* Englewood Cliffs, NJ: Prentice-Hall.

Cooper, J. O., Heron, T. E., & Heward, W. L. (1987). *Applied behavior analysis.* Columbus, OH: Merrill.

Ferster, C. B., & Perrot, M. (1968). *Behavior principles.* New York: Appleton/Century/Crofts.

Gallagher, P. A. (1979). *Teaching students with behavior disorders: Techniques for classroom instruction.* Denver: Love.

Goldstein, A., Sprafkin, R., Gershaw, N., & Klein, P. (1980). *Skill streaming the adolescent. Champaign, IL: Research Press.*

Haring, N. G. (1963). The emotionally disturbed. In S. Kirk & B. Weiner (Eds.), Behavioral research on exceptional children. Washington, DC: Council on Exceptional Children.

Haring, N. G., & Schiefelbusch, R. L. (1967). Methods in special education. New York: McGraw-Hill.

Hewett, F. M., & Taylor, F. D. (1980). The emotionally disturbed child in the classroom: The orchestration of success (2nd ed.). Boston: Allyn & Bacon.

Jones, V. (1985). Adolescents with behavior problems: Strategies for teaching, counseling, and parent involvement. Boston: Allyn & Bacon.

Reisberg, L., & Wolf, R. (1986). Developing a consultation model in special education. Focus on Exceptional Children, 18(9).

Reynolds, G. S. (1961). Behavioral contrast. Journal of the Experimental Analysis of Behavior, 4, 57-71.

Shores, R. E. (1981). Environmental consistency. Project SED teaching training module. Austin, TX: Education Service Center, Region XIII.

POLICIES, COMMUNITY PROGRAMS, AND PARENTS

Thomas Lehning

Individuals with severe behavior disabilities have special needs and require special services from schools and the community in which they live. This chapter focuses on the need for appropriate living arrangements, coordinated service delivery, and related issues. It begins with a brief historical look at the settings in which this population has been served and at the various options available in some communities today. It provides a possible solution and discusses the role of parents, schools, service agencies, and government in a more effective system for meeting the needs of seriously behaviorally disabled individuals.

Key questions include:

1. What types of alternative living settings have proven successful for some severely behaviorally disabled individuals?

2. What major gaps and problems exist in service delivery systems and programs?

3. Where does responsibility for coordinating and administering these services lie?

4. What are the elements of an effective and comprehensive management system for serving this population?

Appropriate Living Arrangements

The Social, Legal, and Historical Context

The clear mandate of current legal, educational, and social policy is to meet the needs of our nation's handicapped students in the most normal environment. In the case of children and youth, "normal" generally connotes living at home with one's family and attending the community school. No matter how great our commitment to this principle, however, there will be some cases in which the home environment is not a satisfactory or practical setting for meeting a child's needs, and alternate residential placements must be found.

For example, children with serious behavior disabilities are often found in conflict with family, peers, school, and the community to such an extent and degree that a satisfactory resolution within the home setting seems very unlikely. There are cases where the parents are unable to nurture or cope with their child, or where the child has affected family stability to the point of provoking a crisis. There are situations in which the family has chosen to give up custody or the state has taken it away. There are also cases where the family could, with appropriate support, continue to meet their child's needs at home; however this support is not currently available in most communities.

Each of these families has different problems, specific needs, and recourse. The type of residential placement and support that SBD individuals and their family members require may vary significantly.

Yet, in the past, the most common alternatives in all such situations were state institutions or juvenile detention. Support systems that might have helped a family to cope and enabled SBD youngsters to remain in their homes, schools, and communities in most instances did not exist. Legal protections were lacking. The result was exclusive and excessive reliance on institutionalization–often reoccurring throughout life.

In the 1960s, changing attitudes toward mental illness and institutions, demands for social leadership from the federal government, and growing support for the principle of normalization gave rise to a national movement for deinstitutionalization. It was based on both constitutional civil rights concerns and the belief services could be delivered more effectively and at a lower cost outside of institutional settings. Over the last two decades, the deinstitutionalization movement has, more than any other single force, altered the way the seriously behaviorally disabled population is viewed and served.

Like similar movements on behalf of other populations with handicapping conditions, the efforts toward deinstitutionalization involved active participation by parents. Working alone and in groups, parents' advocacy has taken many forms. Parents have joined with professionals to lobby for legal changes, brought court cases to challenge unfair treatment, actively interceded with local educational and service agencies to win more appropriate programming, and helped mount public information campaigns.

These changes are evident in the proliferation of state and federal legislation in the last decades, including the Mental Retardation Facilities and Mental Health Center Construction Act of 1963; civil rights legislation establishing rigorous procedures for involuntary commitment and the distribution of funds to develop community based mental health programs;

the Mental Health Systems Act of 1980, which restructured funding through states in an attempt to better coordinate state planning; and the inclusion of "seriously emotionally disturbed" as a handicapping condition to be served under PL 94-142, the Education of the Handicapped Act. The combined impact of the deinstitutionalization movement and the requirements of recent federal and state law has been to halt the overdependence on residential institutions and to return the SBD population to their communities.

Types of Living Arrangements

Instead of a single alternative, deinstitutionalization has fostered the creation of a number of community-centered options. These fall into at least six general categories, currently in varying degrees of implementation nationwide. They are described briefly here, in order from the most to the least restrictive:

Residential Institutions: Although many of the state-supported institutions have been closed or significantly reduced in size, they are still used for short- and long-term residential care of certain behaviorally disabled individuals needing more intensive and highly supervised treatment services. In some cases, assignment to a residential institution or residential school constitutes an out-of-state placement.

Residential Schools: Since implementation of PL 94-142, these are usually private, nonprofit facilities for placement of traditionally hard to place, high-cost populations (e.g. autism, deaf, blind). The reasons for residential school placement of SBD students are similar to those given for other handicapping conditions: Some school districts, especially in rural areas, do not have the resources to provide adequate programming for small populations of students with highly specialized needs. A centralized facility allows the delivery of more complete services by an appropriately trained staff. It also removes students from an enviroment seen by some parents as discriminatory or rejecting. At the schools, children live in dormitories with house parents, attend therapeutic educational programs, and receive specialized therapy and other services from professional support staff.

Group Homes: Group homes offer 24-hour care, training, and treatment in a community-based and more homelike setting. Paid staff act as houseparents, though students usually leave the home to attend school and to receive additional services from community social agencies, such as mental health centers. Six or fewer youngsters are generally assigned to each home in order to maintain a semblance of family atmosphere.

Foster Homes: Short or long-term placement with foster parents may be selected by the state as an alternative living arrangement for children from families that are dysfunctional, abusive, or in crisis. While it may be the most normal option for such children, the foster home rarely has the resources to meet the needs of a seriously behaviorally disabled child. Extensive external support and specialized training are generally needed. As in group homes, children attend community schools and may or may not receive related services from social agencies.

Emergency Housing: Short term, emergency or interim residence may be provided, usually in a communal, dormitory-style facility, to assure a safe and clean living situation while more permanent shelter is being arranged. This alternative provides the individual with emergency removal from a poor living situation and/or a transitional housing arrangement for the homeless SBD.

Supervised Apartments: Apartments are leased in areas convenient to public transportation and provided to handicapped youth and adults. The funding agency, which is usually a division of the Department of Developmental Disabilities, provides case workers who visit the apartments on a weekly basis to assure that all the individuals are adequately maintained. This placement option provides the closest approximation of a fully-integrated community situation.

All these options, taken together, constitute a continuum of residential placements for SBD individuals–if they are accompanied by an appropriate array of community-based support services. Where such community services are available to SBD individuals and their families, more of these children and youth may be able to remain in the home setting, making more restrictive placements unnecessary.

Alternative Living Options: A Critical Need

Although all these residential models have by now been tested, refined, and validated for SBD children and youth, few communities have implemented them. There are few areas which offer the continuum of placement options required to meet this population's needs. Furthermore, the facilities that do exist are often inadequate. Few have staff who are trained to identify or work with the behaviorally disabled. Most are intended to provide medical or nursing services rather than the specialized treatment, rehabilitation, and care required by SBD individuals.

Reductions in federal social program funds since 1981 are associated with the rising number of homeless across the nation. Current estimates of this population range from 250,000 to more than 2 million, and recent studies show that one half to three quarters of all transients in large cities are behaviorally disabled (Municipal League Committee on the Homeless, 1985). Federal shelter funds are targeted for adults, since youth are considered the responsibility of the educational system. Many emergency shelters are legally prevented from accepting minors. As a result, youth have been identified as one of the populations most urgently in need of temporary housing.

Even when funds have been appropriated, programs for the SBD are not easily placed in the community. The location of group and foster homes and other facilities for the behaviorally disabled are often opposed by neighborhood organizations because of fears and lack of understanding of this special population.

Recommendations

It is impossible to examine the need for residential options and the manner in which community-based services are delivered, and not consider that existing resources can be used more effectively in the planning and coordination of services. However, states must also be prepared to make the necessary investment of revenue. Washington and its Department of Social and Health Services have made some excellent recommendations that might assist other states in their planning. Specifically that study recommends that:

1. The State should explore the possibility with the Federal government of revising current Medicaid regulations to "allow the establishment of intermediate care facilities for the SBD."

2. DSHS's Mental Health Division should "examine ways to enhance existing congregate care programs by reimbursing these facilities for offering additional programs for the SBD."

3. The State should "consider developing residential care facilities designed specifically to serve the SBD."

4. The state must find a way to make funding available for communities to develop the residential options necessary to fulfill the state's obligation and commitment to deinstitutionalization (Municipal League, 1985).

It is difficult to foresee any significant new federal resources in the near future in light of current provisions, nevertheless a number of states are moving ahead. Georgia has developed a statewide center network of 24 community-based centers. Colorado provides a model for interagency cooperation. In other words, even in a period of restricted funding, adequate solutions do exist. The need is not to devise entirely new models but to make use of those that have already been developed.

Coordinated Service Delivery

Community-Based Services: A Non-System

The true measure of the success of deinstitutionalization is the adequacy of the replacement options. At present, these options are more of a possibility than a reality in most communities. The promise of deinstitutionalization–of providing humane and effective care within the community–has not been fully achieved. While states have succeeded in reducing their institutionalized populations, too few of the dollars saved by this action have been reinvested in community services. There is a lack of many types of needed services. Programs that offer intensive mental health and rehabilitative services represent the most serious gap in the community mental health delivery system (Johnson, Drake, Orantz, & Brown, 1980).

Furthermore, the existing services are not coordinated. Support is fragmented among multiple organizations addressing only one aspect of an individuals' needs, and rarely are linked to other agencies in a comprehensive system. In reality, mental health/behavioral disabilities services, as currently delivered, constitute a non-system, with no consistent method of meeting all of an individuals' needs and without adequately covering transition from one phase of treatment to the next. Without clear lines of coordination and responsibility, interagency battles over financial responsibility have resulted in the failure of some children to receive the services to which they are entitled under PL 94-142.

As a consequence, youth with behavior disabilities and other handicapping conditions are bouncing among untenable home situations, temporary living settings, crisis centers, and the streets, and between the juvenile justice and social service systems, while their inadequately addressed behavior and emotional disabilities are preventing them from benefiting from their education.

Centralized Responsibility: A Need For Clarification

A problem with many states' service delivery is the absence of clear lines of programmatic, fiscal, and administrative responsibility.

The Education of the Handicapped Act (PL 94-142) constitutes a federal policy that one central state agency must assume overall responsibility for ensuring the availability of appropriate programming and adequate funding for programs for all children who are educationally handicapped. The purpose of this requirement, is to assure a "single line of authority with regard to education so that no child gets lost in the shuffle" (Garrity v. Gallen). Under the Education of the Handicapped Act, it is the state education agency (SEA) which expressly bears this responsibility (20 U.S.C. Sec. 1412(6); 34 C.F.R. Secs. 300.128 and 300.600). This applies even if different agencies may, or do, in fact, actually deliver the services (supra).

Under PL 94-142, the education agency is responsible for services such as alternative living arrangements or family counseling, which are not commonly thought of as related to a child's education, if these services are required for a child to benefit from his/her educational programming, as established in the child's individual education program (IEP).

However, when various agencies are delivering these services, no single agency is assuming overall responsibility. There is a lack of clear and defined agency responsibilities and procedures at all levels to assure collaborative planning and service delivery, and which avoid unnecessary duplication of services and jurisdictional disputes.

Access to Services

Since no single agency oversees and monitors services provided to an individual, no agency has adequate information to document the course of services and resulting outcomes (Municipal League, 1985). This situation creates obstacles to gaining access to all services needed, and it provides no assurances that an individual's needs are being effectively met.

Clarifying Financial Responsibility

A third, and related problem, is the lack of clear assignment of financial responsibility, at times creating situations that are likely in violation of the law. PL 94-142 is quite clear that the educational agency is ultimately responsible for funding all services related to students' educational needs.

Federal regulations (34 C.F.R. Sec. 300.301) do allow the use of joint agreements between agencies to share the costs of residential placement. However, to comply fully with the federal Education of the Handicapped Act, the responsible education agency must be willing and able to pay all costs of IEP programming which the involved noneducation agency is unable or unwilling to pay.

A problem existing in some state systems appears to be that various state agencies providing related services are required by statutory authority to collect costs from families of adequate means. If the service provided is a part of the students' IEP, a violation of the Education of the Handicapped

Act would result.

Courts have taken care to note that "interagency battles over financial responsibility" have resulted in the failure of children to receive services to which they are entitled under the Education of the Handicapped Act. Such "fingerpointing," as the court has called it, cannot be permitted while children's rights "slip between the cracks."

Problems arise because there is no legislation which clearly defines financial responsibility for services that are not on the IEP–services that are not related to education. School districts and SEAs may be reluctant to cooperate with other agencies because of the fear that, as the only agencies with legally defined responsibilities, they will be held accountable for all costs.

Recommendations

A coordinated service delivery system that allows access to services by all SBD individuals who need them should include the following components:

1. *Interagency Agreements.* Comprehensive, formal, legal interagency agreements should be mandated at all levels to clearly delineate responsibility and funding mechanisms. Colorado is one state with an exemplary system of joint interagency planning cooperation that allows children to receive all prescribed services over a period of time without gaps to meet their total needs.

2. *Special Fund.* There should be a special state revenue fund to be used as a supplementary source of funding by all state agencies. In Colorado and Vermont, the state legislatures have created a "superfund" to be used as a supplemental reserve by all agencies to pay for costs actually incurred for students who meet the eligibility criteria for any handicapping condition and need residential placement or any other service which school districts might deem better provided by another agency (e.g. counseling). While no model is totally transportable from one state to another, the experiences of Colorado and Vermont strongly suggest that existing resources in all states can be used more effectively with better planning and coordination of services.

3. *Service Delivery.* There should be a model for service delivery that treats students needing services as an "interagency focus of concern" and that allows educational and social agencies to act as "joint brokers" for student services. Colorado, Vermont, Georgia, Utah, and

Iowa are all examples of states where such models have been successfully implemented.

4. *Advocacy.* Another essential element in coordination is advocacy. Unlike other disability groups, the seriously behaviorally disabled lack a well-organized advocacy network of parents, staff, and volunteers who can intervene on an individual's behalf to ensure that he or she receives appropriate service. This is not a role for government; it is, rather, a service which must come from outside the system. It is a job for concerned citizens and professionals who can provide the leadership and impetus in organizing such an advocacy network, drawing on their own resources or those of a professional advocacy organization.

5. *Case Management System* should be part of any state model. A case manager would be assigned to each individual receiving services and would have responsibility for ensuring that the person is appropriately assessed and referred. Specifically, the case manager would develop an individual plan of service, direct the individual to those services, follow up to ensure that they are provided, and regularly reappraise the mix and level of services required. Such case management programs have worked successfully for other groups, such as the developmentally disabled.

6. *Data base/Accountability.* To assure adequate planning and monitoring of the system, states need to create an interagency data base that documents types, amount, and cost of services provided by each agency and that collects standardized data on individuals served, with appropriate safeguards to protect confidentiality.

Related Issues

Services to Behaviorally Disabled Adults

The other chapters of this book are concerned primarily with the needs of seriously behaviorially disabled children and youth. However, as is evident in the statistics on homelessness cited earlier, the problem of residential options for SBD individuals does not end with the school year. As the Statewide SBD Study (Haring, Jewell, Lehning, Williams, & White, 1986) points out, "Behavior disabilities of the most severe kind tend to be chronic and require continuous assistance and comprehensive management throughout a child's school career and well into adulthood" (p.58). In fact, the needs of behaviorally disabled adults are often more critical than those of the younger handicapped. As imperfect as has been its implementation, PL 94-142 is clear in mandating an array of educational services for handicapped children and youth and in assigning overall responsibility for delivering these services. Behaviorally disabled adults have needs for housing, counseling, medications, and other basic services but they do not enjoy similar protections and guarantees.

There are few mandatory entitlement programs to meet their needs, and no single agency is charged with addressing them. The best that is offered is an uncoordinated "band-aid" approach that is both inefficient and ineffective. The solution to this problem will have to entail an expansion of mandated services and assigned responsibilities along a model similar to that envisioned by the framers of PL 94-142 in regard to education.

Role of Parents

Parents, in particular, should be assisted or taught to play a more prominent advocacy role. The previous lack of strong and effective advocacy organizations has been ascribed to the lack of effective communication between parents and the schools or agencies providing services (Bricker & Caruso, 1979; Marion, 1980). To improve this situation, professionals will have to initiate a conscious program of parent information and support, and of assisting parents to become more active in exercising their rights and responsibilities.

Parents have much to contribute to their children's education and a great investment in its success. Their active participation is a noticeable characteristic of the most outstanding SBD programs nationwide. Furthermore, the participation of parents, legal guardians, or appointed parent surrogates is required under PL 94-142 for all students with handicapping conditions. Systematic cooperation among parents and service providers can be beneficial to all concerned.

One problem that will have to be addressed is the lack of qualified parent surrogates. At present, the person frequently assigned to this role is the state case worker. This creates real or perceived conflicts of interest which prevent the open communication essential to protection of student rights, and it is, moreover, in violation of the requirements of the law. A satisfactory means of identifying and training potential parent surrogates should be a component of the comprehensive management plans developed by each state.

Services to Parents

While calling attention to the need for parent involvement in program improvement and social change, it is important to acknowledge that the task of parenting a seriously behaviorally disabled child is a stressful and demanding one. Just as the regular class teacher needs the assistance of outside specialists to successfully meet the needs of handicapped students in the least restrictive environment, families need support in the stressful task of providing care for the SBD child living at home. One of the most important supports may be the opportunity to have someone else look after the child for a period, whether for a few hours, a weekend, or a more extended period of time. "Respite care" is often the most critical factor in avoiding more restrictive placements. It may be provided in a number of ways: by an individual support worker in the home; at a "respite home," which, similar to a foster home, has been approved and contracted for the task; at other residential programs, including schools, institutions, and group homes; or, in some communities, at special respite care centers established for this purpose exclusively.

Other support services which may be needed by parents include opportunities for networking and mutual support, training in rights and responsibilities and in advocacy methods, referrals to service agencies, and information on topics related to the disability and effective intervention. Many states have developed guidelines and procedures for implementing such a system but few have been used. Such support services are frequently provided by ongoing advocacy organization–another reason why such organizations are important in meeting handicapped individuals' needs.

Agencies at all levels should support research efforts to examine support services for parents of SBD children. There is much to be learned about strategies for assisting the families of these individuals.

Summary

The deinstitutionalization movement and subsequent changes in laws, social attitudes, and public policy have been successful in greatly reducing the numbers of seriously behaviorally disabled individuals confined inappropriately to residential institutions. However, an effective community-based service delivery system has failed to materialize. What exists is actually a "non-system" of fragmented, uncoordinated services in which far too many individuals are inadequately served or not served at all.

One of the most pressing current needs is that of alternative living arrangements for SBD children, youth, and adults. Although proven models exist, few states and communities offer the full continuum of residential options that are necessary to meet the range of individual needs within the SBD population. The more restrictive end of this continuum includes residential institutions and residential schools; less restrictive alternatives such as group homes, foster homes, supervised apartments, and emergency housing facilities should also be widely available.

Other elements of an effective service delivery system include:

1. Clearly assigned responsibility for overall coordination and planning by a single agency.

2. Legal agreements between this agency and all others involved in service delivery which spell out the roles and relationships of each.

3. A case management system, that enables proper assessment, referrals to services, and follow-ups.

4. A state "superfund" or other source(s) of financial support for services that are needed but not clearly within a specific agency's mandate.

5. A comprehensive management plan.

The goal must be to ensure that each SBD individual receives the array of services necessary to meet his/her individual needs. A few states already have comprehensive and effective service delivery systems in place. To achieve comparable programs in other states will require the organization of an advocacy network of parents, professionals, and other dedicated volunteers.

References

Bricker, D., & Caruso, V. (1979). Family involvement: A critical component of early intervention. *Exceptional Children, 46*(2), 108-116.

Garrity v. Gallen, 522 F. Supp. 171 (D.N.H. 1981).

Haring, N. G., Jewell, J. P., Lehning, T. W., Williams, G. J., & White, O. R. (1986). *Serious behavior disabilities: A study of statewide identification and service delivery to children and youth.* Olympia, WA: Office of the Superintendent of Public Instruction.

Johnson, G. W., Drake, H. M., Orantz, R., & Brown, T. R. (1980). *An assessment of the community adjustment and service needs of former state hospital patients: A study of deinstitutionalization.* Olympia, WA: Department of Health and Social Services.

Marion, R. L. (1980). Communicating with parents of culturally diverse exceptional children. *Exceptional Children, 46*(8), 616-623.

Municipal League Committee on the Homeless (1985). *The crisis on our streets: The plight of the homeless mentally ill in Seattle.* Seattle, WA: Author.